THE PROPHETS
AND THEIR TIMES

THE PROPHETS
AND THEIR TIMES

By

J. M. POWIS SMITH

SECOND EDITION REVISED BY
WILLIAM A. IRWIN

THE UNIVERSITY OF CHICAGO PRESS

CHICAGO & LONDON

International Standard Book Number: 0-226-76356-0

THE UNIVERSITY OF CHICAGO PRESS, CHICAGO 60637
The University of Chicago Press, Ltd., London

PREFACE TO THE FIRST EDITION

THE prophets are perennially interesting. They represent the religion of Israel at its best. They were the spokesmen of the progressive idealism of their day, the organs of a noble discontent with the established order, the heralds of a golden age.

New books on the prophets are always in order. Each generation needs their message. That message, however, is not easily comprehended in its fulness. The words of one age are not intelligible to the citizens of another, without interpretation. When to the difference in time and circumstance there is added a difference in race, language, and culture, the difficulty of understanding is greatly increased.

The purpose of this book is not to preach the message of the prophets to the men of today. It is rather to show as clearly as possible what the prophets were trying to do and say in their own generation. To this end a knowledge of the historical background of their work is necessary. The prophets were students of their times. They were vitally concerned in all that was going on in the political and the social world. They sought to guide the course of events into the right channels. Hence no understanding of their work is possible apart from a knowledge of what was going on in the world about them. The more accurately the conditions amid which they worked are known, the more complete will be our appreciation of their message.

The world of the prophets was always changing. New forces and new personalities were constantly coming to the fore. Our knowledge of that world has been greatly enriched in recent decades by the discovery and decipherment of cuneiform and hieroglyphic records. Discoveries are always in progress. Each new find changes the situation for us and makes necessary modifications in our interpretations. The recent reading of documents regarding the fall of Nineveh is a case in point. We not merely have to change the date of that event, but we must re-write the history of the last decade of the Assyrian Empire. That involves changes in the reading of contemporary Hebrew history. Such things call for new books on prophecy.

In recent years the study of the prophets has concerned itself increasingly with the psychology of prophecy. That study is as yet in its infancy; but much may be expected of it. Some use has been made of that approach to the prophets in this book. Limitations of space and the necessarily somewhat precarious character of the results of much of that study thus far have precluded giving it larger recognition in this handbook. But careful work in that field will produce much fruit.

My obligations to the world of scholars, past and present, are too numerous to mention, but are none the less profoundly and gratefully realized. No one man is sufficient for these things. If this interpretation of the prophets has any special value, it is largely due to what has been learned from my predecessors. May the reader join me in a vote of thanks to them.

University of Chicago   J. M. Powis Smith
Christmas Eve, 1924

PREFACE TO THE SECOND EDITION

IT IS with grave misgivings that one lays violent hands on the work of a great scholar. More particularly, if bound to his memory with ties of the spirit in the succeeding relations of student, then friend, and later for a too brief period of years as colleague, will such an iconoclast feel rather that he should put his shoes from off his feet and stand in reverence. I must plead, then, in extenuation of my present audacity that the task here made public was undertaken at the suggestion and request of the University of Chicago Press, who, looking forward to a new printing of Dr. Smith's *The Prophets and Their Times*, rightly sensed that the fifteen-year interval since its publication had witnessed considerable progress in Old Testament study. But my hesitation was further allayed by the fact that in his own copy, which through the generosity of Mrs. Smith I possess in my library, there are in his own hand marginal notes of changes and corrections to be embodied in the revision, which to our inestimable loss he himself was not permitted to carry through. I have thus visible assurance, in addition to my memory of his constant striving from the better to the best, that I have but acted in accordance with what he would himself have wished.

The proper limits of such a revision are a matter of delicate discrimination. Fortunately for the major problems the issue was of clear-cut objectivity. The chapter on Ezekiel, for example, synchronizing almost exactly as it did with the publication of Herrmann's commentary and Hölscher's study of this prophet, was clearly outdated by the intensive work that has since ensued. In many matters, however, decision was much less certain. It will be seen that at times I have made bold to question or even to reverse the interpretation Dr. Smith presented. Obviously, I may not claim that in so doing I have put forward the view that his ever active mind would now have reached if he were yet with us. But I make bold to hope that I have at least been true to his spirit, and that in some humble way I may have contributed to the continuing usefulness of this little book in the service of those high ends to which his career was dedicated.

It is pleasant to confess indebtedness to my colleagues in the Oriental Institute—a comradeship whose rich resources have been at my call without stint. Naturally I have drawn most upon the assistance of my associates in the field of Old Testament studies—Drs. R. A. Bowman and S. I. Feigin. But I have not been backward in availing myself of the immense historical resources of Professor A. T. Olmstead, and the fruit of years of careful study of ancient Babylonia possessed by Drs. G. G. Cameron and Waldo H. Dubberstein. Nor may I neglect to mention the toil of my friend and student, Mr. Joseph L. Mihelic, to whose care in checking references such measure of accuracy as this revision may possess is largely due. While credit for any merits of the work must be given in generous measure to these, obviously they may not be held accountable for the mistakes, from which it is too much to hope that I have been immune.

It will be seen that the work of revision has been most extensive in connection with the problem of Ezekiel, just now mentioned. In fact, except for a citation from the first edition, the chapter is entirely rewritten. But, further, the Old Testament specialist will soon discover that I have therein made bold to take a line differing from all previous solutions of the riddle of this book. However, the fact is that there exists no treatment of the problem so commending itself by soundness of method and cogency of result as to command my allegiance. The criticism of the Book of Ezekiel stands at this moment in complete chaos, proof of which is abundantly provided by detailed comparison of recent studies. There is absolutely no body of "assured results," save the meager agreement that the book is composite and that Ezekiel began his ministry in Palestine. I have, then, had no recourse but to present my own conclusions, matured through many years of special study given to this problem. Obviously I have laid myself open to criticism; for there is no one on whose agreement and support I may depend, beyond perhaps minor points, save my own students, many of whom are now Old Testament teachers in their own rights. And this situation is aggravated by the fact that I have not presented my evidence. For that let me claim the right of being my own first critic. It has been less than fair to my colleagues in Old Testament study, whoever of them far or near may see this work, to have put forth conclusions so diverse from the usual but with no more of supporting evidence than the meager and actually minor notes to be found in my chapter. Yet I can only crave indulgence on the grounds that it was impossible to argue the case in the limits of a chapter: it is the task of an entire book; and to have sought even to sketch the grounds of my conviction could not possibly have been fair to the position which I hope to put before the scholarly world at some later time.

In one further matter I have been guilty of refusing the well-worn path. I have set myself against the prevailing view that the prophets were ecstatics. But, happily, I am at this point not so much alone. The considerable bibliography, which I have appended at the appropriate point, though claiming no completeness will serve to indicate what to my mind is a growing conviction among Old Testament scholars.

The matter is of high importance, not merely for its historic interest, but rather, as it seems to me, for its basic relevance in our approach to Hebrew prophecy and our understanding of its religious meaning and abiding significance. The study of the prophets is today more than a sequestered academic indulgence; the problem of their inspiration and revelation is basic to some of the crucial issues of this troubled time. Striking as is the fact that they lived through a time very like our own, and worked out their convictions of the awful reality of the righteousness of God through a tragedy as deep as ours, yet we should err in overlooking the present relevance of the source and validity of their knowledge of God.

One need not emphasize the fact that the violent threats to human freedom which we witness today are basically ideological. Under our eyes the ancient heresy is revived that man is properly a slave, dependent for his rule on a superman, and for his direction on a superknowledge—more specifically, a supernatural knowledge. It is in opposition to this that we see the significance of Protestantism, which on the background of several great expansive movements of medieval times came as a profound liberation of the human spirit. But it did not spring full born; a movement of such transforming proportions demands time to grow and mature. However, for our special concern of the moment it is important to realize that in the larger atmosphere of that wonderful new day biblical criticism had its birth; and biblical criticism has been in a most intimate way interwoven with the essence and life of Protestantism and the evolution of its thought. The profound contributions to theological thinking of roughly the last hundred years have been induced in the first instance by the work of the biblical scholar breaking ancient errors and building a structure biblical theology and divine revelation in harmony with the truth that his researches made clear.

But freedom's battle is never finally won; it must be fought afresh on new battlefields of each succeeding age. More especially today, when the new enemy is that very old foe—authoritarianism—from which the Protestant Reformation signalized our liberation and successive centuries of biblical work have buttressed our freedom, must the biblical worker assume his age-old responsibility for religious thought. From an increasing number of sources, ostensibly Protestant not less than Roman Catholic, we witness militant movements or trends of thought which threaten as their ultimate outcome nothing less than the re-enslavement of man, body and spirit, to dogmas of the superman or the superknowledge.

It is once more the primeval strife of Marduk and Tiamat, of God and Chaos. And its weapons are, as always, primarily those of the spirit. It would be absurd to claim that the issue rests finally in the hands of the biblical scholar. As the attack comes from many quarters, so for the defense none of us alone is sufficient. But the biblical worker has something to say in his own right about the basic claims of the authoritarians, by whatever name they may choose to be known. At their assumption of a supernatural revelation, as these words are commonly understood, he scoffs. Indeed, he has scoffed so effectively that the ignorant have supposed he denies divine revelation *in toto*. Nothing could, however, be farther from fact; the biblical scholar is most of all in a position to know the reality of the process which under his examination he sees taking place in ancient Israel—a process so wonderful that no less words than divine revelation are adequate to describe it.

Though for Jewish thought the high attainment of divine revelation came in the Pentateuch, Christianity has rather been drawn to the work of the prophets, who in some mysterious way seemed in themselves to bridge the gulf between the seen and the unseen. Their constant asseveration, "Thus saith the Lord," could well lend verisimilitude to such a claim. But, as well, of some of them remarkable stories are preserved. Isaiah saw the Lord seated on his throne and heard his words; before the astounded Ezekiel the heavens were opened, and he saw visions of God; and what may one say of the mystic effect of the revelations of Daniel, with their tantalizing glimpse of "a time, times, and half a time"? However this may be, the mood of Old Testament study of the past twenty-five years has lent aid and encouragement to the notion of a unique revelation through the prophetic experience. For we have been addicted to the idea of a peculiar prophetic psychology: in the trance state they heard voices and saw spiritual realities, which, then, on their recovery of normal consciousness they announced as the word of God. Psychology in a measure worked its own cure, for we were assured that the trance is no source of valid knowledge; all that the ecstatic brought out of his vision he had first taken into it. But more recently, as noted above, we have moved farther away from this sort of explanation of the great prophets. Even this shabby basis for a doctrine of supernatural revelation is now crumbling away.

We should have preserved a better balance if we had kept in mind that the sages of Israel were the first to enunciate a rational explanation of divine inspiration; indeed, they studied it so carefully and well that theirs remains to this day the one acceptable account of this

mystery. They phrased it in poetry; but the meaning is
so clear that we need not belittle it with bald prose.
They presented the figure of Wisdom, of whom they
wrote,

> The Lord possessed me in the beginning of his way,
> Before his works of old.
> I was set up from everlasting, from the beginning,
> Before the earth was. . . . .
>
> Wisdom hath builded her house;
> She hath hewn out her seven pillars;
> She hath killed her beasts; she hath mingled her wine;
> She hath also furnished her table:
> She hath sent forth her maidens;
> She crieth upon the highest places of the city;
> Whoso is simple, let him turn in hither.
> As for him that is void of understanding, she saith to him,
> Come, eat of my bread
> And drink of the wine which I have mingled.
> Leave off, ye simple ones, and live;
> And walk in the way of understanding.

It is remarkable how with their limited resources for
the study of history they were able to trace this reality
across long ages of human quest. The biblical scholar
today has the advantage of the fruitful story of the centuries since their time; he is equipped also to know the
thousands of years that preceded them far better than
their wildest dreams might have hoped. And this re-
source but quickens his amazed admiration for their
insight. It is just this divine Wisdom—call it by whatever name sounds best to one's peculiar mental furnish-
ing—which is the supreme fact of all the centuries.
The prophets saw it too; for them the Lord was su-

preme not so much above and beyond as *in* and *through* history. Where men were striving and suffering and dying, there was he among them, uttering his voice with power and bringing to pass new things. He used dictators to work his sovereign purposes, and made the wrath of men to praise him. And this is the steadying and sustaining reality for our days, so like theirs: "The Lord reigneth; let the earth rejoice!" But it is a reality that becomes more immediate and intimate—far more meaningful and energizing for us at this moment—when it is understood that the voice of God, which was so clear for them, was just the same voice, speaking in the same ways, as that we hear today through the thunder and the storm and the earthquake of a world in flames, though because of our dulness of ears we hear it less clearly than they.

> By terrible things thou wilt answer us in righteousness,
> O God of our salvation,
> Thou that art the confidence of all the ends of the earth;
> And of them that are afar off upon the sea.

W. A. IRWIN

UNIVERSITY OF CHICAGO

TABLE OF CONTENTS

CHAPTER I

THE SONS OF THE PROPHETS

THE term "sons of the prophets" is one easily misunderstood. In reality it implies nothing as to the family relationships of the prophets. It is an example of idiom occurring frequently in the Old Testament. When Noah is called "a son of five hundred years,"[1] we understand that he was five hundred years old; when Saul characterized David as "a son of death,"[2] he meant that David ought to be slain; and when the sage spoke of "the son of a fool,"[3] he was not predicating the folly of the father, but rather that of the son. Similarly, the "sons of God" in Gen. 6:2 are simply "divine beings," beings possessing the characteristics or essence of divinity; even as "son of man" when applied to Ezekiel emphasizes his humanity in contrast to the deity of God who speaks to him. In like manner, "sons of the prophets" are persons endowed with the spirit of the prophets,[4] and not at all sons of prophets according to the flesh. Thus the term "sons of the prophets" is used in the early literature to denote the body of prophets as a whole. When Amos said, "I am not a prophet, nor the son of a prophet,"[5] he was

[1] Gen. 5:32; cf. Jonah 4:10.   [2] I Sam. 20:31.

[3] Prov. 10:1; 17:25; 19:13.

[4] Cf. "son of valour" in I Sam. 18:17, meaning "a valiant man," and "son of worth" in I Kings 1:52, meaning "a worthy man."

[5] Amos 7:14.

1

repudiating the entire prophetic movement of his day, with which he refused to be classified.

These sons of the prophets represent the earliest stage in the history of prophecy in Israel. They were a gregarious folk, living and working in groups or communities. When Saul left Samuel, after receiving the announcement of and anointing for his kingship, he met a company of the "sons of the prophets" on the road, prophesying as they went along;[6] when David fled from Saul to Naioth in Ramah, he found himself in the midst of a group of "sons of the prophets";[7] when Elisha helped one of the "sons of the prophets" who had lost a borrowed axe, a community of them was engaged in the task of enlarging the living quarters of the group;[8] when Ahab sought the counsel of the prophets of Yahweh regarding his proposed campaign against Ramoth Gilead, they came together four hundred strong and spoke as one man;[9] when Elisha lost his leader, Elijah, he was supported by groups of the sons of the prophets at Bethel, at Jericho, and at Gilgal;[10] and when Jezebel was persecuting the prophets, Obadiah hid a hundred of them in caves.[11]

What constituted these men prophets? We are told that the prophet was in olden times called a "seer."[12] That is the title given to Samuel and to Gad, one of David's prophets,[13] and later applied to prophets in

[6] I Sam. 10:5 ff.
[7] I Sam. 19:20.
[8] II Kings 6:1–7.
[9] I Kings 22:6.
[10] II Kings 2:3–18; 4:38 ff.; cf. 4:1 and 9:1.
[11] I Kings 18:4.
[12] I Sam. 9:9 (cf. vss. 10 f., 18 f.).
[13] II Sam. 24:11.

general.[14] This means that they were credited with the power to see things hidden from the eye of the common man. It was said of Samuel, for example, "everything that he says surely comes to pass."[15] When Ahab and Jehoshaphat desired to know in advance whether or not their campaign against Ramoth Gilead was to be successful, they called together the prophets of Yahweh and inquired of them.[16] It is repeatedly stated of the leaders of Israel that they "enquired of Yahweh" before undertaking some enterprise or making some important decision.[17] There were various ways of doing this, but the prophet's oracle was one of the most important.

The same belief in the prophet as one who was in a certain measure in the confidence of Yahweh is reflected in the word "prophet" itself. This is a Greek word meaning "one who speaks for, or on behalf of, another." It never conveys in and of itself, but only in later development of the word for Biblical usage, the idea of foretelling or prediction. The Hebrew word for "prophet" is accurately translated by the Greek equivalent. The sense of the Hebrew word (*nâvî*) is clearly brought out in two passages. In Exod. 4:10–16 we find Moses striving to escape the hard task to which Yahweh is calling him. His first excuse is that he is not skilled in public speech, and so is not fitted to be an

[14] II Sam. 15:27; Amos 7:12; Isa. 29:10; 30:10; Mic. 3:7; II Kings 17:13; I Chron. 9:22; 21:9; 25:5; 26:28; 29:29; II Chron. 9:29; 12:15; 16:7, 10; 19:2; 29:30; 33:18; 35:15.

[15] I Sam. 9:6.   [16] I Kings 22:6 f.

[17] E.g., I Sam. 22:5 ff.; 23:9–12; 30:7 f.; II Sam. 5:23–25; 21:1.

ambassador to the pharaoh. Yahweh assures him that he will go with him. "I will be with thy mouth, and teach thee what thou shalt say." Moses is still unwilling; so Yahweh relieves him of the responsibility of speech, and tells him that Aaron his brother shall speak for him. The way in which he phrases this assurance is noticeable:

Is not Aaron the Levite your brother? I know that he can speak well. . . . . And you shall speak to him and put words in his mouth: and I will be with your mouth and with his mouth and teach you what you shall do. And he shall be your spokesman unto the people; and he shall be to you instead of a mouth and you shall be to him instead of God [4:14–16].

This idea of a spokesman on behalf of another is identified with the conception of the prophet in the other passage to which reference has been made, Exod. 7:1, 2:

And Yahweh said to Moses, "See, I have made you as God to Pharaoh; and Aaron your brother shall be your spokesman [Heb. *nâvî'*, 'prophet']. You shall speak all that I command you; and Aaron your brother shall speak unto Pharaoh."

In the light of these and similar statements,[18] it is quite clear that the prophet was looked upon as one who declared the will of Yahweh to the people.

The prophet, however, was not thought of as in a state of continual inspiration. His divine illumination all too often faded into the light of common day. He was thought of rather as one who was susceptible of impressions from the world of the unseen, and so constituted an easy channel of communication between

[18] Cf. Jer. 1:9; Deut. 18:18.

two worlds. The coming of the "divine afflatus" upon the prophet was not subject to his own volition, but when it came he was a helpless victim of its power. The usual phrases indicative of the reception of the prophetic message are: "The hand of Yahweh was upon," or "came upon," or "fell upon," such and such a man;[19] and "the spirit of God came upon," or "rested," or "spake by," or "fell upon," the prophet.[20] The descent of the "hand of Yahweh" or the "spirit of Yahweh" upon a man or group of men transported them beyond the bounds of normal procedure. They were plunged into an ecstatic state in which they seemed to lose consciousness of the external world. When Saul upon his departure from Samuel met a company of prophets coming down from the high place and prophesying as they came along, he also was seized upon by the spirit of prophecy and was turned into another man, prophesying as the rest of the group were doing.[21] Later, when Saul and David had become estranged, Saul sent messengers to seize David at Naioth in Ramah; but the messengers found Samuel and a band of prophets prophesying around David, and they themselves were seized by the contagion of the prophetic spirit, and they too began to prophesy. This same experience befell two more bands of Saul's messengers. Then Saul went himself in person; but the

[19] I Kings 18:46; II Kings 3:15; Ezek. 1:3; 3:14; 8:1; 33:22; 37:1.

[20] Num. 11:25 f., 29; 24:2; I Sam. 10:6, 10; 11:6; 16:13; II Sam. 23:2; II Kings 2:9, 15, 16; Isa. 48:16; 61:1; Joel 2:28 f.; Ezek. 2:2; 11:5; II Chron. 24:20.

[21] I Sam. 10:5–13.

prophetic frenzy was no respecter of persons, and Saul found himself prophesying like the rest of the company. The description of his conduct on that occasion is significant because it tells not only what Saul did, but shows that his conduct was just like that of all the rest. "And he stripped off his clothes, and he also prophesied before Samuel and lay down naked all that day and all that night."[22] These two cases and the story of the four hundred prophets in the days of Ahab seem to indicate something like mass prophecy, in which what we call "mob psychology" played a large part. A similar ecstatic state seems to have overpowered Balaam when he was urged by Balak to curse Israel but could utter nothing but blessings:

The spirit of God came upon him. And he took up his parable and said:

> "The saying of Balaam the son of Beor,
> And the saying of the man whose eye is opened;
> The saying of him who hears the words of God,
> Who sees the vision of the Almighty,
> Fallen down, yet with opened eyes. . . . ."[23]

This same ecstatic condition is found elsewhere, as in the case of the unknown prophet of Byblos about 1100 B.C., who intervened in a state of frenzy in behalf of Wen-Amon, the Egyptian envoy to the court of Byblos.[24] The Mohammedan dervishes likewise are at times wrought up to a similar pitch of frenzied ecstasy. That this ecstatic state was characteristic of early

[22] I Sam. 19:19–24.   [23] Num. 24:2–4.

[24] See J. M. Powis Smith, *The Prophet and His Problems* (1914), pp. 12 ff.

prophecy is attested by the fact that the word for "prophesy" is used to describe the conduct of Saul after the "evil spirit from God" came upon him and transformed him into a lunatic;[25] and by the further fact that the word for "prophesy" and that for "insane," "crazy," parallel each other in Jer. 29:26. When one of the sons of the prophets was commissioned by Elisha to go to Ramoth Gilead and anoint Jehu king of Israel, Jehu's captains upon his return to their company wanted to know who the "mad fellow" was who had summoned him from the midst of their council of war.[26] Still further, as in the case of the dervish, so in that of the prophet, this state of prophetic ecstasy could be self-induced. Upon a critical occasion, when Jehoram, of Israel, and Jehoshaphat, of Judah, were in great need of divine help, they applied to Elisha for his prophetic aid. Elisha protested, but finally yielded to their wish, saying: " 'But now, bring me a minstrel.' And it came to pass that when the minstrel played the hand of Yahweh came upon him [viz., Elisha], and he said, 'Thus says Yahweh.' "[27] That prophecy waited upon music, at least at times, is also seen from the fact that the company of prophets whom Saul met coming down from the high place was equipped with "a psaltery, and a timbrel, and a pipe, and a harp," to the strains of which they were prophesying.[28]

These early prophets were recognizable, not only by

[25] I Sam. 18:10.

[26] II Kings 9:11.

[27] II Kings 3:1–19.

[28] I Sam. 10:5.

their strange conduct, but also by certain external
signs. Their manner of life in general was, at least in
some cases, patterned after the nomad's way of living.
Elijah was a typical nomad, living in seclusion on the
margin of the desert and flitting from place to place
with uncanny speed.[29] His later reincarnation, John
the Baptist, who perhaps modeled his way of living
after the traditional conception of Elijah, "had his
raiment of camel's hair, and a leathern girdle about
his loins; and his meat was locusts and wild honey."[30]
It seems practically certain that the early professional
prophets were marked or branded in some way so as to
indicate their calling to the eye. In I Kings 20:35–43
one of the "sons of the prophets" is represented as having disguised himself in order to entrap Ahab into self-
condemnation. When Ahab had put himself upon record, the prophet removed "the headband away from
his eyes, and the king of Israel discerned that he was
of the prophets." The king did not apparently recognize his person, but only his class. The headband thus
would seem to have covered up some brand upon the
forehead or some peculiar tonsure that characterized
prophets as such. The prevalence of the use of such
marks by the prophets is attested by Zech. 13:4–6,
where false prophets are charged with wearing "a
hairy mantle to deceive" and with branding their
hands in some way characteristic of the prophets.

How did these prophets obtain their living? It is

[29] For the standards of life cherished by the nomads see the story of
the Rechabites in Jer. 35:1–11.

[30] Matt. 3:4.

quite evident that they expected pay for their services, and were in the habit of receiving it. When Saul's servant proposed that Samuel, the seer, should be consulted with reference to the finding of the lost asses, Saul made objection on the ground that they had nothing with which to reward the seer for his services:

Saul said to his servant, "But behold, if we go, what shall we bring the man? for the bread is spent in our vessels, and there is no present to bring to the man of God. What have we?" And the servant answered Saul again and said, "Behold, I have here at hand the fourth part of a shekel of silver: that will I give to the man of God to tell us our way."

The small amount of the proposed gift[31] is significant of the value placed upon the seer's service. In like manner, when Jeroboam's son fell ill, the king sent his wife to consult Ahijah, the prophet, regarding the outcome of the sickness, and he instructed her to take with her as a gift to the prophet "ten loaves, and biscuits, and a cruse of honey."[32] When the king of Syria wished to know through Elisha how his own sickness was to terminate, he, too, sent a messenger with a present to the prophet; but it was a present worthy of a king.[33] Elisha steadfastly refused reward when Naaman, the Syrian, wished to show gratitude for his healing from leprosy, though Gehazi, Elisha's servant, was not so self-denying.[34] The general opinion of the times with reference to the prophets' desire for money is vividly illustrated

[31] I Sam. 9:7, 8. A quarter of a shekel was worth about 15 cents; but its purchasing power today is far less than it was in ancient times.

[32] I Kings 14:3.

[33] II Kings 8:7-9.   [34] II Kings 5:15-27.

by the story in Amos 7:10–17. When Amos announced the approaching downfall of the house of Jeroboam, the chief priest at Bethel sent word to the king charging Amos with conspiracy against him, and then suggested in insinuating and insulting language that Amos go back home to Judah, where such preaching would be heartily welcomed and be richly rewarded, for disaster threatening Israel would be good news in Judah. This stirred Amos to a denial of any connection between himself and the professional prophets of his day. They might be, and doubtless were, actuated by self-seeking motives, but he was driven to his work by the power of the spirit of Yahweh.

As we look back upon the facts here gathered regarding the prophetic movement in early Israel, we cannot escape the conviction that these forerunners of the great prophets were to a great extent like prophets and seers in non-Hebraic countries.[35] There is the same ecstatic frenzy, the same type of soothsaying, or foretelling, and the same tendency to commercialize their calling. No historical movement, however, is to be judged by its mere beginnings, but rather by its outcome. What did it ultimately contribute to human betterment? Prophecy may safely permit itself to be estimated by the same standard. The prophecy of early Israel met the needs of its day; that age was not yet ready for anything more exalted. This early prophetic movement already revealed some characteristics that were to mark the entire history of prophecy. It

35 See Smith, *op. cit.*, pp. 3–35.

represented the conviction that the course of history was in the hand of God, who had a purpose and plan for his people. It believed that this divine plan was from time to time revealed step by step to certain men who were in the confidence of God. It, therefore, sought with all its power to lead the people and the leaders to follow in the path indicated by the prophets. Prophecy's predominant interest from the start was in the progress of the community or nation, rather than in that of the individual. Individuals were of significance only in so far as they vitally affected the life of the people as a whole. It is noteworthy how many times in early Israel prophecy is brought into connection with events and persons of national significance. The first reference to the prophetic movement in its organized form speaks of the company of the prophets as coming down from the "hill of God," where there was "a garrison of the Philistines."[36] It is not, perhaps, assuming too much to suppose that their prophesying at that particular time was closely connected with the presence of the hated invaders. The prophets were keenly interested in the varying fortunes of the early monarchy and did not shrink from engaging actively in political affairs, helping to make and unmake kings as circumstances required. The names of Deborah, Samuel, Gad, Nathan, Ahijah, Jehu ben Hanani, Elijah, Elisha, and Micaiah ben Imlah all recall scenes in which national interests were involved; and, if these great leaders were engaged in political activities,

[36] I Sam. 10:5.

it is evident that the mass of their prophetic followers would be at least interested in similar matters. In the times of Saul and Ahab, at any rate, the masses of the prophetic movement were involved in the political situation.

There is no sharp break between the early prophets and the great prophets of later times. The transition from early prophecy to later was a process of normal, natural growth. The prophets grew with the nation. As the nation was more and more drawn into the whirl of international politics, the outlook of the prophets widened, their faith deepened, and the nature of their prophesying gradually underwent a transformation. Certain fundamental characteristics were retained to the end, but one has only to compare the mad fellows of Saul's day with the serious thoughtfulness and rational methods of men such as Habakkuk and Jeremiah to realize the immense distance that separates Israel's great prophecy from its crude beginnings. The study of the psychology of prophecy has been an important source of enhancement of our understanding of the Old Testament through these last twenty-five years, leading to results, among others, such as already sketched in this chapter in regard to the ecstatic character of the movement in Saul's days. The superficial similarity of this to incidents like Isaiah's great experience related in the sixth chapter of his Book was immediately apparent; so there arose a tendency to regard prophecy as essentially an aspect of abnormal psychology, to be understood only in the light of trance experiences. But the striking fact of our prophetic books is how little of this is actually recorded. Apart from this narrative in the Book of Isaiah, and several features of the Book of Ezekiel which must be seriously qualified by the discussion of that Book to which we shall presently go on, there is practically nothing that carries an a priori presumption of ecstatic experience. It must be demonstrated that Zechariah's revelations are anything more than a literary device, and one would be blind to the patent meaning of the account who would postulate ecstasy of Amos' "visions."[37] Jeremiah's "call"[38] is but the deep experience of religious awakening of a serious-minded adolescent; and elsewhere the ecstatic experience can be claimed only by a process of reading in one's theory rather than accepting the plain meanings of the account. Moreover, it has long been seen that it is a *reductio ad absurdum* to claim that every prophetic utterance was preceded by a trance. As a result of all this there has grown up in recent years a notable reserve in regard to the ecstatic element in the canonical prophets.[39] It

[37] Amos 7:1-9; 8:1-3; 9:1-4; cf. Artur Weiser, *Die Profetie des Amos* (1929).

[38] Jer. 1:1-19.

[39] See, e.g., T. H. Robinson, *Prophecy and the Prophets in Ancient Israel* (1925), p. 45, and *History of Israel* (1932), pp. 368 f., 405 f.; W. O. E. Oesterley and T. H. Robinson, *Hebrew Religion* (1930), p. 193; Elmer A. Leslie, *Old Testament Religion in the Light of Its Canaanite Background* (1936), pp. 167 f.; L. E. Binns, *The Book of the Prophet Jeremiah* (1919), p. xxxvi, § 4; T. H. Robinson and Friedrich Horst, *Die zwölf kleinen Propheten* (1936-38); cf., too, A. Bertholet, *Hesekiel* (1936), pp. xvi-xvii; A. Heschel, *Die Prophetie* (1936), pp. 26 f.; A. Bentzen, *Daniel* (1937), pp. iv-v.; J. Lindblom, "Die Religion der Propheten und die

would appear that we are, instead, to understand them
as great religious thinkers and leaders. At the most
they were mystics rather than ecstatics, as such possessing close interrelations with the religious experience
through all subsequent ages; and of some of them even
this measure of unusual experience seems rare, if ex-
istent. Briefly, the psychology of the canonical prophets was a normal religious psychology. And their inspiration was of a rich and varied source; poetic fervor,
moral earnestness and intolerance, quiet musing, in-
tellectual clarity, political acumen, even at times a
stubborn conservatism and fear of change or an opposite radicalism, love of country and of one's people,
but all touched and sublimated by a certainty of the
reality and righteousness of God—here is the elemental
stuff of the prophetic thinking which crystallized in the
incomparable utterances of our Books of the Prophets,
and made of their times one of the great epochs in the
history of the human spirit. The prophets felt themselves to be in a very real sense partners with Yahweh
in his great work, they expected to hear his voice of
inspiration and instruction, and they heard it.

Mystik," *Zeitschrift für die alttestamentliche Wissenschaft*, LVII (1939),
65 f.; J. E. McFadyen, *The People and the Book* (1925), pp. 206–8;
W. F. Albright, *From the Stone Age to Christianity* (1940), pp. 234,
238–40; Norman W. Porteous, in *Record and Revelation* (1938), pp. 225–
37.

CHAPTER II

PROPHETIC LEADERS AND THE UNITED KINGDOM

IN THIS chapter we shall consider the work of four prominent prophets whose activity fell in the years of the united kingdom and in the period of preparation for it. These leaders were individuals who worked in more or less close co-operation with the great company of the sons of the prophets, but by their individual initiative and force took an outstanding position among their fellows, and so left their names permanently impressed upon the memory of their people.

The first of these was a woman, Deborah, the wife of Lapidoth,[1] one of the few women to function as a religious leader in Israel.[2] Her lot was cast in troublous times.[3] The nomadic Hebrews had come in from the

---

[1] Judg. 4:4.

[2] The title "prophetess" is applied elsewhere to the following women only: Miriam (Exod. 15:20), the individual mentioned in Isa. 8:3, Huldah (II Kings 22:14), and Noadiah (Neh. 6:14). But a considerable class of women as well, apparently some sort of workers of magic, are described in Ezek. 13:17 by a form of the Hebrew verb "to prophesy."

[3] The story of her influence is contained in Judges, chaps. 4 and 5. The fifth chapter is generally regarded as one of the earliest documents preserved in the Old Testament. It is a paean of triumph over the defeat of the embattled Canaanites at the hands of the people of Israel. It is great poetry and invaluable for history. The fourth chapter of Judges is a prose narrative, dealing, at least in part, with the same situa-

15

desert regions in such numbers and had taken possession of so much Canaanitish territory that they were
fast becoming a menace to the Canaanites. The Canaanites were therefore restricting their expansion and
pressing them hard, striving to render them impotent.
At this juncture Deborah took action. She was evidently a well-known woman. She was in the habit of
seating herself beneath a tree and there announcing
oracles upon all sorts of questions brought to her for

---

tion as that celebrated in chap. 5. But it is of later origin and is apparently a composite narrative. The differences between chaps. 4 and 5
are most naturally accounted for on that basis. In chap. 4 the leader of
the Canaanites is Jabin, king of Canaan, while Sisera is his commander-
in-chief; but in chap. 5 Sisera is evidently presented as king in his own
right and Jabin is not mentioned. As a matter of fact, except for the
period of the Egyptian domination, we know of no such unity in pre-
Israelite Canaan as to make a "king of Canaan" a possibility. In chap.
5 all the tribes around the plain of Esdraelon are represented as engaged in the conflict, while in chap. 4 only Zebulon and Naphtali
participate. In chap. 5 Sisera receives his deathblow while awake and
standing up, but in chap. 4 he is slain while lying down asleep. According to chap. 5, the battle was fought in the plain of Esdraelon, near
Taanach and Megiddo (Judg. 5:19); but chap. 4 places the struggle
at the foot of Mount Tabor (Judg. 4:12-14), 15-20 miles farther north
and east as the bird flies. From facts such as these it is generally con-
cluded, not only that the prose story has received some later editorial
touching-up, but also that the narrative is the result of the mixture and
confusion of two separate accounts. One of these was apparently a record of the battle also recorded in Josh. 11:1-15, where Jabin again
appears as the leader of the Canaanites. The other was a later narrative
of the struggle recounted in chap. 5. The situation out of which the
song of Deborah arose is quite clear. For further discussion of this
question see the commentaries on Judges, by George F. Moore (1895),
G. A. Cooke (1913), E. L. Curtis (1913), and C. F. Burney (1918).
Of. W. F. Albright, *Bulletin of American Schools of Oriental Research*,
No. 62 (1936), pp. 20-31.

answer.[4] Her ability in such matters had obtained for her great prestige throughout the surrounding country. As she saw the pitiable plight to which her people were being reduced, she resolved to risk all upon a great move. She therefore selected the best available leader, Barak, the son of Abinoam, from Kedesh-Naphtali, and commissioned him in the name of Yahweh to raise a force and strike for freedom. The confidence placed by Barak in Deborah as the representative and mouth-piece of Yahweh was shared by the people at large, and in the power of the faith in Yahweh which she inspired a decisive defeat was inflicted upon the Canaanites. The fact that the Kishon overflowed its banks at this very time and helped the Israelites rout the foe made the defeat more complete, and gave the Israelites re-newed assurance that they were acting in line with the will of Yahweh and that he was co-operating with them.

The contribution of Deborah, the prophetess, was that she saw that it was time to act, that she chose the right leader for the action, and that she stimulated the faith and courage of Israel to the winning-point. She created the morale needed for the situation. That hers was no easy task is quite evident. The song not only sounds the praises of the loyal Israelites who risked their lives and property by joining in the effort for freedom, but it also calls down curses upon those who should have responded to the call for aid but did not. Some of the recalcitrants were in a position to realize

Judg. 4:4, 5.

the situation vividly and to reap richly of the fruits of the victory; but they were cowards. Reuben, Gilead, Dan, and Asher are chided for their indifference and failure to co-operate; but against Meroz the poet's wrath blazes forth fiercely, for Meroz was right in the heart of the oppressed region and had much to gain; but nothing moved Meroz to action:

> "Curse ye Meroz," said the angel of Yahweh,
> "Curse ye bitterly the inhabitants thereof,
>   Because they came not to the help of Yahweh,
>   To the help of Yahweh against the mighty."

The struggle represented a movement for political independence, a desire for economic liberty to expand, and a confidence in Yahweh as willing and able to obtain for his people all that they needed and desired. Deborah stood forth as the embodiment of both patriotism and religion. The victory seems to have had far-reaching consequences in the Hebrew struggle with the Canaanites. We know of no further attempts of this nature to subjugate Israel.

Conditions in Israel had changed by the time of the appearance of Samuel, the next outstanding figure among the prophets.[5] The role of oppressor, relin-

---

[5] The account of Samuel's life is given in the first Book of Samuel. It is not, however, a single continuous story. The Books of Samuel are, like the Hexateuch, a composite product. General agreement obtains among scholars upon this proposition; but there is much variation of opinion upon the detailed working-out of the process of analysis into the original sources. But again, there is close agreement as to what is early and what is late in the narratives of the life and work of Samuel; and that is all that concerns us here. The early narratives concerning

quished by the Canaanites, was now taken by the Philistines, an Aegean people who had settled on the Maritime Plain and bade fair to overrun all Palestine. Samuel's task was that of inspiring and organizing the Hebrews to undertake the struggle with the Philistines for independence.

The danger from the Canaanites was probably a thing of the past by the time of Samuel's birth. While he was growing up, a new foe had appeared upon the

Samuel are quite generally accepted as the following: I Sam. 9:1— 10:16; 16:1–13; 25:1. However, there has developed recently a skepticism as to the historical worth of 9:1—10:16; it is seen that this section contains largely legendary material and inaccurate interpretations that are out of harmony with the certainly reliable accounts in subsequent chapters. And the story of Samuel's annointing David in 16:1–13 is dubious from several points of view. This leaves us with very little historical material of the first order upon which to base an interpretation of Samuel—in fact nothing but 25:1, which tells us that he died and was buried! Under the circumstances we must have recourse to the next layer of materials and select from them what seems most likely to be approximately trustworthy. This later matter includes I Samuel, chaps. 1–3; 7:1–17; 8:1–22; 11:14 f.; chap. 15; 19:18–24. See for a discussion of these questions the commentaries on Samuel by H. P. Smith (1899), A. R. S. Kennedy (1905), W. Caspari (1926), and also J. A. Bewer, *The Literature of the Old Testament* (1933); S. R. Driver, *Introduction to the Literature of the Old Testament* (1914); W. O. E. Oesterley and T. H. Robinson, *Introduction to the Books of the Old Testament* (1934); O. Eissfeldt, *Einleitung in das Alte Testament* (1934); H. Gressmann, *Die älteste Geschichtsschreibung und Prophetie Israels* ("Die Schriften des Alten Testaments," Vol. II, No. 1), pp. 1 ff.; A. Lods, *Israel from the Beginning to the Middle of the Eighth Century B.C.* (1932), pp. 352–56; G. B. Gray, *A Critical Introduction to the Old Testament* (1913); S. A. Cook, *Critical Notes on Old Testament History* (1913); Richard Press, "Der Prophet Samuel: Eine traditionsgeschichtliche Untersuchung," *Zeitschrift für die alttestamentliche Wissenschaft,* LVI (1938), 177–225.

scene in the person of the Philistines.[6] They were an aggressive people, and they rapidly made for themselves a large place in Palestine. They were apparently in a fair way to reduce their Israelite neighbors to vassalage. Indeed, we are told in I Sam. 13:19–22 that the Philistine oppression had proceeded so far that the making of agricultural implements and weapons of war had been prohibited by them in Israel, so that the trade of "smith" had fallen into abeyance among the Hebrews. Another narrative, which is probably based upon old records regarding the Ark,[7] tells of two defeats of the Hebrews by the Philistines in the second of which the Ark was captured and carried off into Philistine territory. When pestilence broke out among the Philistines, it was naturally attributed to the anger of the foreign god whose shrine had been thus desecrated; and so the Ark was returned by the Philistines with offerings of propitiation. Amid stirring events like this the young Samuel grew up. These disasters and accompanying acts of oppression constituted the themes of conversation among the groups of patriotic Hebrews surrounding him. Such events fed the fires of his youthful patriotism and did much to arouse in him the spirit of prophecy.

The fact that Samuel made a deep impression upon

[6] For a good history of the Philistines see R. A. Stewart Macalister, *The Philistines—Their History and Civilization* ("Schweich Lectures" [1911]; London: Oxford University Press, 1913). Cf. H. R. Hall in *Cambridge Ancient History*, II (1926), chap. xii.

[7] I Sam. 4:1—6:21.

his times is shown by the large amount of traditional material that gathered about his name and has been perpetuated unto this day. Samuel, chapters 1–3, seems to be a section from a collection of legendary lives of the prophets, made, perhaps, somewhere about the time of the Deuteronomic reform under King Josiah. Here we are told of the birth of Samuel in answer to the agonizing prayer of Hannah, his mother, and her vow to dedicate her boy, if her prayer is granted, to the service of Yahweh in his temple at Shiloh. Loyal to her vow, she takes the child at the earliest possible moment that he can dispense with his mother's care and leaves him in the sanctuary at Shiloh under the care of Eli, the priest. Her mother-love found touching expression in the making of a little mantle or cloak every year which she took to her child upon the occasion of the annual pilgrimage to the festival at Shiloh. Samuel, meantime, "grew in favour both with Yahweh and also with men." Finally, while still a boy, he received his first message from Yahweh in the form of an announcement of the overthrow of Eli and his house on account of the sins of Eli's two sons, Hophni and Phinehas. This wonderful child

. . . . grew and Yahweh was with him, and did let none of his words fall to the ground. And all Israel from Dan even to Beersheba knew that Samuel was established as a prophet of Yahweh. And Yahweh appeared again in Shiloh; for Yahweh revealed himself to Samuel in Shiloh in the word of Yahweh. And the word of Samuel came to all Israel.[8]

[8] I Sam. 3:19—4:1a.

Not only so, but chapter 7 goes on to tell of a miraculous overthrow of the Philistines at Mizpeh, as a result of which

. . . . the Philistines were subdued, and they came no more into the border of Israel, and the hand of Yahweh was against the Philistines all the days of Samuel; and the cities which the Philistines had taken from Israel were restored to Israel from Ekron even unto Gath; and the borders thereof did Israel deliver out of the hands of the Philistines.[9]

Thus Samuel is made the deliverer of his people once for all from the power of the oppressor.

Much of the foregoing narrative is lacking in historical verisimilitude. At two points, in particular, it is subject to correction on the basis of earlier narratives. Samuel did not expel the Philistines from the territory of Israel, for that great task was left for the young King Saul to enter upon. Indeed, we are told that "there was sore war against the Philistines all the days of Saul";[10] and Saul's last fight with the Philistines brought him defeat and death.[11] Not until the reign of David were the Philistines finally brought to terms.[12] In like manner the early influence of Samuel is greatly magnified. Instead of "the word of Samuel" coming "to all Israel," he seems to have been known at first throughout only a quite limited area. We read in I Sam. 7:16 f. that Samuel's home was at Ramah and that from there he went out annually on a circuit that included Bethel, Gilgal, and Mizpeh, at which points

9 I Sam. 7:13–14.   11 I Sam. 31:1–6.

10 I Sam. 14:52.   12 II Sam. 8:1; 23:9–17.

he "judged Israel." These names, with Shiloh added, represent a territory at the most not more than 20 miles from north to south and 2 miles from east to west. Not only so, but when Saul's servant spoke to him of Samuel as a seer who could tell him what had become of the lost asses, Saul apparently was hearing about Samuel for the first time[13]—and that notwithstanding the fact that Saul's home at Gibeah was but a short distance from Samuel's headquarters. This would certainly be inconceivable if Samuel had occupied such a place in the public mind as the later stories assign to him.

At another point, also, the later records seem to misrepresent Samuel. The desire on the part of Israel for a king is represented as having displeased Samuel to such a degree that Yahweh had to overrule him and order him to comply with the people's request.[14] The chapter in which this point of view appears was written by an author who disapproved of the institution of the monarchy and wrote against the background of a long history of the monarchy in Israel. There are three accounts of the anointing of Saul as king. In the first, he is selected by Samuel privately, at the instigation of Yahweh, is anointed secretly, and accepts reluctantly, being distrustful of his prestige and his influence over the people.[15] In the second account, Samuel is represented as having summoned all the tribes of Israel unto Mizpeh, where he casts lots until the lot falls upon

[13] I Sam. 9:5 ff., 18 f.

[14] I Sam. 8:1–22.   [15] Sam. 9:1—10:9.

Saul, who, when found hiding among the baggage, is dragged forth and anointed publicly amid the acclamations of the people.[16] This is quite evidently a part of the later tradition, for it shows Samuel as holding the same attitude of hostility to the monarchy as was seen in I Samuel, chapter 8. In the third record, Saul is seen as a bold patriot who rises to the occasion when a call comes from the men of Jabesh Gilead for help against the Ammonites, who are about to devastate their city. Saul sends out a ringing challenge to the surrounding country that meets with a hearty response, organizes the volunteers into three divisions, falls suddenly upon the Ammonites from three directions, and utterly routs them. In grateful enthusiasm the people hail Saul as king and proceed to Gilgal, where they "made him king before Yahweh," and rejoiced greatly.[17] Samuel appears here after the victory as the one who proposes the public ratification of Saul's kingship.[18] This note is in such close keeping with the point of view in I Sam. 10:25–27 that it is quite generally looked upon as an editorial addition made to bring this narrative of anointing into harmony with the one in 1 Sam. 10:17–27. In the first and third of these coronation stories the anointing of Saul grows directly out of the disturbed political and military situation, and both of them may be essentially correct. In the first, Samuel fires the young patriot with a holy and patriotic zeal to deliver his people. In the third, the oppor-

[16] I Sam. 10:17–27.

[17] I Sam. 11:1–11, 15.   [18] I Sam. 11:12–14.

tunity presents itself to strike a telling blow for liberty
and for Yahweh; and Saul rushes to the defense of
Jabesh Gilead and thus earns his position as king. The
first story in which Samuel anoints Saul in private may
possibly be due to the growth of prophetic tradition
which claimed for itself all the honor it could. There
are elements in the story that look like the work of the
later prophetic mind; but, in the absence of positive
proof to the contrary, we may well allow Samuel credit
for initiating in Saul's mind the dream of freeing his
people from their oppressors.

The next occasion upon which we meet Samuel is in
connection with the rejection of Saul as king. Of this
event there are also two accounts. In I Samuel, chapter
13, Saul is repudiated by Samuel for a reason that does
not clearly appear. In I Samuel, chapter 15, the rejection is based upon the fact that Saul has not carried out
faithfully the command of Yahweh to exterminate the
Amalekites. But the explanation of the rejection given
in I Sam. 13:7b–15a is that Saul, after mustering his
forces for an attack upon the Philistines, grew impatient over Samuel's failure to keep his appointment,
and so proceeded to offer the sacrifices necessary before
launching battle against the foe without waiting longer
for the delinquent prophet. At this juncture Samuel
appeared and proceeded to read Saul out of the kingship. The reason given is that Saul has "not kept the
commandment" of Yahweh. If the fact that he had
sacrificed with his own hands constituted his offense in
the eyes of this narrator, then he must have written
very late; for other laymen are represented as offering

sacrifice without offense, e.g., David, Solomon, and Elijah. There was no law against the offering of sacrifice by a layman until the adoption of the Deuteronomic Code in the days of King Josiah. Hence these verses in chapter 13 are rightly treated as of late origin by most modern interpreters.[19] The story of the rejection in chapter 15 is to the effect that Samuel communicated to Saul the order of Yahweh that he should destroy Amalek, leaving neither human being nor animal alive, but devoting the whole people and all that they possessed as a *herem* to Yahweh. Saul, however, brought back some of the livestock as spoil and led the captive King Agag in triumph back to Gilgal. There he encountered Samuel, who rebuked him for his disregard of the divine command, saying to him:

> Does Yahweh delight in burnt offerings and sacrifices
> As in hearkening to the voice of Yahweh?
> Verily, to hearken is better than sacrifice,
> To give heed than the fat of rams.
> For disobedience is as the sin of divination,
> And presumption is as the guilt of the teraphim.
> Because thou hast rejected the word of Yahweh,
> He has rejected thee from being king over Israel.[20]

Thereupon Samuel "hewed Agag in pieces before Yahweh in Gilgal." The point of view and spirit of this narrative are primitive enough, surely, to warrant relatively early origin. There is every reason to suppose that here we are in touch with reality—that a

[19] So, e.g., H. P. Smith, Kennedy, Caspari, *op. cit.*, and the commentaries of K. Budde and W. Nowack, *ad loc.;* but cf. Eissfeldt, *op. cit.*, p. 308; R. Kittel, *Geschichte des Volkes Israel*, II (1925), 86.

[20] I Sam. 15:22, 23.

vivid picture of the thought and feeling of Samuel's day is flashed before us. It seems altogether reasonable to accept the attack upon Amalek and the disagreement between Samuel and Saul as to the treatment of the spoil and the captive king as actual historical facts. This account, in any case, attests the fact that Saul lost the powerful support of Samuel, who absented himself from the court of Saul for the rest of his days.

In I Sam. 16:1–13, Samuel is represented as going to the home of Jesse, the Bethlehemite, and there anointing David, one of Jesse's sons, as king of Israel in place of Saul. Scholars in general rightly regard this section as of later origin.[21] It grew out of the later feeling with reference to David. David must be Yahweh's anointed, and Samuel of all men must anoint him. The only other contact of Samuel with David is related in I Sam. 19:18–24, but this, too, is a product of the later prophetic tradition.[22] Samuel's farewell speech[23] upon the anointing of Saul is also to be assigned to a later homilizing spirit. The attitude of hostility toward the monarchy in itself is here again attributed to Samuel without due warrant. But the challenge that Samuel is made to throw out to his people—to the effect that he defies anyone to accuse him of what we today call "grafting"—is doubtless grounded upon a sound tradition. Samuel was too true a patriot to have sought to enrich himself at the expense of his fellow-citizens.

[21] See Budde, H. P. Smith, Kennedy, Kittel, Dhorme, Cornill, and Nowack, *loc. cit.*

[22] See commentaries, *ad loc.*

[23] I Samuel, chap. 12.

The great merit of Samuel was that he saw the need of his times, found the man capable of meeting that need, and inspired in him the courage and faith necessary for the successful accomplishment of his task. The importance of his contribution to the history of Israel is shown by the large amount of tradition that gathered about his name. It is impossible with any appreciable degree of accuracy to sift the legendary from the historically valid in the mass of later tradition; but it is clear that Samuel did so great a work in his own day that the memory of it grew with succeeding generations. The two characteristics that may safely be predicated of him are his vital faith in his people's God and his keen political insight. These two qualities combined to make him a leader and a prophet.

The prophet Gad was a contemporary and an adviser of David, both before and after he became king His name appears only twice in the Books of Samuel. The first reference to him represents him as urging David to stay no longer in Mizpeh in the land of Moab,[24] whither he had fled to escape the wrath of Saul, but to return to the land of Judah.[25] This shows that Gad had cast in his lot with David and against Saul and that he was therefore a faithful supporter not driven away by the hard lot of David during the last years of King Saul. The second appearance of Gad is after David had taken the census of all Israel. Now he comes forward as a spokesman of Yahweh's wrath

[24] Reading with the Syriac text "Mizpeh" instead of "the hold" as in Hebrew; see commentaries, *ad loc.*

[25] I Sam. 22:5.

against the king.[26] The narrative in which Gad figures is quite naïve in its thought of Yahweh. Yahweh is said to have been angered against Israel (though no occasion is cited for his wrath), so he stirred up David to take a census of his people. This David arranged to carry out, though the wise Joab and his subordinate officers counseled him against what was evidently thought of as an impious procedure. No sooner was the census complete than David's conscience smote him for his wickedness. Just at this juncture the prophet Gad, David's seer, felt himself inspired to speak to David in the name of Yahweh, offering him a choice of seven years of famine, or three months of defeat and pursuit at the hands of his enemies, or three days of pestilence. David selects the pestilence, which forthwith falls upon the people, carrying off seventy thousand men. David saw the angel of Yahweh that had charge of the work of destruction and besought him for mercy upon Israel. Thereupon Gad again appeared in David's presence and instructed him to build an altar to Yahweh on the threshing floor of Araunah the Jebusite, where he had seen the angel. Upon David's doing so and offering upon his altar burnt offerings and peace offerings, "Yahweh was entreated for the land and the plague was stayed from upon Israel."

This narrative is placed at a late date by most interpreters.[27] But there are elements in it that prevent us from putting it too late. The conception of Yahweh

[26] II Sam. 24:11–14.

[27] So, e.g., H. P. Smith, Kennedy, Budde, Nowack, and Caspari, *op. cit.*

here is quite unmoralized. He inspires David to undertake an enterprise,[28] and then punishes him through
his people for undertaking it. But the conception of
prophecy is relatively early. Gad is not afraid of the
king; he dares to appear in opposition to his course of
action and to serve as the mouthpiece of Yahweh's
wrath. But he utters no protest against the punishment
of the people for the offense of their king, and he bids
the king seek forgiveness through ritualistic measures.
In both of these respects Gad is far behind the standpoint of the great prophets of the eighth century B.C.
His criticism of the king, however, like that of Samuel,
prepared the way for the liberty accorded his greater
successors.

The last prophet of the Davidic age was Nathan.
Unfortunately, little of the material concerning him
can successfully claim an early origin. The story in II
Sam. 7:1–17 of Nathan's counsel to David, given as
the word of Yahweh, that he should not proceed to the
erection of a temple to Yahweh, but should leave that
task for his son, is quite generally assigned to the
seventh century B.C. or even later.[29] This means that it
is of but modest historical validity for the times and
events of which it purports to tell. A similar judgment
is generally passed upon the parable of the ewe lamb
which Nathan is said to have related to David after his

---

[28] Cf. the changed point of view in I Chron. 21:1.

[29] So, e.g., Kennedy, H. P. Smith, Budde, Kittel, Nowack, Caspari, *op. cit.;* also C. Cornill, *Introduction to the Canonical Books of the
Old Testament* (1907), p. 197.

sin with Bathsheba and his murder of Uriah.[30] But it is important to recognize the claims attributed to Nathan in this narrative. Just as Samuel, in his dealings with Saul, so Nathan as the representative of Yahweh sets himself above the king, calling him to account for his evil conduct. In this we have one of the great features of Hebrew prophecy. For them there was no doctrine that "the king could do no wrong"; the king was not above divine law, but, on the contrary, his responsible position made him amenable more than the average to the laws of God. And the prophets as spokesmen of Yahweh did not flinch from reproving and denouncing royal sinners, even though at risk and, in some cases, at the actual price of their lives. This reckless courage of the prophets of Israel in their service of truth is one of their priceless bequests to later ages. There remains, then, of the narrative regarding Nathan, to be safely ranked as early, only the statement in II Sam. 12:25 that he was responsible for giving Solomon the name Jedidiah, meaning "beloved of Yahweh," and the account in I Kings, chapter 1, of the proceedings connected with the accession of Solomon.

The narrative of Solomon's acquisition of the throne of Israel is vivid and natural, bearing the marks of its writer's close familiarity with the actual course of

[30] II Sam. 12:1–14. So, e.g., H. P. Smith, Budde, and Nowack; but Kennedy argues for an earlier date; and Caspari holds that the passage is basically early but expanded with Deuteronomic material. There is no reasonable basis for doubting a genuine historic nucleus in the story.

events. When David was near his end, Adonijah, his eldest son, took steps to assure himself of the possession of his father's throne by getting himself anointed and acclaimed king by a powerful group even while David was yet alive. But he reckoned without his host. Nathan, the prophet, learned of what was going on and hastened to Bathsheba, the mother of Solomon, and urged her to seek an interview with David and to remind him of his pledge to her that Solomon should succeed him upon the throne. Bathsheba carried out her instructions and told her story to David as directed. She was scarcely through when Nathan was announced. He took up the story of what Adonijah had done, reminded the king of his promise to Solomon's mother, and gently challenged the king to make good. The spirit of the dying king responded to this appeal with something of its old fire, and orders were given for the anointing of Solomon by Zadok the priest and Nathan the prophet. The result was that the movement of Adonijah collapsed and Solomon was firmly established on the throne. This story shows that Nathan had long had influence with David and that he had made common cause with Bathsheba and Solomon to the end that Solomon should reign in his father's stead.

The story speaks eloquently of the place that Nathan held in David's court. He had evidently been in the close confidence of the king for years. He was familiar with all the intrigues that were going on as the old king's strength failed. He himself knew the tricks of the politician's trade, and he did not hesitate to bring to bear upon David's mind and heart all the influence at his control. Solomon was quite evidently not the choice of all the people; Adonijah had a strong following; but the prestige of David's will and the influence of the aged prophet and the priest of the royal shrine were too much for Adonijah to overcome. Whether there were any strong or adequate moral or religious motives operative in Nathan's mind in these maneuvers we have no means of knowing. But the presumption is that Nathan was dominated by genuinely prophetic motives, which were not only political or patriotic but also profoundly religious.

CHAPTER III

PROPHECY AND THE SYRIAN WARS

THE newly born kingdom of Saul grew to manhood under King David, expanded to its full development under Solomon, and suffered disintegration under Rehoboam. The reign of Solomon swept Israel out into the stream of world-politics. Solomon's many foreign brides were the pledges of good faith in as many treaties. Solomon also encouraged foreign commerce, starting a sea trade on the Red Sea from a port in Edom to the land of Ophir,[1] in ships manned by Phoenician sailors, and building a "navy of Tarshish,"[2] which made the round trip in a period of three years. Not only did he trade by sea, but he also became a royal horse-merchant, trading in horses between Egypt and the northern kingdoms. One of the thrilling results of recent archeological work has been the discovery on the mound of Megiddo— hence close by one of the branches of the great ancient road through Palestine to the north—of a complex of buildings dated certainly to the time of Solomon and by their features identified as a stable capable of accommodating some three hundred horses. In a remarkable way the discovery has corroborated the brief

[1] I Kings 9:26; 10:11.   [2] I Kings 10:22.

statement in I Kings 10:28–29.[3] He was also a great builder, being credited with the erection of the Temple and of the even greater palace[4] and with the rebuilding and fortification of Gezer, Bethhoron the Lower, Hazor, Megiddo, where his huge palace-fortress compound with its parade ground was uncovered by excavators,[5] and the wall of Jerusalem.[6] All this activity and expenditure made necessary a heavy tax upon all the people and a large amount of forced labor.[7] In all this

[3] See P. L. O. Guy, *New Light from Armageddon* (1931), pp. 37–48; J. H. Breasted, *The Oriental Institute* ("University of Chicago Survey," Vol. XII [1933]), p. 255 and Figs. 125–26; R. S. Lamon and G. M. Shipton, *Megiddo* (1939), pp. 32–47.

[4] I Kings 6:38; 7:1.

[5] Lamon and Shipton, *op. cit.*, pp. 8–61.

[6] I Kings 9:15 ff.

[7] I Kings 5:13–18; 9:15–23; 11:26 ff. The Lucianic text of the Septuagint adds materials here that are not in the Hebrew text. The flight of Jeroboam in the latter is placed immediately after his interview with Ahijah, the implication being that Solomon had heard of this meeting and had sought to arrest Jeroboam. Nothing is said of any overt movement toward the revolt at this time. The Lucianic account comes directly after 12:24 and makes Jeroboam to have organized a rebellion, at the head of a force of three hundred chariots. When Solomon sought to kill him he took refuge in Egypt, whence he returned after the death of Solomon to organize revolt against Rehoboam. In the midst of these activities he is met by a prophet, named Shemaiah, who prophesies the disruption and promises Jeroboam the kingship of the ten tribes. For a critical attack upon the value of the Lucianic text see E. Meyer, *Die Israeliten und ihrer Nachbarstämme* (1906), pp. 363–70; and B. Stade and F. Schwally, *The Books of Kings* ("Sacred Books of the Old Testament," [1904]), p. 130. For a critical defense see A. T. Olmstead, *American Journal of Semitic Languages and Literatures*, XXX (1913), 15 ff.

Solomon was following the example of the great kings of the Orient and especially the pharaohs of Egypt. The burden was certainly heavy notwithstanding that Solomon was a shrewd businessman, and, as well, we know from recent investigation of a very rich source of wealth exploited by him: nothing less, indeed, than copper, and perhaps iron, mines in the land of Edom south of the Dead Sea.[8] And Solomon's interest in Ezion-Geber, at the head of the Gulf of Akabah, was not confined to its relation to his shipping; for excavation of the ancient mound has revealed ancient copper-smelting works from his time.[9] Evidently, the ore from farther up the valley, as well as, perhaps, some of the plentiful supply near the head of the gulf was carried down to the metal works in the ancient port and there refined.

Taxation is never popular, and forced labor is always resented. It is only what might be expected, therefore, when we find that rebellion broke out in

[8] Nelson Glueck, "King Solomon's Copper Mines," *Illustrated London News*, July 7, 1934; "Explorations in Eastern Palestine," *Annual of American Schools of Oriental Research*, Vol. XV (1935); "The Recently Discovered Ore Disposits in Eastern Palestine" and "Report on Specimens of Ore and Slag from Eastern Palestine," *Bulletin of American Schools of Oriental Research*, No. 63 (1936), pp. 4–8; *The Other Side of the Jordan* (1940), chap. iii.

[9] N. Glueck, "King Solomon's Naval Base at Ezion Geber," *Illustrated London News*, July 30, 1938; "The First Campaign at Tel el-Kheleifeh (Ezion Geber, Elath)," *Bulletin of American Schools of Oriental Research*, No. 71 (1938); "The Topography and History of Ezion Geber and Elath," *Bulletin of American Schools of Oriental Research*, Vol. LXXII (1938); "The Second Campaign at Tel el-Kheleifeh," *Bulletin of American Schools of Oriental Research*, No. 75 (1939); *The Other Side of the Jordan*, chap. iv.

Solomon's own day. The leader of the movement was Jeroboam, one of Solomon's overseers of his levy or *corvée*. The rebellion was unsuccessful, and Jeroboam had to flee to Egypt until the death of Solomon.[10]

Either before his flight to Egypt, or soon after his return, Jeroboam encountered the prophet Ahijah, of Shiloh. Ahijah had put on a new cloak for the occasion. This he stripped off and rent into fragments, handing ten of them to Jeroboam, saying: "Take thee ten pieces: for thus says Yahweh the God of Israel, 'Behold, I will rend the kingdom out of the hand of Solomon, and will give ten tribes to thee.' "[11] There is no adequate reason for doubting the participation of the prophets in the revolt of Jeroboam. They were always vitally interested in the welfare of their people and the conduct of their kings. It is almost inconceivable that a great movement like this should have taken place in Israel and the prophets have kept silence throughout its progress. This was precisely the sort of thing most likely to arouse them to frenzy. As Samuel was behind Saul and David, and as Nathan supported Solomon, so in all probability prophecy in the person of Ahijah cast in its lot with Jeroboam. It is hardly likely that in that day an aspirant for the throne would have proceeded far without the support of some recognized representative of Yahweh. The prophets would almost inevitably be in opposition to the continuation of Solomon's general policy. They were enthusiastic supporters of the ideals of the nomadic life and looked

10 See n. 7, p. 35.   11 I Kings 11:29–32.

with hostility upon the increasing luxury and effeminacy of the civilized life in Canaan. They would certainly be outraged by the presence of the shrines for foreign gods in Jerusalem which Solomon had provided for his imported wives. It is not at all likely that Ahijah's support of Jeroboam was an invention of later prophetic writers, when we recall that these later prophets denounced the disruption as directly contrary to the will of Yahweh.[12] We therefore are fairly safe in accepting this record of Ahijah's participation in the revolt as essentially correct.[13] Ahijah appears in action again only in I Kings 14:1 ff. where he predicts the death of Jeroboam's boy. This may possibly be symptomatic of a later breach between Jeroboam and Ahijah, but here conjecture only is possible.[14]

The next prophetic name appears in the reign of Baasha and is that of Jehu, son of Hanani.[15] The narrative regarding him is late; and all that can safely be inferred from the story is the name of the prophet and perhaps the fact that he was a hostile critic of King Baasha. The outstanding fact in Baasha's reign is that

[12] See Hos. 8:4; 13:11; I Kings, chap. 13, and 14:1–18.

[13] But see, per contra, H. P. Smith, *Old Testament History* (1903), pp. 177 ff., where no allusion is made to Ahijah; similar silence is observed by B. Stade, *Geschichte* (1887), pp. 344 ff.; A. T. Olmstead (*History of Palestine and Syria* [1931], p. 351) accepts the Lucianic account, frankly attributing Jeroboam's seditious behavior to suggestion by the prophet Shemaiah.

[14] The narratives concerning Ahijah have been greatly expanded by later Deuteronomic editors. The oldest materials are confined to I Kings 11:26–32a, and 14:1–6, 17 f.

[15] I Kings 16:1–7.

his attacks upon Judah led Asa, king of Judah, to hire the aid of Benhadad, king of Syria; and so Syria began the series of attacks upon Israel which opened the long-drawn-out struggle between Syria and Israel.

Our next known prophets are found in the reign of Ahab, in the first half of the ninth century B.C. Ahab's father, Omri, had begun to make a large place for Israel among the small kings of western Asia.   It is significant that the Assyrian inscriptions spoke of Israel as "the land of Omri" long after Omri's death.[16] Omri left a strong kingdom to his son, and Ahab proceeded to make it stronger and richer. He made an alliance with Phoenicia by marrying Jezebel, the daughter of Ethbaal, king of Sidon; and Judah also was in alliance with him either voluntarily or as a vassal.[17] His relations with Syria seem to have varied greatly. At times peace prevailed between the two peoples, at other times they were fighting fiercely against each other, and at still other times they are found fighting as allies against a common foe.

It is fairly safe to say that the outstanding interest of Ahab was in the foreign relations of his kingdom. His alliances with Syria, Phoenica, and Judah and his frequent wars make that clear. The great antagonist during most of his reign was Syria. He inherited war with Syria from his father, and the alliances with Phoenicia and Judah were probably aimed directly at her. The

---

[16] Adad-nirari III (810–782 B.C.) and Tiglath-Pileser III (746–728 B.C.) both speak of Israel by that name.

[17] I Kings 22:2 ff.

Old Testament record of the Syrian wars is almost certainly incomplete. The insolent message of Benhadad in I Kings 20:3 f. presupposes the subservience of Israel, which certainly could not have been counted upon or acknowledged unless previous events had put Israel in the power of Syria. Two battles are recorded in I Kings, chapter 20, between Ahab and Benhadad, both of which resulted in Benhadad's defeat. After the second defeat a treaty of peace was made between them, by the terms of which Benhadad restored to Ahab certain cities which Omri had been compelled to hand over to Syria, and also gave Israel the right to certain trading privileges in Damascus.[18] These battles may perhaps be put fairly early in the reign of Ahab, though we have only the name of the Syrian king to guide us as to the date.[19]

However, in 854 B.C.[20] a new and greater enemy appeared in western Asia, viz., Shalmaneser III, king of

[18] I Kings 20:34.

[19] See D. D. Luckenbill, "Benhadad and Hadadezer," *American Journal of Semitic Languages and Literatures*, XXVII (1910), 267–84.

[20] For the chronology of this period see Emil Forrer, *Mitteilungen der Vorderasiatischen-Gesellschaft*, Vol. XX, No. 3 (Leipzig, 1916). But Forrer has changed the year 854 B.C. for the battle of Ḳarḳar to 853 B.C.; and this has been widely followed (e.g., by Sidney Smith in *Cambridge Ancient History*, III [1925], 22). This change is due to his misunderstanding of the data for 789–785 B.C. in the Assyrian Chronicle. A more plausible explanation of these data is given by A. T. Olmstead in "The Assyrian Chronicle," *Journal of the American Oriental Society*, XXXIV (1915), 344 f. (see in particular p. 363, n. 4), of which Forrer seems to have been ignorant. Forrer's conclusions have been challenged by Olmstead (*ibid.*, XLI [1921], 374, n. 61, and *Archiv für Orientforschung*, V [1928–29], 30).

Assyria. The Old Testament record is silent about him and his doings. But he must have filled the minds of the kings of the Mediterranean coastlands of western Asia to the exclusion of all lesser interests. Our knowledge of him is obtained from his own inscriptions. In his great Monolith Inscription, he records a battle against twelve kings at Ḳarḳar, and among the twelve he lists Ahab, of Israel. The narrative runs as follows:

I departed from Argana and advanced to Ḳarḳar. Ḳarḳar, his royal city, I destroyed, devastated, and burned with fire. Twelve hundred chariots, twelve hundred riding-horses, and twenty thousand soldiers of Hadad-Ezer of Damascus; seven hundred chariots, seven hundred riding-horses, and ten thousand soldiers of Irhuleni of Hamath; two thousand chariots and ten thousand soldiers of Ahab of Israel; five hundred soldiers of the Quaeans, one thousand soldiers of the Muṣrians, ten chariots and ten thousand soldiers of the Irqanateans; two hundred soldiers of Matin-ba'al of Arvad; two hundred soldiers of the Usanatians; thirty chariots and ten thousand soldiers of Aduni-balu of the Shianians; one thousand camels of Gindubu the Arabian . . . . ten thousand soldiers of Basa, son of Ruhubi, the Ammonite: these twelve kings came to his aid. To make war and battle they came against me. With the splendid forces which Ashur, the lord, had given; with the powerful weapons which Nergal who goes before me had presented, I fought with them. From Ḳarḳar to Gilzan I accomplished their overthrow. Fourteen thousand soldiers, their fighting men I brought low with my weapons.[21]

[21] The entire inscription will be found in R. W. Rogers, *Cuneiform Parallels to the Old Testament* (1926); D. D. Luckenbill, *Ancient Records of Assyria* (1926); R. F. Harper, *Assyrian and Babylonian Literature* (1901). For the correct location of Ḳarḳar (as against the earlier view) see R. Dussaud, *Topographie historique de la Syrie antique et médiéval* (1927), p. 242; also M. Monmarche, *Les Guides bleus: Syrie-Palestine* (1932), p. 281, and the map "Lattiquie-Hama" (at pp. 246–47); see, too, the map "Alep," issued by Bureau Topographique des Troupes français du Levant (1931).

The victory of which Shalmaneser lays claim was evidently a very dubious one; for he returned to Assyria at once and did not follow up his success as a normal victor would have done. Not only so, but he found it necessary to confront this same coalition of kings again in 850, 849, and 845 B.C. The peoples of the western coastlands were fighting for their very existence and fighting what was inevitably a losing battle in the outcome. Ahab's name does not appear among the combatants after 854 B.C. His death probably occurred before the campaign of 850 B.C.

In addition to these great struggles, Ahab fought also against Mesha, king of Moab. Omri had made Moab subject to Israel; but, in the middle of Ahab's reign, Mesha led a successful revolt, and Moab broke away from Israel. This conflict is recorded on Mesha's Inscription, commonly known as the Moabite Stone.[22] This revolt is either a different one from that recorded in II Kings 3:4 ff., or else the latter passage has dated it incorrectly, which is probably the case. The last conflict in which Ahab fought was the attack upon Ramoth Gilead in which he lost his life.[23] Here he was fighting against Hadadezer, of Syria, with whom in 854 B.C. he had been allied against Assyria.

Looking back upon the record of the score of years during which Ahab led Israel, it is obvious that he was an active, courageous, forceful, and statesman-like

[22] See S. R. Driver, *Notes on the Hebrew Text of the Books of Samuel* (2d ed., 1913), pp. lxxxiv–xciv, and W. H. Bennett, *The Moabite Stone* (1911); George A. Barton, *Archaeology and the Bible* (1937), p. 460.

[23] I Kings, chap. 22.

king. Our oldest narratives reflect a clear recognition of those qualities. He fought hard to gain his independence from Syria, and he cultivated the friendship of his neighbors from the point of view of strengthening Israel for this task. But when the greater danger of an Assyrian conquest loomed up, he put aside his own plans for a while and threw himself heartily and effectively into the effort to drive back Shalmaneser. It is clear from the record that, next to Hadadezer himself, Ahab was the most powerful of the allied kings. This joint undertaking of the allies was by all odds the most important interest in each of the lands involved. It was doubtless from a regard for the interests of this movement that Ahab dealt so generously with Benhadad after defeating him at the battle of Aphek. Ahab was engaged in a series of great struggles that must have occupied all his thought and energy and have strained the resources of his kingdom to the utmost. The very existence of the kingdom was at stake.

The prophets of the period were, of course, deeply interested in the course of events. Patriotism and religion were always closely allied. It is natural, therefore, that prophets are reported to have given the king the benefit of their counsel in connection with his battles against Benhadad.[24] But the broad outlook of Ahab was not shared by all the prophets, and one of them did not hesitate to denounce him after the battle of Aphek for having spared Benhadad when he had had him in his power.[25] Again, when Ahab was organ-

[24] I Kings 20:22, 28.   [25] I Kings 20:35-43.

izing his final campaign against Ramoth Gilead, there was a difference of opinion among the prophets. Four hundred of them *en masse* urged Ahab on to the fray, assuring him that Yahweh would lead him on to victory.[26] But Micaiah ben Imlah was of the contrary opinion. It seems that this prophet had established a reputation for hostility to the royal policy prior to this occasion;[27] and, as Ahab had expected, he threw cold water upon the enterprise and foretold the death of Ahab himself.[28]   But a most interesting thing is Micaiah's attitude toward the other four hundred prophets. He does not shrink from saying to the king that these prophetic advisers of his have been inspired by Yahweh to tell him a lie.[29] Inspired liars! What a strange collocation of terms! Incidentally, this representation shows what a low moral standard prevailed in Israel when this kind of procedure could be predicated of Yahweh. But, on the other hand, Micaiah shows some power of discernment here in that he recognizes that these prophets are quite honest and sincere in their counsel. They are prophesying out of their own inmost convictions, believing that it is the will of Yahweh to give victory to his people. If this diagnosis of their opinion was correct, then, strictly speaking, they could not rightly be accused as false prophets; they were not deliberately misleading Ahab; they were giving him the best judgment of which they were capable; indeed, they were speaking to him the

[26] I Kings 22:5, 6.   [28] I Kings 22:17, 18, 28.

[27] I Kings 22:8.   [29] I Kings 22:19–23.

word of God! If Micaiah was correct, the deceiver here was Yahweh himself, not the prophetic group. Trying to see things as they were, we may perhaps say that it was a case of two different types of patriots. The four hundred prophets were small-minded, narrowly patriotic people who saw nothing but the fact that Ramoth Gilead, an Israelitish town, was in the hands of the Syrians; and they thought that this was a good opportunity to recover what belonged to them. Micaiah, however, perhaps realized that this war of aggression on the part of Israel was a foolish thing, coming at a time when it was necessary that preparations should be going on for another joint defense against the rapacious Assyrians. It certainly was no time for the Syrian states to be engaging in internecine strife and expending the human and material resources that were to be so much needed against the Assyrian in the immediate future.

However, the incident is remarkable for certain aspects that reveal the advance of religious thought in Israel in the ninth century B.C. Why did Jehoshaphat, devout servant of Yahweh as he undoubtedly was, look on unconvinced while the four hundred official prophets of Yahweh employed all their devices to satisfy him and Ahab that their God looked with favor on the projected attack on Ramoth Gilead? Do we not detect here some growing disapproval among better elements of the Hebrew people of the irrational excesses of ecstatic prophecy? Does Jehoshaphat not seem to reason, "I can't believe that divine revelation comes by such absurd and senseless conduct. If Yahweh be so great

as we believe, surely his word must come to men in
some more appropriate way"? But, further, Micaiah's
reply to the officer who had gone to bring him into the
court is noteworthy. To the request that he bring some
pleasant message he retorted, "As Yahweh lives, what
Yahweh says to me will I speak." Now the officer had
no thought of requesting Micaiah to deceive the king
with a smooth assurance which he knew would not
accord with the course of events; but rather he voiced
the common belief of the time that the prophets were
great magicians, that utterance of their oracle carried
in it mighty power for its accomplishment. So he was
merely asking Micaiah to work a spell for the success of
the allied adventure. But the prophet repudiates all
this; he is but the spokesman of God and has no power
but to declare God's will. Here we are to recognize the
dawning of a real conception of divine revelation, such
as was to be so important in the succeeding course of
Israel's religious development.

The outstanding prophets of Ahab's reign and the
immediately following period, according to the records
in the Books of Kings, were Elijah and Elisha. These
two men receive an extraordinary amount of attention, and are credited with extraordinary deeds. But,
when the narratives regarding them are seen in the
cold light of criticism, grave doubt as to their his-
toricity arises. It appears at once that Elijah and
Elisha are both credited with deeds that are strangely
alike. Both bring to life again a dead child who was
the only son of his mother.[30] Both fill the failing oil

[30] I Kings 17:17 ff.; II Kings 4:17 ff.

cruse of a widow.[31] Both at the time of their death are described as "the chariots of Israel and the horsemen thereof."[32] Both are given credit for the anointing of Jehu and Hazael of Syria.[33] And both alike are made responsible for the extermination of Baalism—Elijah through the slaughter on Mount Carmel and Elisha through the bloody work of Jehu.

Not only so, but the narratives are full of legendary and folklore elements, so that they give the impression of sagas rather than of historical narratives. Elisha makes iron to swim.[34] Ahab sends an embassy to "all the nations" and puts them under oath that Elijah is not in hiding in their dominions. No king in the ancient world was in a position to do such a thing, let alone the king of such a small people as Israel. Elijah is fed by ravens at the brook Cherith,[35] just as Semiramis—according to a legend to Askelon—was exposed as a child in the desert and fed by doves with curdled milk, and as Romulus and Remus of ancient Rome were fed by wolves. Elijah traveled for forty days and forty nights to Mount Horeb without food, and saw and heard wonders upon his arrival.[36] Incidentally, we wonder why he was so long upon the journey—Horeb was but eleven days' journey from Kadesh.[37] Elisha calls down a curse upon the heads of little children who

[31] I Kings 17:14–16; II Kings 4:1 ff.

[32] II Kings 2:12; 13:14.

[33] I Kings 19:15 f.; II Kings 8:13; 9:1–10.

[34] II Kings 6:1–7.   [36] I Kings 19:1–18.

[35] I Kings 17:1–6.   [37] Deut. 1:2.

make fun of his bald head, and straightway she-bears come out of the woods and tear and rend forty of them.[38] Elijah calls down fire from the heavens upon the heads of two successive companies of soldiers sent to seize him and they are consumed.[39] Elijah on the top of Mount Carmel is able to get an abundance of water in a time of severe and long-continued drought.[40] Elijah finds a glorious ending by being translated to the celestial regions in a chariot of fire.[41] And Elisha's dead body has such miraculous potency that, when another dead man was put into Elisha's tomb, the new-comer at once sprang to his feet.[42] There is a far greater proportion of this kind of material in the Elijah-Elisha stories than is found anywhere else in the prophetic writings of the Old Testament.

Narratives of this kind may quite easily have sprung into being very soon after the times of Elijah and Elisha. No great lapse of time is needed for the origin of such tales. It was a credulous and superstitious age. Stories of the marvelous would find ready credence. We need only observe similar phenomena in recent times to realize this. The doings and sayings of Washington and Lincoln have been enlarged upon and glorified in most unhistorical fashion.[43] In our own day

[38] II Kings 2:23–25.

[39] II Kings 1:9 ff.   [41] II Kings 2:1–12.

[40] I Kings 18:19 ff., 33–35.   [42] II Kings 13:21.

[43] See S. G. Fisher, "The Legendary and Myth-making Processes in Histories of the American Revolution," *Proceedings of the American Philosophical Society*, LI (1912), 53–76; C. A. Manning, "Yermak Timofeyevitch in Russian Folk Poetry," *Journal of the American Oriental Society*, XLIII, 206–15.

we have only to think of the stories current in England in the autumn of 1914 to the effect that Russian troops had been sent on their way through England to take their place beside the Allies upon the Western front, though not a single Russian regiment ever set foot upon English soil. A still closer parallel to our stories is the tale of the angelic bowmen who intervened between the retreating English and the attacking Germans at Mons in 1914. Though that tale has been traced to its creator, who has declared it to be a work of his literary imagination,[44] it was believed by multitudes and still finds its defenders. But the fact that the Elijah and Elisha narratives may have arisen at a relatively early date does not give them the right to be accepted at their face value. Not their age but their character is against them. They are largely the product of the luxuriant and uncritical imagination of their times.

The stories make Ahab out to have been a persecutor of the prophets of Yahweh and his worshipers. But Ahab's children carried names compounded with the name Yahweh, viz., Joram, Ahaziah, Joash, and Athaliah. These were Jezebel's children, too! Children named after Yahweh are the most convincing evidence that Ahab honored Yahweh as his god. Not only so, but there were flourishing prophetical groups in Bethel and Jericho in Ahab's day and after his death.[45] When Ahab started out upon his final campaign he was able to summon four hundred prophets of Yahweh

[44] Arthur Machen, *The Bowmen and Other Legends of the War* (London, 1915).

[45] II Kings 2:3, 5, 7, 15.

to give him counsel.[46] Micaiah ben Imlah was known to be hostile to Ahab; yet Ahab did not kill him, but called him into consultation. On the other hand, the worshipers of Baal could all be assembled in a single temple in Samaria shortly after Ahab's death.[47] Ahab's hostility toward Yahweh, therefore, would seem to have been a nonexistent thing, and his zeal for the Baalim to have been greatly magnified.

Yet, if these narratives come from a period fairly close to the times that they purport to describe, there must be some elements of truth and reality in what they report. Ithobaal, father of Jezebel, really was priest-king of Sidon in the ninth century B.C. There actually was a famine lasting for a year or more in Phoenicia in the reign of Ithobaal, according to Menander of Ephesus.[48] The gathering of the prophets and priests of Baal on Mount Carmel in a time of drought for the purpose of making intercession to the Baal for relief from the drought and famine is quite in keeping with ancient practice. The hatred of Elijah against the Baalim rings true to prophetic form and probably rests upon a basis of fact. The nomadic and somewhat ecstatic character of Elijah is likewise to be credited to a sound tradition.

Elijah's opposition to Ahab as presented in the traditions centered around two things, viz., Ahab's attitude toward the Baalim and his seizure of Naboth's vineyard. It was a case of the practical statesman con-

[46] I Kings 22:6.   [47] II Kings 10:18 ff.

[48] See Josephus *Contra Apion* i. 18 and *Antiquities of the Jews* viii. 13. 2.

fronted by an out-and-out idealist and religious enthusiast. Ahab, whose policy of alliance with his neighbors was doubtless well thought out and had large ends
in view, could not respond to the prophet's desires and
initiate a persecution looking toward the extermination
of Baalism from Israel, without breaking off his alliance
with Phoenicia, at least, and perhaps also with other
Canaanitish and Syrian powers. But these alliances
were vital to the success of the larger aims that Ahab
had in mind and were not to be lightly broken upon
the word of a mere long-haired "prophet" from the
desert. It may be that Ahab's support of Baalism went
no farther than an amiable tolerance and a provision
for the religious needs of his Phoenician wife. But this
was too much for the enthusiast and idealist who would
have had Ahab forego everything in the world but his
undiluted loyalty to his own people and to Yahweh the
God of Israel. Prophecy was a conservative force in
Israel, standing for loyalty to the ideals of the nomadic
life of days gone by, hostile to the advance of civilization and culture, and intolerant of the worship in
Israel of any other god but Yahweh.[49] Elijah was a
typical embodiment of this conservatism.

The Naboth episode is made responsible by tradition for the fall of Ahab's dynasty.[50] This crime may
with reasonable safety be charged up against Ahab and
Jezebel. It was the type of action all too common with
oriental despots. Ahab was unduly influenced by his

[49] See J. M. Powis Smith, "The Conservatism of Early Prophecy,"
American Journal of Theology, XXIII, 290–99.

[50] I Kings 21:19; II Kings 9:36 f.

Phoenician wife so that he permitted her the use of power which she did not fail to use to the utmost. If the course of events is faithfully depicted in the narrative, it is not at all unlikely that Ahab knew nothing of the scheme of Jezebel until it was accomplished and he was in enjoyment of the ill-gotten spoil. In any case there was here a conflict between two opposing types of government—that of the typical autocrat over against that of the sturdy democrat. Naboth was but standing up for the maintenance of his long-recognized family rights, while Ahab through Jezebel cast rights to the winds and so acted as to obtain his wish without scruple. And further, the conflict between two types of social organization that had become increasingly acute since the establishment of the kingship here comes into open and violent expression. The Hebrews had inherited from the desert their groupings in tribe, clan, and family; but this structure of the community was not adapted to conditions of life in Palestine with the individualism encouraged by peasant and commercial life. Moreover, the Canaanites, from whom they learned so much, had long abandoned this primitive organization for a more practical structure under kings, princes, army leaders, and financial lords of various sorts. This was the influence that began to surround David as soon as he established his capital in Jerusalem, and it increasingly characterized the Hebrew kingship, both north and south. Naturally, the old aristocracy of tribe and clan resented these upstart lords of the court or the commercial world; and conservative elements found sanction for their opposition in Yahweh's traditional desert origin. There is, then, no reason to suppose that the principles at stake in the Naboth episode were not old; and Elijah's share in it seems almost predetermined by his nomadic leanings. It is difficult for us to feel any serious concern about the issue in this aspect; Israel steadily fell away from its primitive social structure while its religious life grew richer.[51] But as champion of the rights of the humble against brutal exploitation by the powerful, Elijah was in harmony with the spirit and attitude of Hebrew prophecy from the first, and in a remarkable way he anticipated the social and moral earnestness that was to find unparalleled expression in the great writing prophets of a hundred or more years later.

Elijah's personality and work clearly left a deep impression upon the consciousness of his generation. The degree to which his life has been idealized and glorified in the traditions is of itself a testimony to the importance of his contribution to his times. We may not be able to follow the tradition in its enthusiastic glorification of Elijah and accredit to him all the wonders of these legends; but we must recognize that he was an outstanding figure in his day, that he did not shrink from antagonizing the mighty king, Ahab, and that, while he may not have been alert to the dangers of the international situation, he was keenly alive to the necessity of justice to the common man and of unswerving loyalty to Yahweh as the God of the nomadic fathers, who required of their sons the same simplicity of life and sincerity of worship that had characterized the pioneers.

[51] See A. Causse, *Du groupe ethnique à la communauté religieuse* (1937); Louis Wallis, *God and the Social Process* (1935).

In so far as he is not a pale reflection of Elijah, Elisha appears as a strong supporter of Israel in its war with Syria. His contribution to the struggle by way of advice and stimulation of faith in Yahweh did much to keep up the morale of the king and his people. He differed apparently from Elijah, not only in his manner of life, but also in his attitude toward the movements of his day. Elijah was essentially conservative and almost reactionary in principle; Elisha was sympathetic toward the progress of his day and helpful in the solution of practical problems. He died a loyal patriot, in his last hours giving encouragement and stimulus to the king for the struggle against Syria. Notwithstanding this seeming reversal of the policy of Elijah, there was really a great unanimity in the objectives of the two men. Both alike strove valiantly against the menace of Baalism; and it will be recalled how Elisha fulfilled the two latter commissions that were given to Elijah in the theophany at Horeb—the overthrow of the House of Ahab and the deposition of Ben-Hadad of Damascus. However heartily we may re-echo the deprecation by Hosea a hundred years later of the bloody methods followed in Jehu's successful revolt, yet it must be recognized that, in the way in which the moderating influence of the ages makes even the wrath of men to serve the purposes of God, this petty upstart princeling, in fulfilling the policy of his protagonists Elijah and Elisha, insured the ultimate deliverance of Israel from the iniquities of Baalism and Yahweh's sole reign as Israel's God.

CHAPTER IV

AMOS AND HOSEA

THE disaster that befell Israel and Ahab at Ramoth Gilead was but the beginning of a long period of depression. In the days of Jehu, Damascus seems to have had its own way with Israel. "In those days Yahweh began to cut Israel short; from Jordan eastward, all the land of Gilead, the Gadites, and the Reubenites, and the Manassites, from Aroer, which is by the river Arnon, even Gilead and Bashan."[1] Not only so, but the armies of Assyria were frequent visitors in the Westland. In 849, 846, and again in 842 B.C. Shalmaneser III invaded this region and fought with its allied forces. Indeed, in 842 B.C. Jehu was forced to pay tribute to Shalmaneser, as we learn from Shalmaneser's Obelisk Inscription, where he pictures Hebrews kneeling before him and says: "Tribute of Iaua [Jehu], son of Omri (mar Humri). Silver, gold, a golden bowl, a golden beaker, golden goblets, pitchers of gold, lead, staves for the hand of the king, javelins, I received from him."[2] In 839 B.C. Shalmaneser again attacked Damascus and defeated Hazael, receiving tribute also from Tyre, Sidon, and Byblos.

The depths to which Israel had sunk in the days of Jehoahaz are reflected in this Hebrew statement re-

[1] II Kings 10:32 f.

[2] D. D. Luckenbill, *Ancient Records of Assyria* (1926), I, 211.

garding the king of Syria: "Neither did he leave of the people to Jehoahaz but fifty horsemen, and ten chariots, and ten thousand footmen; for the king of Syria had destroyed them and had made them like the dust by threshing."[3] But, finally, "Yahweh gave Israel a saviour, so that they went out from under the hand of the Syrians."[4] This "saviour" was none other than the Assyrian king. Adad-nirari IV (810–782 B.C.) of Assyria was an energetic sovereign. He declares in one of his inscriptions:

> From the shore of the Euphrates out, I subdued the land of the Hittites, the whole of Amurru, Tyre, Sidon, the land of Omri, Edom and Philistia as far as the great western sea. Taxes and tribute I laid upon them. To the land of Damascus I drew nigh. I shut up Mari, king of Damascus, in Damascus, his residential city. Fear before the splendor of Asshur, his lord, overcame him; he seized my feet and became subject to me.[5]

That meant the end to all trouble for Israel from Syria; and for the next half-century Assyria was quiescent in the Westland. It was a period of weakness and internal strife in Assyria herself, and consequently, as she was unable to push her conquests, the Westland was left undisturbed. Joash, of Israel, and Jeroboam II utilized this opportunity to recover Israel's lost territory. The result was that by the latter part of Jeroboam's reign Israel was in a highly prosperous and supremely confident condition. The Kings narrative

[3] II Kings 13:7.   [4] II Kings 13:5.

[5] Nimrud Inscription; see R. F. Harper, *Assyrian and Babylonian Literature* (1901), pp. 51–52; Luckenbill, *op. cit.*, pp. 262–63.

thus describes and explains the good fortune of Israel:

He restored the border of Israel from the entering of Hamath unto the sea of the plain, according to the word of Yahweh, God of Israel, which he spoke through his servant Jonah, the son of Amittai, the prophet, who was from Gath-hepher. For Yahweh saw the affliction of Israel that it was very severe; for there was not any restrained nor any released, nor any help for Israel. But Yahweh had not said that he would blot out the name of Israel from under the heavens; so he saved them by the hand of Jeroboam, the son of Joash.[6]

Jeroboam is here evidently thought of as the "saviour" mentioned in II Kings 13:5; but Jeroboam could have done little had it not been for Adad-nirari, who cleared Syria out of his way.

Into the midst of this blazing sunshine of prosperity came Amos, of Tekoa, thundering forth denunciation and disaster.[7] Amos was a shepherd,[8] who watched his flocks as they grazed on the sunny slopes of the hills, 10 miles or so to the south of Jerusalem. Quite likely he spent many days in sight of the Dead Sea with all its waste and desolation, so suggestive and burdened with so terrible a tradition from the distant past. He also describes himself as a dresser of sycamore trees.[9]

[6] II Kings 14:25–27.

[7] The appearance of Amos as a prophet may be placed about 750 B.C. For a full discussion of the date see W. R. Harper, *Amos and Hosea* ("International Critical Commentary" [1905]), pp. cii–civ; R. S. Cripps, *The Book of Amos* (1929); Julian Morgenstern, *Amos Studies* (1936–38); Artur Weiser, *Die Prophetie des Amos* (1929). On Amos and Hosea see also T. H. Robinson, *Die zwölf kleinen Propheten: Hosea bis Mica* (1936).

[8] Amos 1:1; 7:14 f.   [9] Amos 7:14.

The sycamore does not grow at an elevation of more than 1,000 feet; and since Tekoa is almost 3,000 feet above sea level, Amos must have owned or worked in some fields located at a considerable distance from Tekoa. But his occupations afforded him much time and food for thought. As an owner of sheep, he had occasion from time to time to visit the great markets of Judah and Israel in order to sell the products of his flock. From such excursions into the great commercial centers he returned to the solitudes of his mountain home, his mind filled with new and strange sights and his heart burdened with a heavy load of grief over what he saw.

It is significant that Amos refused to allow himself to be called a "prophet." He clearly realized that the "prophets" of his day were in bad repute and that he must separate himself sharply from them if he would not be misunderstood. The nature of the misunderstanding is quite clear from the slur of Amaziah, the chief priest at Bethel, when he urged Amos to return home, saying:

> O seer! Go away; flee to the land of Judah;
> And eat bread there, and there prophesy!
> But at Bethel do not prophesy again;
> For the king's sanctuary, and the royal palace are here![10]

The implication of this was that Amos was like the rest of the prophets of the day who were prophets for revenue only. Amaziah told Amos that he was in the wrong place to obtain reward for that kind of a message; he should go back home and preach it to the

[10] Amos 7:12 f.

people of Judah; they would be glad to hear such
threats against Israel and would pay him well for his
message. Amos indignantly repudiated the implied
charge and declared himself genuinely called of Yahweh to the task of prophecy. Thereupon he proceeded
to prophesy with a vengeance, saying to Amaziah:

> Your wife will play the harlot in the city;
> Your sons and your daughters will fall by the sword;
> Your land will be distributed by measure;
> And you yourself will die upon an unclean soil;
> And Israel will be entirely carried into exile.[11]

The facts that brought Amos to this conclusion regarding Israel were the social wrongs that he saw
rampant there. It was a "post-war" period, when,
even as here, the rich seem to have been getting richer
and the poor poorer. It was the great merit of Amos
that he insisted upon fundamental morality as the supreme thing in human relations with God. There was
no lack of ritualistic splendor in Israel; but in the eyes
of Amos this was little better than an insult to Yahweh
as long as justice was not operative between man and
man. Amos was himself a poor man, or at most a man
of moderate means. He understood the trials of the
poor, and he felt their burdens. It was out of a deep
sympathy with men of his own kind that he spoke
words of indignation and scorn against the rich oppressor. He returns to this subject again and again, never
wearying of denouncing the conscienceless rich:

> Thus has Yahweh said:
> "For three transgressions of Israel,—
> Yea, for four, I will not turn it aside;

[11] Amos 7:17.

> Because they sell the righteous for silver,
> And the needy for a pair of sandals—
> Those trampling upon the head of the poor—
> And they turn aside the way of the lowly;
> And father and son walk in collusion;
> So that they profane my holy name.
> And they spread out pawned garments beside every altar;
> And they drink the wine of the condemned in the house of their god."[12]

And again:

> Hear this, you who trample upon the needy,
> And cause the lowly of the land to cease, saying,
> "How long until the new moon pass that we may sell grain,
> And the Sabbath that we may display wheat,—
> Diminishing the ephah and enlarging the shekel,
> And perverting treacherous scales—
> That we may buy the poor for silver,
> And the needy for a pair of sandals,
> And that we may sell the refuse grain?"[13]

The sensuous wives of the rich oppressors are roughly addressed thus:

> Hear this word, you cows of Bashan,
> You who are on the mount of Samaria,
> Who oppress the weak, who crush the needy,
> Who say to their lords, "Bring that we may drink."

> The Lord God has sworn by his holiness,
> That there are days coming upon you,
> When they will drag you away with hooks,
> And what is left of you with fish-hooks;
> And through the breaches you will go, each straight ahead,
> And you will be cast upon the refuse heap.[14]

[12] Amos 2:6–8.   [13] Amos 8:4–6.   [14] Amos 4:1–3.

Amos not only found fault with the social order in Israel, saying that the rich were using all kinds of devious methods to get the better of the poor, but he also denounced the type of worship prevalent in his day. There was no lack of rich ceremonial worship in the way of sacrifices and offerings and splendid accouterments. But the spirit of true worship was entirely lacking. The difficulty was not that the worshipers were not wholly sincere and devout in the practice of the ritual, such as it was; but that, while zealous in the practice of ceremonial, they were living lives that lacked the fundamental moral qualities without which no worship, however elaborate, could be pleasing to Yahweh:

> "Come to Bethel—and transgress!
> To Gilgal—and multiply transgression!
> And bring your sacrifices every morning,
> Every three days—your tithes!
> And burn a thank-offering of leaven,
> And proclaim voluntary offerings—publish them
>   abroad!
> For so do you love to do, O children of Israel."
>   It is the oracle of the Lord Yahweh.[15]

And:

> For thus says Yahweh to the house of Israel:
> "Seek me, that you may live!
> But seek not Bethel,
> And do not enter Gilgal,
> Nor pass over to Beer-sheba!
> For Gilgal will surely be carried into exile.
> And Bethel will become a nonentity.

[15] Amos 4:4 f.

> Seek Yahweh, that you may live,
> Lest fire flash forth upon the house of Joseph
> And consume, with no one to quench it in Bethel."[16]

And further:

> "I hate, I loathe your feasts,
> And I will not accept your sacred conventicles;
> Though you offer me your burnt-offerings
> And your sacrifices, I will not accept them;
> Nor will I look favorably upon the sacrifice of your
>   fatlings.
> Put away from me the noise of your songs;
> Nor will I listen to the melody of your harps.
> But let justice roll down like waters,
> And righteousness like a perennial stream.
> Was it sacrifice and offerings that you brought me
> In the wilderness during forty years, O house of Israel?"[17]

It may hardly be supposed that Amos would have done away with sacrifice and ritual entirely if he could; he had not arrived at a conception of religion as purely ethical or theological and abstract. It was not ritual as such to which he objected, but rather the practice of ritual by people who believed that thereby they set in motion magical forces and insured for themselves well-being and happiness. Amos would not have had them give up ritual; but he did insist that their ceremonial should be the expression of a devout and humble faith in a God who demanded first of all moral character and social justice. The religion of Amos claimed the whole life and was not satisfied with any partial control.

One of the most striking aspects of the thought of Amos is his denunciation of the neighboring peoples.

---

[16] Amos 5:4–6.   [17] Amos 5:21–25.

His list of the foreign nations upon whom he announces the doom of Yahweh includes Damascus, Philistia, Ammon, and Moab.[18] This interest of prophecy in outside nations was not wholly new with Amos. The traditions represent Elijah and Elisha as thinking of Yahweh as having some control over the internal affairs of Damascus. The J document in Genesis assigns the creation of the world to Yahweh. That did not imply a monotheistic conception, for in the ancient Semitic world national gods were commonly looked upon by their own peoples as responsible for the creation. The westward movements of Assyria in the ninth century also did much toward the enlargement of the Hebrew thought of God.[19] The international policy of Omri and Ahab, made necessary by the imminence of the Assyrian peril, involved at least a sympathetic tolerance of the gods of the allies of Israel; and the actual conquest of the western states in general and of Israel in particular by Shalmaneser must have made necessary to the theologically minded a new adjustment of their ideas to fit the new facts. A loyal worshiper of Yahweh could not long endure the thought that Yahweh was inferior in power to the Assyrian gods. The only escape from this conclusion was to make Yahweh

[18] The similar oracles against Tyre, Edom, and Judah are probably not to be attributed to Amos himself but to later editors. For the discussion of these questions see W. R. Harper, Cripps, Morgenstern, Weiser, *op. cit.;* but as defending their genuineness see F. C. Eiselen, *The Prophetic Books of the Old Testament*, II (1923), 407 ff.

[19] See George A. Smith's chapter, "The Influence of Assyria upon Prophecy," in *The Book of the Twelve Prophets*, I (1928), pp. 41–54.

supreme over Assyria itself and to regard the movements of Assyria as a part of the plan of Yahweh for the
conduct of his world. The Assyrian thus became ultimately for Hebrew thinkers the chastening rod of Yahweh's wrath against Israel, his own people. This process of enlargement of the scope of Yahweh's activity
was already under way when Amos appeared as prophet. He used it effectively for his own prophetic purposes. It is an open question as to the extent to which
these oracles against Israel's neighbors were motivated
by wrongs committed against Israel by these peoples.
In the case of Moab, at least, apparently, the offense
for which punishment is threatened was a wrong of
Moab against Edom. The date of this barbarity is unknown, but it may well have been in connection with
the invasion of Moab by Israel, with Judah and Edom
as allies.[20] If so, a crime against an ally of Israel would
be only one degree less keenly felt than one against
Israel herself. However that may be, it is clear that
Amos resents in Yahweh's name the brutality of the
offenses he charges against these peoples. He was here
the mouthpiece of broad humanitarian principles for
the violation of which he threatened the peoples with
destruction. It is significant that this broadening of the
God-idea appeared in close connection with ethical
considerations, for in the domain of ethics there are no
national barriers. As a matter of record, it should be
said in this connection that Israel's achievement in
monotheism, as well as its arrival at the thought of
personal immortality, was by way of the ethical neces-

[20] II Kings 3:4–27.

sities of the passing centuries. When monotheism came it was an ethical monotheism, and when immortality was reached it was an ethical immortality.

How did Amos arrive at his conviction that Israel was doomed to punishment and exile? Not by way of an intimate knowledge of or keen insight into the course of international politics. As a matter of fact, Amos did not name the agent through whom this punishment was to be executed. It is not at all likely that he knew. The kingdom of Israel in his day was more prosperous and powerful under Jeroboam II than it had been at any previous period. Assyria was suffering a continuous decline of power from the time of Adad-nirari's death in 782 B.C. until the accession of Tiglath-Pileser in 746 B.C. Between 782 and 772 B.C. Shalmaneser IV fought six campaigns against the kingdom of Urartu to the northwest of Assyria. Argistis, king of the Kaldi of Urartu, at one time was so successful that he pressed south to a point within three or four days' march of Nineveh. The successes of Urartu greatly encouraged the western states that were vitally interested in the outcome of the contest, if they were not even in league with Urartu. So Shalmaneser found it necessary to march west and attack Damascus in 773 B.C. His successor, Ashur-dan III, fought against Hadrach in central Syria, in 772 and 765; and his successor was on the defensive against an attack upon Arpad in northern Syria by the Kaldi, of Urartu, in 754 B.C. That was the last of Assyria's foreign wars until the appearance of Tiglath-Pileser. Consequently, Assyria was in no condition to be regarded by any observer as an imminent peril to her neighbors about 750 B.C. Nor was the situation in Egypt at that time any more threatening to western Asia. The Twenty-second Dynasty was drawing to a close and was powerless both at home and abroad. Internal schisms paralyzed the strength of Egypt, and the pharaohs found themselves powerless to engage in campaigns in Asia. Amos clearly expected the calamity to come from the north;[21] but whether he thought of Assyria, Urartu, or the wild hordes of the more distant north we have no means of knowing. The only thing of which he seems to have been certain was that Yahweh was about to punish Israel for its sins. His certainty, therefore, had its sure basis in his conviction of the justice of Yahweh. The agent through whom that justice should find expression he did not need to know. It was enough that justice would be done by Yahweh, the God of justice.

The message of Amos was in direct opposition to the prevailing thought of his age. His contemporaries were confident of the happiness of the future, in their command, as they believed, of mighty superhuman forces. Through their performance of the accepted ritual they would insure that on the great "Day of Yahweh" their god would come among them with blessing of basket and store, with increase of flocks and herds and of human kind, and would manifest his favor upon Israel in mighty overthrow of all enemies. This was a type of thought well established in Israel and had become the orthodox hope of the generations. Scholars in recent years have become aware of the wide prevalence of this sort of hope through the Near East and

[21] Amos 5:27; 6:7, 14; 7:17.

its high significance in Israel's life. They recognize it as a part of the prevalent cult of the dying and rising god, which in turn was an expression in myth and ritual of the annual pulsations of vital activity through the succeeding seasons—of growth and decay in vegetation and procreation and stagnation in animal life. Through the ritual re-enactment of this life-cycle the ancient worshiper believed he could assist, if not indeed absolutely determine, the annual return of life and all the well-being this great occasion entailed.[22] But to Amos such hopes and expectations were groundless; yet he seized upon the popular expectation of the coming of Yahweh, who as supreme righteousness could come to a sinning people only in stern judgment. The Day of Yahweh was indeed coming; but what a different Day! Not blessing and joy, but disaster and mourning were to be its outstanding characteristics. Israel's religious guides were wholly mistaken!

> Alas, for those who long for the Day of Yahweh!
> Wherefore, then, is your Day of Yahweh?
> It is darkness, and not light.
> It is as though a man were fleeing from a lion,
> And a bear met him;
> And he went into a house and laid his hand upon the wall,
> And a serpent bit him.
> Is not the Day of Yahweh darkness, and not light;
> Yea, deep darkness, with no brightness in it?[23]

[22] There is a large and growing literature on this subject. The reader will probably find the most satisfactory presentation of the matter in the two volumes put out by S. H. Hooke, *Myth and Ritual* (1933) and *The Labyrinth* (1935). For an earlier view cf. H. Gressmann, *Der Ursprung der israelitisch-jüdischen Eschatologie* (1905), pp. 142–58; and J. M. Powis Smith, *The Prophet and His Problems* (1914), pp. 3–35.

[23] Amos 5:18–20.

And even as the premillennialists of the present day
are looking for the end of the world to come at almost
any moment, so it is probable that Amos did not put
his coming Day of Yahweh far away. He rather seems
to have been living in the shadow of its speedy approach. He did not make the mistake of attempting to
fix the date upon which the great Day should dawn,
but the vision of its retributive justice was the domi-
nant thought in his mind.

Did Amos forswear all hope? Was there nothing in
store for Israel but a certain fiery form of judgment? It
is hardly credible that a prophet would have put himself to such pains, if he had seen nothing ahead but ruin
for the people to whom he preached. Why should any
man preach, if he saw no possibility of pointing out a
way of salvation? Amos must have had some future for
Israel in mind. He preached judgment in order to turn
Israel away from her sins and to lead her into the way
of escape. He put forth a few suggestions of deliverance, always conditioned upon right conduct and a
genuinely religious attitude.[24] But there is no confident
portrayal of a glorious future.[25] The persistent note is
one of tragedy. It will throw some light upon this to
recall that Amos was not a citizen of the northern
kingdom, but of Judah. He was engaging in a praise-
worthy mission when he crossed the border and began
prophesying to Israel; but he could perhaps contem-

[24] Amos 5:4–6, 14 f.

[25] The closing passage of the book, 9:8b–15, is quite generally regarded as a later addition; see W. R. Harper, *op. cit.;* Robinson, *op. cit.*,
p. 2.

plate the downfall of Israel with less emotion than would have been possible for an Israelite proper. From the point of view of his faith in Yahweh, he could always fall back upon his own people and look to them to carry on Yahweh's work in the world and to serve as the recipients of Yahweh's blessings.

A few years after the appearance of Amos in Israel, Hosea came forth from the ranks of Israel itself. He was the prophet of the decline and fall of northern Israel and the only one of the writing prophets to spring from the soil of that kingdom. His prophetic career probably ran parallel with the end of Jeroboam's reign and the chaotic conditions that followed in Israel down to the accession of Pekah in 736 B.C.[26] During this period, the Assyrian Empire was reasserting itself in western Asia. In 746 B.C. Tiglath-Pileser seized the throne of Assyria and inaugurated a new era of power. During the first ten years of his reign he was engaged in constant warfare against the peoples of the north, the south, and the west. But he was consistently successful and finally made Assyria master of the world, bringing the peoples of Babylonia, Urartu, and the states of western Asia to acknowledge and submit to Assyria's power. In 738 B.C. Menahem, of Israel, paid tribute to Assyria.[27] But as in the case of Amos, so in that of Hosea, his judgment as to the disaster await-

[26] Hos. 7:3–9; 8:4; for a full discussion of the date see W. R. Harper, *op. cit.*, pp. cxli f.; Eiselen, *op. cit.*, II, 365–68; J. M. Powis Smith, *Amos, Hosea, and Micah* (1914), pp. 75–77.

[27] II Kings 15:19 f.; the king "Pul" of this passage is generally regarded as being identical with Tiglath-Pileser.

ing Israel was not based upon observation of the growing power of Assyria. He does, indeed, mention Assyria as a punitive agency; but he also mentions Egypt,
and during this period Egypt was absolutely powerless.[28] The Twenty-second Dynasty came to a futile
ending in 745 B.C., and the Twenty-third Dynasty
ushered in "the total dissolution of the Egyptian
State."[29] Hosea's message was based not upon political
considerations primarily, but upon moral and religious
convictions.

The personal life of Hosea, in whatever way it may
be understood, had much to do with his prophetic activity. The facts regarding it are to be found in Hosea,
chapters 1 and 3. The story there told has been treated
both as allegory and as the actual personal experience of
Hosea.[30] This latter view is today generally accepted.
But we still differ as to the sense in which this personal
history is to be understood. For a brief period in the
nineteenth century, it seemed as though the view
would carry the day that Hosea had fallen in love with
a charming young woman and married her, only to
find out later that she was untrue to him and was
presenting him with children that were not his own.

[28] Assyria is mentioned in Hos. 5:13; 7:11; 8:9; 9:3; 10:6; 11:5;
12:1; Egypt appears in 7:11, 16; 9:3, 6; 12:1. Both countries are
looked upon as places of exile in 9:3, 6; 10:6.

[29] J. H. Breasted, *History of Egypt* (1924), pp. 539–45.

[30] For the history of the interpretation of Hosea's marriage see W. R.
Harper, *op. cit.*, pp. cxliii ff. and 208 ff. For a discussion and refutation
of the allegorical interpretation see Hans Schmidt in *Zeitschrift für die
alttestamentliche Wissenschaft*, XLII, 245 f. Cf., too, Budde in *Theologische Studien und Kritiken* (1925), pp. 1 ff., and Robinson, *op. cit.*, p. 7.

In the midst of this tragic situation, Hosea discovered that this was Yahweh's method of awakening in him the spirit of prophecy, for he, through this experience, was brought to understand that Israel had treated Yahweh just as Gomer was treating Hosea. Thereupon he put his wife under restraint and in separation from himself, in order that she might come to realize her great guilt and be taken back upon repentance into Hosea's family circle, even as Israel because of its sins must go into exile for punishment preparatory to restoration to Yahweh's favor.[31]

Attractive as this view is, there are certain obstacles in the way of its complete success in explaining all the data. It is not at all surprising then that scholars reverted frankly to the older view that Gomer was a well-known prostitute whom Hosea married for prophetic reasons. But more recently, with our growing understanding of the continuing influence of the Canaanite cults on Israel's religious practice,[32] we have come to recognize that the situation was scarcely as crass as that; indeed, for the standards of the time it was not abnormal. The class of temple women of Babylonia have long been known; we are coming to recognize that a similar institution existed in Palestine as a normal part of the Canaanite religion, hence also adopted by Israel. They were, by theological dogma,

---

[31] For an eloquent exposition of this view see G. A. Smith, *Book of the Twelve Prophets*, I (1928), 241 ff.; and also W. R. Harper, *op. cit.*, pp. 206–24.

[32] See Elmer A. Leslie, *Old Testament Religion in the Light of Its Canaanite Background* (1936).

the wives of the god. They were not at all prostitutes in the revolting modern sense of that word; though it enhances our appraisal of their morals little to admit that they were "religious prostitutes"; on the contrary, the entire institution becomes the more hideous and wicked, but not so for the eighth century B.C.; rather, they were members of an honored profession. There was then no stigma on Hosea in "taking" such a woman. And while we demand that a prophet must be in advance of the standards of his day, it is unreasonable that we expect him to measure up to the level of our heritage, enriched as it has been by the spiritual discovery of hosts of just such religious pioneers as he.

So there was no obstacle to Hosea's taking this woman into his home. But still the modern reader will naturally put the issue the other way about: With all Israel to choose from, why did he pick on one of these women? Obviously, there are two answers. It is apparent that he did this for the religious object lesson he intended to work out with the woman; for a further understanding of this we must delay until we have studied the incident, if, indeed, it will even then become fully evident. But as well we must reckon with a probability of the simple, elemental fact that Hosea liked, if not really loved, Gomer; there was some charm about her person or bearing that attracted him. And since by the thinking of the time she was a reputable woman, there was no reason why he should hold aloof from her.

It is necessary in an approach to the episode to inquire first as to the significance of the parallel stories already mentioned, those of chapters 1 and 3. Most diverse views are held as to their relation. A common interpretation is that sketched above, that makes the incidents of chapter 3 the sequel to those of chapter 1;[33] her immorality finally brought Gomer to complete destitution, and there Hosea found her in the slave market and brought her home as related in chapter 3. Others, again, would ignore the entire chapter as but a spurious and inaccurate repetition of chapter 1. Still others, recalling the diverse form of narratives in the prophetic books, hold that both are valid accounts of the one episode; chapter 1 being the "third person" narrative and chapter 3 the "first person".[34] But, indeed, this interpretation strains or ignores the facts. A careful examination reveals that the two are not the same incident. First of all, chapter 3 tells specifically that it is a second episode; Hosea is commanded "Go, again, love a woman . . . . an adulteress."[35] Further, the woman is never mentioned by name, although the one in chapter 1 is Gomer bath Diblaim; and the descriptions of the two are distinct. Gomer is "a harlotrous wife" (Heb. *'esheth zenunim*), but the woman in chapter 3 is "an adulteress" (Heb. *mena'epheth*); it is

[33] Cf., too, Budde, *op. cit.*, and in *Theologische Blätter* (1935), cols. 337–42.

[34] See Robinson, *op. cit.*, pp. 15–16; O. Eissfeldt, *Einleitung in das Alte Testament* (1934), pp. 431–34; but against this see Budde, *Theologische Studien und Kritiken* (1925), pp. 56 f., and *Theologische Blätter* (1934), col. 337.

[35] Hos. 3:1. For a defense of the punctuation taking the adverb "again" not with "the Lord said" but with the going and loving, see Budde in *Theologische Studien und Kritiken* (1925), pp. 57–58.

but a mark of our unfamiliarity with Hebrew social
standards that we have loosely equated the two. Then
the purport of the two episodes is quite diverse; that of
chapter 1 finds its meaning in the birth and symbolic
naming of the children. But in chapter 3 there are no
children, and the incident is significant only in the relations of Hosea with the woman. These are not duplicate narratives, whichever view of the duplication is
preferred; they are records of two distinct incidents in
the prophet's career. That one is in the third person
and the other in the first is an interesting fact, but
without bearing on the interpretation. But these considerations, except the first, have equal cogency against
the view that the incident in chapter 3 is the sequel, in
some way, of that in chapter 1. The women are entirely distinct; the incidents are unrelated save only
that both the women are, for our thinking, of be-
smirched honor. The astonishing fact then appears
that Hosea contracted such a dubious union not once,
but twice. Still worse, it will seem, the second woman
cannot be defended on the basis of the standards of
ancient Israel; without qualification she was a bad
woman; she was an adulteress.

And why did Hosea choose such a notorious character? The answer is made clear in verse 1: because
she typified the conduct of Israel. Just as she was un-
faithful to the husband who loved her, so Israel had
turned from Yahweh to other gods. Accordingly, he
brought her home, warning her that she must abandon
her evil ways and be for him alone.[36] Then he explains

[36] It is a strange fact of the exegesis of the Book of Hosea that almost
uniformly the text of 3:3 is tampered with. There is not a scrap of

that similarly Israel shall live "many days without
king, or prince, or sacrifice, or sacred pillar, or ephod
or teraphim"—the marks and accompaniment of the
pagan cults of Canaan. The text does not make clear
how this is to come about, but from other passages we
may understand the threat to the nation expressed
here.

We have noted that the union with Gomer (chap. 1)
finds its meaning in the naming of her children. This is
sun-clear from the narrative. They foreshadowed
bloody retribution on Israel's reigning house, and divine rejection of the nation as slave children whom God
would not recognize for rightful heirs of his bounty.[37]

So now we can understand the significance of
Hosea's choice of a "harlotrous woman" for this protracted drama. It would have been meaningless otherwise; the children of an ordinary Israelitish woman
would not have fulfilled the character demanded by
his symbolism. But Gomer, a woman of the shrine, a
"wife of a strange god,"[38] obviously bore "harlotrous
children," that is, they too were children of the god,
though there is no reason to doubt they were actually

---

manuscript or versional support for the course taken but only the views
of the several expositors as to what the verse should say; surely, a
strange reversal of all proper criticism and exegesis!

[37] The names Lo-ruhammah and Lo-ammi carry an allusion to the
legal procedure in the ancient Orient whereby the child of a slave
mother became an heir of his free father only if recognized by him as his
child; more specifically, if he said, "My son" (see Johns, *Babylonian and
Assyrian Laws, Contracts and Letters*, p. 135).

[38] Cf. Mal. 2:11.

Hosea's.[39] So they symbolized effectively Israel in its engrossment with these pagan cults, still more in its faith that by these cults all their increase, even that of their families, came about. It is then this basic disloyalty of Israel that Hosea undertakes to represent in his strange "marriage," and his conviction of divine rejection and coming punishment. Indeed, this should always have been clear to us, for it is just what Hosea tells us in 2:2–4. After an interruption that every expositor of the book recognizes to be spurious (1:10— 2:1) he goes on immediately describing Israel as the pagan mother of the Israelites upon whom then Yahweh will have no mercy.[40]

The nature of Israel's disloyalty is clearly brought out:

> For she said, "I will go after my lovers,
> Who give me my bread and my water,
> My wool, and my flax, my oil and my drink."
> Therefore, behold, I will hedge up her way with thorns,
> So that she will not find her paths.
> And she will pursue her lovers,
> But not overtake them;
> And she will seek them,
> But will not find them.

[39] Observe they were born "to him" (vs. 3). Exegesis has gone astray in its effort to attach meaning to the omission of this phrase in regard to the second and third children; this is purely stylistic.

[40] Much of the current notion of the tragedy of Hosea's home bases in these verses, taking them as a valid account of unfaithfulness practiced by Gomer. There can be no reasonable doubt that Robinson is right (*op. cit.*, pp. 8–9) in seeing here another aspect of Hosea's figurative imagery: Israel is conceived in a combination of the collective and the individual, with the Israelites urged to protest to their mother Israel her unfaithfulness.

And she will say, "I will go back to my first husband,
For it was better with me then than now."
And she did not know
That it was I who gave her
The corn and the new wine and the oil;
And that I increased her silver
And the gold which they made into the Baal.
Therefore I will take back my corn in its time,
And my new wine in its season;
And I will rescue my wool and my flax
So that she cannot cover her nakedness.
And now I will expose her shame to the eyes of her lovers;
And none can deliver her from my hand.
And I will bring to an end all her mirth,
Her feasts, her new moons, and her sabbaths,
And all her fixed seasons.
And I will lay waste her vines and her fig trees,
Whereof she said, "They are my hire,
Which my lovers have given me."
And I will make them a wilderness,
And the beasts of the field shall devour them.
And I will visit upon her the days of the Baalim,
To whom she sacrificed,
And she put on her nose-ring and her necklace,
And went after her lovers;
But she forgot me! It is the oracle of Yahweh.[41]

Words like these reveal a strange situation. Yahweh
even now in the eighth century B.C. has not yet come to
be thought of by northern Israel as the God of the soil
and its products. This was the struggle into which
Elijah had thrown himself a century before. But it was
of still earlier date. There is every reason to accept the
statements of the writers in the Book of Judges, though

[41] Hos. 2:5–13.

late, that as soon as Israel entered the land they came under the seductive influence of the Canaanite cults;[42] and it is the persistence of this situation that Hosea here almost at the close of the history of the northern kingdom so vividly portrays. Israel was under the necessity of learning agriculture from the Canaanites, the older settlers of the land; and for them the cult of the Baalim and Ashtaroth[43] was an indispensable part of agriculture—indeed, a most important part. And this Baalistic religion, it is now clear,[44] was the local expression of the myth and ritual of the god who died and rose again, to which reference has already been made. It was in essence one with the cult of Osiris and Isis in Egypt or of Tammuz[45] and Ishtar in Babylonia; in fact the Biblical name of the goddess Ashtoreth is but another form of Ishtar. And the familiar myth of Demeter and Persephone in Greece is a part of this same cycle of thinking, pervasive throughout the Near East —indeed, in variant forms throughout the world. The Canaanites, then, believed, and Israel learned to believe also, that by the enactment and celebration of the episodes of the death and resurrection of Baal they brought about the revival of the life-process after its stagnation in the drought of summer; by this means the autumn rains came with their reviving of vegetation; by this, too, animals reproduced, and children were

[42] See Graham and May, *Culture and Conscience* (1936), chaps. iv–v; Leslie, *op. cit.*, pp. 106 f.

[43] Cf. Judges 2:13, etc.

[44] See Leslie, *op. cit.*, pp. 23 f.   [45] Cf. Ezek. 8:14.

born to man. It seems strange, yet it was inevitable, that Israel should come to a syncretism, actually identifying Yahweh with Baal, or at times carrying over much of Baalistic thought and practice into their worship of their national God. So at many shrines, and apparently at the royal center in Bethel, Yahweh was worshiped with the paganisms of Baal.

Allusions to this faith and practice, which were the background and environment of the work of all the pre-Exilic prophets, are especially numerous and clear in the Book of Hosea.[46] And there is no difficulty in tracing them in the passage just now quoted. We see first the ritual quest of the dead god, through finding whom the worshiper secured bread and water, wool and flax and oil and drink. But also the public indecencies that were an integral part of the cultus are more than hinted at; for this they supposed they received as "hire" from "lovers," the fruit of the vine and fig tree; these ritual "marriages" were accompanied by adornment and feastings. But the emphasis of Hosea is that all this is prostitution of the worst sort; it is attributing to immoral, pagan gods what is really the gift of Yahweh; or, not less reprehensible, thinking of Yahweh in revolting pagan concepts. And so, just like Elijah, he threatens that the gifts of the soil will be withheld until the truth is understood; but also the nation will suffer some disaster which he describes as exposing her shame in the eyes of her lovers.

But there were immense spiritual values in the cult

[46] Cf. May, "The Fertility Cult in Hosea," *American Journal of Semitic Languages and Literatures*, XLVIII, 73–98.

of the dying god, though by primitive thought submerged under a mass of revolting paganisms and indecencies. Here was the profound sacrament of the ancient world that a god should die in order that his people might have life—a faith that, sublimated and purified, became central in Christianity. It is of the significance of Hosea not alone that he combated the iniquities of the popular cult but also that he had the inspired genius to recognize the truth imbedded therein. This yearning of the Divine over his people had but meager expression by previous thinkers in Israel; they were rather impressed with the power of God. But Hosea has left us remarkable expressions of it; and from his time onward the concept of the love of God comes to characterize Israel's theology. It is no accident that a thinker just a little later enjoined his people, "Thou shalt love the Lord thy God with all thy heart and with all thy soul and with all thy strength."[47] Hosea's words are scarcely less impressive:

When Israel was a child, then I loved him, and called my son out of Egypt. . . . . I taught Israel to walk; I took them on my arms. . . . . I drew them with cords of a man and with the bands of love. . . . . How shall I give thee up, Ephraim? How shall I cast thee off Israel? How shall I make thee as Admah? How shall I set thee as Zeboiim? My heart is turned within me, my compassions are kindled together. I will not execute the fierceness of mine anger, I will not return to destroy Ephraim; for I am God and not man.[48]

Hosea's message centers in the thought of God. Amos had been vitally concerned about the wrongs

[47] Deut. 6:5.   [48] Hos. 11:1–9.

done to man by his fellow-man; Hosea is equally concerned about the misconceptions of God prevailing in
the popular cultus. Amos objected to cultus as a wholly unsatisfactory substitute for righteousness; Hosea
sees in the cultus of the time a gross misrepresentation
of God. He was the first known prophet to attack image worship.[49] His conception of God was too spiritual
to permit so crass a representation of Yahweh as an
idol in human or animal form. He derided the idea
that men by their own hands could make God.[50] That
an ox or a calf should symbolize Yahweh to his people
was for Hosea an intolerable thought. How absurd
such materialistic thinking seemed to him appears from
the scorn he put into words in the phrase, "men kissing
calves!"[51] It was because of all such pagan concepts
and the immoral practices which expressed them that
Hosea came to the firm conviction that the people and
their official guides in religion knew nothing about
God. He reverted to this thought repeatedly:

My people are destroyed for lack of knowledge;
Because you have rejected knowledge,
I too will reject you that you shall not be priest of mine;
And since you have forgotten the law of your God,
I too will forget your children.[52]

Harlotry, and wine and new wine take away the understanding,
My people consults its tree,
And its staff informs it.
For a harlotrous spirit has led them astray,
And they have played the harlot away from their God.[53]

[49] Hos. 4:12, 17; 11:2; 14:3.   [50] Hos. 8:6; 14:3.
[51] Hos. 4:11, 12. See also Hos. 4:14; 5:4; 6:6; 8:9 f.
[52] Hos. 13:2; cf. 8:5 f.; 10:5 f.   [53] Hos. 4:6.

Hosea displayed keen insight in this diagnosis of Israel's sin. He grasped the whole ethical and religious
problem in one comprehensive view. All Israel's sin
and trouble were traced back by him to one single
cause, viz., the failure of Israel to understand aright
the character of Yahweh. If they would but learn to
know Yahweh aright, the cultus would be rightly used
and interpreted; the social order would be relieved of
its abuses; and the foreign policy of Israel would be
wisely conceived and conducted.

The political situation in Israel was a matter of
great concern to Hosea. He was living in the midst of
the troubled times following the death of Jeroboam.
One king followed another in rapid succession. The
air was surcharged with conspiracy all the time. He
looked for the massacre by Jehu at Jezreel to be
avenged upon Jehu's family.[54] He declared the mur-
derers who succeeded one another upon the throne to
be kings lacking the divine ordination to their office.[55]
He boldly denounced the king and court for the un-
blushing sensuality of their conduct.[56] Indeed, he considered the very institution of kingship sinful—a part
of Israel's tragic history through which she fell away
from her high calling and destiny. The nation was of
old called in the person of Jacob and given a divine
charter of conduct, to do justice and kindness. But
they entered the land, and turned from their simple
ways; they became rich in business, then their entire
life grew corrupt. They built wealthy shrines with or-

[54] Hos. 1:4 f.   [55] Hos. 8:4.   [56] Hos. 7:3–7.

nate and licentious cultus; and social oppression grew with selfishness. In opposition to the will of God they made a king—a sin for which they were still paying in the brutalities of the upstart monarchs of Hosea's own days. Their predicament was leading them further along the path of error into scheming and negotiations with Egypt and Assyria. For all this, disaster would come; and in the end Israel would once again dwell in tents—a prediction which it is difficult to say whether Hosea regarded as a threat or a promise.[57]

The text of Hosea as it now stands contains glowing pictures of the prosperity and glory in store for Israel after her punishment is past.[58] But these passages are in all probability the product of later editors.[59] Hosea was not without hope. He could not have preached to his people had he known that such preaching was futile and final and that complete destruction was inevitable for his people. All his work constituted a great effort to turn Israel's mind toward repentance, in order that escape from complete destruction might be found. He seems to have regarded national disaster as a certainty. But he looked for Israel to turn through this hard discipline to a humble faith and allegiance to her God, as in the days of old before the blandishments of Canaanite luxury had corrupted her life. If the text of the book as we now have it is arranged in approximately the order in which Hosea uttered his oracles,

[57] Cf. Hos. 8:4, 14; 9:10–17; 10:1–3 f.; 12:4–10; 13:8–12.

[58] Hos. 1:10—2:1; 2:14–16, 18–23; 3:5; 11:11.

[59] See the commentaries of W. R. Harper, Nowack, and Marti; but cf. E. Sellin, *Zwölfprophetenbuch* (1923), and Robinson, *op. cit.*

it is of interest to see that Hosea's last message pleads with Israel to turn her back upon the sins of the past and seek earnestly the forgiveness of Yahweh:

Turn, O Israel, unto Yahweh, your God;
For you have stumbled through your guilt.
Take with you words and return unto Yahweh,
Say unto him, "Pardon all our guilt,
And take away our sin;
That we may requite thee the fruit of our lips.
Assyria will not save us;
Upon horses we will not ride;
Nor will we say again to the work of our hands, Our God."[60]

[60] Hos. 14:1-3. There is no need to deny these words to Hosea; they are in close accord with the whole tenor of his message.

CHAPTER V

THE ASSYRIAN PERIL: FROM TIGLATH-PILESER TO SARGON

WITH the accession of Tiglath-Pileser to the Assyrian throne in 746 B.C., the empire took on new life. Tiglath-Pileser at once began active operations against his country's foes, and in 746–745 B.C. drove out the Aramean tribes that had encroached upon the eastern borders of Assyria between the Lower Zab and the Uknu rivers. In 744 B.C. he started west toward Syria, but, after crossing the Euphrates in his march upon Arpad, he learned that Sardur III, of Urartu, had crossed the mountains and descended upon the upper valley of the Euphrates. This intervention of Urartu at a critical juncture in the history of Syria probably was due to deliberate cooperation between Syria and Urartu against Assyria. Tiglath-Pileser at once returned across the Euphrates and administered a decisive defeat to Sardur III. For the next three years Tiglath-Pileser campaigned continuously in northern Syria, and in 741 B.C. overthrew Arpad. Thereupon Damascus, Tyre, and other states of north Syria submitted to him, and the whole region was organized as a province of the Assyrian Empire. At the same time, the leading states of central Syria paid him tribute. In 738 B.C. hostilities broke out in central Syria which called Tiglath-Pileser west again.

He devastated Hamath and reduced it to a province of Assyria. On this occasion, he received tribute from Menahem, of Israel.

At the same time, the peoples of Urartu were making trouble for Assyria. In 739 and 736 B.C. Tiglath-Pileser conducted campaigns against Urartu in the region to the south of Lake Van and restored the power and prestige of Assyria there. In 735 B.C. he attacked Turuspa, the capital city of Urartu, partly destroying it and devastating the whole land of Urartu. But the states of Syria rallied once more to the aid of Urartu, their ally, and Tiglath-Pileser was called west again in 735–734 B.C.

King Uzziah, of Judah, had died in 751 B.C.[1] In that same year the call to prophesy had come to Isaiah, of Jerusalem (Isa. 6:1).[2] This call came in the form of a vision in the Temple at Jerusalem. The writing-down of this experience may very well have followed at a somewhat later date; perhaps upon some occasion when he was challenged by the opposition to give proof of his right to prophesy. In that case his initial experience would be somewhat colored in the telling by the succeeding experience of his prophetic activity. This would account in part for the gloomy outlook of his

[1] A. T. Olmstead, *History of Palestine and Syria* (1931), p. 417; but T. H. Robinson (*History of Israel*, pp. 462–63) says 744 B.C.

[2] The best commentaries on Isaiah are G. B. Gray (1912), G. W. Wade (1911), J. Skinner (1915), O. C. Whitehouse (1905), Bernhard Duhm (3d ed., 1914), Karl Marti (1900), George Adam Smith (1927), and Otto Procksch (1930); cf. also T. K. Cheyne, *Introduction to the Book of Isaiah* (1895). An excellent survey of literature on Isaiah is furnished by Kemper Fullerton, *Harvard Theological Review*, VI (1913), 478–520.

vision. The content of the vision is very clear. The consciousness of the glory and majesty of Yahweh as very God overwhelms Isaiah to such a point that he feels himself doomed to destruction because he has seen what no mortal may look upon and live. The term "holy" affirmed by the seraphs does not here connote a moral idea, but a metaphysical one; for it is the name applied to the very essence of deity itself as distinguished from humanity. Thereupon one of the seraphs touches Isaiah's lips with a live coal taken from the altar and assures him that this act has cleansed him from impurity and put him in harmony with the exalted Yahweh. Immediately Isaiah hears a voice crying:

Whom shall I send forth, and who will go for us?

To this call he instantly responds:

Here am I! Send me.

The commission is then laid upon Isaiah to go and preach to his people, though he is assured, in the same breath, that the people will not listen to him and will be unable to understand him. To Isaiah's protesting question as to the length of such a ministry, the answer is given that it must continue until his people are totally destroyed. That a call such as that should come to a young man seems almost incredible. How could anyone dream of preaching if he were assured in advance that his work would be totally in vain? [3] The call, which

---

[3] The last phrase of vs. 13 is lacking from the Greek version and is thus clearly marked as a very late addition to the text of Isaiah. It is probable that vss. 12 and 13 are wholly late, even though they do not hold hope, as vs. 13 does; see Duhm and Marti, *op. cit.;* but, contra, Procksch, *op. cit.*

Isaiah came to interpret in this gloomy way early in his career, even if he did not originally so conceive it, has a very important bearing upon the question as to whether Isaiah preached the messianic hope or not. There was nothing of messianism involved in his call. He felt himself charged with a message of unavailing denunciation and threatening. Overwhelming destruction is in store for Judah; but the means of the punishment is not yet clearly envisaged, as was the case also with Amos and Hosea.

The early preaching of Isaiah, in the years before the outbreak of the Syro-Ephraimitish War, was to a great extent a continuation and repetition of the message of his predecessors, Amos and Hosea. The similarity of his preaching to that of Amos would almost suggest the dependence of Isaiah upon the work of that older prophet. The sermons of Isaiah that belonged to this period are (1) "The Terror of the Coming Day of Yahweh";[4] (2) "The Fall of Judah's Wicked Leaders";[5] (3) "The Frivolity and Sensuality of the Women of Wealth";[6] (4) "The Parable of the Unprofitable Vineyard";[7] (5) "The Ruin of Samaria."[8] In these sermons Isaiah emphasizes the sin of Israel as it finds expression in idolatry, soothsaying, militarism, pride and vainglory, materialism, sensuality, impoverishment of the poor, drunkenness, skepticism, bribery, and perversion of justice. The emphasis upon ingratitude in the parable of the Vineyard recalls Hosea's demand for love and

---

[4] Isa. 2:6–21   [5] Isa. 3:1–15.   [6] Isa. 3:16–24.

[7] Isa. 5:1–7.   [8] Isa. 9:8—10:4 and 5:25–29.

loyalty toward Yahweh. The form of 9:8—10:4, with
its strophes ending in a recurring refrain and its threat
of downfall for Samaria, reminds us of the similar series
of refrains in Amos 4:4–11. Amos' conception of the
Day of Yahweh comes back with increased intensity in
Isaiah's picture of its terrors. The character of the
women whom Isaiah denounces suggests the epithet
"kine of Bashan," which Amos applied to the same
women;[9] and the crimes of the rich against which
Isaiah protests are the same as those exposed by
Amos.[10] The punishment threatened by Isaiah is a
vague and terrible catastrophe sent by Yahweh, as it
was in Amos, and not a specific and human event to be
mediated by some historical agent. Isaiah's thought of
the Remnant is again related to that of Amos[11] and belongs to this earliest period of his career. The name
Shear-jashub[12] was antecedent to the Syro-Ephraimitish War. It had probably been given the boy at his
birth, and had been the occasion of one or more sermons at that time. The structure of the name shows
that the emphasis was on the Remnant-idea and not
upon the "return." Indeed, it is probable that the
original form of the name was Shear-jesheb, and that it
meant "a remnant will abide," not "will return."[13] In
any case, the thought is that a mere remnant will survive the terrible disaster of the Day of Yahweh. It is a

[9] Amos 4:1.

[11] Amos 5:3–6, 15.

[10] Cf., e.g., Amos 2:6–8 and Isa. 3:14 f.

[12] Isa. 7:3.

[13] See J. M. Powis Smith, "Shear-jashub," *Zeitschrift für die alttestamentliche Wissenschaft*, XXIV (1914), 219–24.

word of punishment, not of promise. This message of Isaiah's youth, with all its dire disaster, is addressed to both kingdoms. Amos and Hosea had been primarily, if not exclusively, interested in northern Israel; but Isaiah was concerned quite as much with Judah as with Israel. He did not shrink from announcing the destruction of his own nation. Nothing could demonstrate more conclusively the absolute self-sufficiency of Isaiah's God; he is not dependent upon any nation in the slightest degree. Nor could anything prove more clearly the great outreach of Isaiah's faith; though the people of Yahweh perish at his hand, Yahweh himself will continue to be God.

A new aspect of the social and political situation presented itself with the approach of the Syro-Ephraimitish invasion of Judah. This war was an inheritance of Ahaz from Jotham, his father.[14] Apparently, a great coalition movement of the western states against Assyria was under way. In this movement Damascus and Samaria, at least, were involved. Judah had evidently refused to co-operate in the revolt, and was either neutral or pro-Assyrian.[15] Menahem, of Samaria, had made terms with Assyria in 738 B.C. His son, Pekahiah, probably continued the policy of submission to Assyria; but after two years he was assassinated by Pekah, who quite evidently was anti-Assyrian and perhaps pro-Urartu in his politics. This brought on the attack upon

[14] II Kings 15:37.

[15] Cf. the loyalty of Panammu II and Bar-rekub, kings of Sam'al, to Tiglath-Pileser, when Ya'udi was fighting him; see the inscription of Bar-rekub in G. A. Cooke's *North Semitic Inscriptions* (1903), pp. 171 ff.

Judah. When the army of Damascus had joined forces with that of Samaria upon the soil of Israel, and a state bordering upon panic had seized the minds of the people of Judah and their king,[16] the conviction came to Isaiah that he must speak the will of Yahweh to his king. Accompanied by his little son, Shear-jesheb, he encountered Ahaz, who was on a tour of inspection of the water supply of Jerusalem in anticipation of the threatened siege of the city. The message of Isaiah was to the effect that Ahaz should take heart and not be dismayed by two such futile foes as Rezin and Pekah. Though they were seeking to split Judah by internal factions[17] and to set up a new king who would be favorable to their interests, their plans were doomed to failure.[18] It was a call to unwavering faith in Yahweh. "If you do not believe, you will not be established."[19]

This first oracle did not accomplish its purpose. Therefore, a second was given to Ahaz, either on the same day or at some other time. The challenge came to him to ask for the performance of a miracle, no matter how extraordinary it might be, and it should be done for him as a demonstration of the fact that the

[16] Isa. 7:2.

[17] On the meaning of Isa. 7:6 see A. Brux, *American Journal of Semitic Languages and Literatures*, XXXIX (1922), 68–71.

[18] The second half of 7:8 is a gloss by a later hand, wholly lacking in force if regarded as original.

[19] In the Hebrew there is a clever play upon words which cannot be satisfactorily carried over into English. George Adam Smith (*The Book of Isaiah*) with the use of a north-England word gives the rendering, "If ye have not faith, ye cannot have staith."

prophet was actually speaking the mind of Yahweh. Suppose Ahaz had accepted this offer, what then? But Ahaz declined, alleging his unwillingness to subject Yahweh to such a test. It is quite probable that Ahaz had gone so far in his own policy that he was afraid to risk the acceptance of the prophet's challenge. It might turn out that the prophet could do what he promised, and then Ahaz would be in an embarrassing position! On the other hand, what stupendous faith was involved in such a challenge on the part of Isaiah—a faith that stopped at nothing. After all, Isaiah was but calling upon Ahaz to exercise a trust in Yahweh that was puny as compared with Isaiah's own robust and gigantic faith. However, when Ahaz declined to choose a miracle, Isaiah proceeded to give him a "sign" from Yahweh himself:

> Behold, a young woman is with child and will bear a son and will call his name "Immanuel." For before the lad knows how to reject the bad and choose the good, the land on account of whose two kings you are in terror will be deserted.[20]

This is one of the most famous passages of the entire Old Testament; and it is doubtful if any has occasioned a more voluminous literature of interpretation.[21] The views presented have been diverse and contradictory;

[20] Isa. 7:14, 16. Vs. 15 is here omitted as a gloss; see Duhm's commentary, *ad. loc.*, and J. M. Powis Smith, *American Journal of Semitic Languages and Literatures*, XL (1924), 292–94. The verse interrupts the close connection between vss. 14 and 16 and is best accounted for as an attempt on the part of a later reader to fix more definitely the date before which the prediction was to be fulfilled.

[21] For a sketch of the history of exegesis of the passage see G. B. Gray, *The Book of Isaiah*, pp. 133–36.

and as yet no approximation to agreement is apparent. Recent advances in our knowledge of the ancient East render it highly probable, however, that Isaiah is here alluding to an element of that large body of folklore and legend, which, less official than mythology, yet exerted an immense influence on the thinking of peoples of the ancient world. Just as Amos had employed the popular expectation of the Day of Yahweh, so Isaiah here uses that of the Wonder Child,[22] to which we have come to recognize reference in not a few other passages of the Old Testament. Isaiah, then, urges his policy on Ahaz with the assurance that the child is soon to be born through whom, in popular belief, the golden age is to be ushered in. But in this case he will be so much the more marvelous that this glorious eventuality will not await the intervention of his mature powers but will attend even his early infancy. Thus the prophet is consistent with his first oracle in this crisis (vs. 4), promising that nothing is to be feared from the invading kings of Aram and Israel. However, for Ahaz personally there is no such assurance; he had lacked the sustaining faith demanded by the crisis (vs. 9). In certain forms of the legend the child deposes the reigning monarch and rules in his place. And this would seem to be Isaiah's thought here; for, while Judah is to be delivered through removal of the two invading kings

---

[22] See R. Kittel, *Die hellenistische Mysterienreligion und das Alte Testament* (1924). The view is not new; see Gray (*op. cit.*) and Procksch (*op. cit.*), who disapprove.

(vs. 16), the Lord will bring on Ahaz and his people[23] and his father's house—the entire royal family—"days that have not come."

A third oracle given in connection with the Syro-Ephraimitish War is contained in Isa. 8:1-4. It is, in fact, the sequel of the Immanuel prediction. He was bidden by Yahweh to prepare a document, inscribing thereon in easily legible characters the four words, lemăhēr shălăl hăsh băz, i.e., "for swift is spoil, speedy is prey." Two well-known men were called as witnesses of the agreement that Isaiah made with some woman described as "the prophetess," whose identity is not obvious, though recent interpretation tends to deny that she was his wife;[24] we have no basis elsewhere for supposing that the wife of a prophet was called "the prophetess." It is probable rather that the incident parallels Hosea's alliances discussed in the previous chapter. Then almost a year later when their son was born, Isaiah bestowed upon him the foregoing name. The boy and the episode together gave great prominence to Isaiah's prophecy of the overthrow of Damascus and Samaria. All three of the oracles considered must have been uttered before Isaiah became aware of the fact that Ahaz had summoned Assyria to his aid.[25]

[23] While "people" here suggests the people of Judah as a whole, the word in Hebrew frequently connotes smaller groups, notably personal retainers.

[24] See May, American Journal of Semitic Languages and Literatures, XLVIII, 87; cf. also Raven quoted by Delitsch in Biblical Commentary on the Prophecies of Isaiah, ad. loc.

[25] II Kings 16:7 ff. Tiglath-Pileser's own account of his campaign against Damascus and Samaria is contained in his Annals and in an-

Isaiah's desire was to encourage Ahaz to put his trust in Yahweh and not to make application to Tiglath-Pileser, of Assyria, for aid. As we know from II Kings 16:7, Ahaz took the apparently more practical course of appeal to Assyria. But was it in reality any more practical? By calling in Tiglath-Pileser, Ahaz put himself and his country under vassalage to Assyria, with the accompanying necessity of paying tribute. This obligation was responsible for much of Judah's later trouble. Had Ahaz heeded Isaiah, he would have had to put up a stiff resistance for a few months to the invaders, it is true; but Tiglath-Pileser would ultimately have come to his aid on his own account, for the Assyrian would not have been long ignorant of the fact that the whole northern movement was anti-Assyrian in its scope and purpose. Tiglath-Pileser could have been trusted to look out for Assyria's interests; and Judah would have been under no obligation to the great king. On the whole, the obligation would have lain the other way. Isaiah was not so impractical a dreamer, on this occasion, at least, as might appear. As it was, Tiglath-Pileser came west and punished the rebels severely. Israel lost her territory east of the Jordan,[26] the population of which was deported to As-

---

other small inscription; see S. A. B. Mercer, *Extra-biblical Sources* (1913), pp. 38–40; R. W. Rogers, *Cuneiform Parallels to the Old Testament* (1926), pp. 316–21; George A. Barton, *Archaeology and the Bible* (1937), pp. 464 f.; D. D. Luckenbill, *Ancient Records of Assyria* (1926), I, 276, 279–80, 287, 292–93.

[26] II Kings 15:29.

syria,[27] and Judah paid heavily for the relief she obtained through Assyria.

When the prophet learned that Ahaz had disregarded the repeated assurance from Yahweh, in that he had called upon Tiglath-Pileser for help, the whole tone of his prophecy changed. One good reason why Isaiah so strenuously objected to the Assyrian alliance lay in the fact that it involved a recognition of the Assyrian gods and so involved disloyalty to Yahweh, as well as a heavy burden of tribute to be paid by the common people of the land.[28] That Isaiah's objections were well grounded is clear from the record in II Kings 16:7–18. Immediately after Ahaz returned from Damascus, whither he had gone to pay his respects to Tiglath-Pileser, he went to inspect the new altar that he had ordered to be built in the Temple at Jerusalem. This was a duplicate of an altar to the Assyrian king,[29] which he had seen at Damascus; and it was erected on the site of the old altar of Yahweh, which was displaced and reduced in rank. This, with other accessory changes, was all done "because of the king of Assyria." The robbery and impoverishment of Yahweh's Temple in order that the king and gods of Assyria might receive the tribute demanded by them and the displacement of Yahweh's altar by one that acknowl-

[27] For Tiglath-Pileser's account of this see Mercer, *op. cit.*, p. 40.

[28] What the narrator in Kings euphemistically calls "a present," Tiglath-Pileser in his Nimrod Inscription lists as "tribute" (see R. F. Harper, *Assyrian and Babylonian Literature* [1901], p. 57; Luckenbill, *op. cit.*, pp. 287–93).

[29] See Olmstead, *op. cit.*, p. 452.

edged the supremacy of the Assyrian cults were more than Isaiah's loyalty to Yahweh could contemplate with equanimity.

To the days immediately following Isaiah's discovery of the faithless policy of King Ahaz probably belong the fragments of his prophecy now imbedded in Isa. 7:17–25 and 8:5–22. In these utterances Isaiah expressed his conviction that Ahaz, by rejecting the call to trust in Yahweh only, has prepared for himself and his people a terrible disaster from which there can be no escape:

> Inasmuch as this people has rejected
> The waters of Shiloach that run smoothly;[30]
> Therefore, behold, the Lord will bring up upon them
> The waters of the River that are mighty and many;[31]
> And it will rise over all its channels,
> And run over all its banks;
> And it will sweep on into Judah, an overflowing flood,
> And will reach up to the neck.[32]

In Isa. 8:11–18 we find some words that were apparently spoken by Isaiah to a group of his followers and supporters. The precise date of their utterance is unknown, but it was prior to 721 B.C., when Samaria fell, and it may have closed Isaiah's activity in connec-

[30] The Hebrew text adds here an unintelligible phrase, saying something about "joy" and "Rezin, the son of Remaliah."

[31] The Hebrew text adds here "the king of Assyria and all his glory," which is probably a correct interpretation of Isaiah's thought by a later editor.

[32] Isa. 8:6–8a. The Hebrew adds here a clause that is clearly a later comment: "And the spreading out of his wings will fill the breadth of thy land, O Immanuel."

tion with the Syro-Ephraimitish War. Its position in
the text, at least, points to such a connection. The
exact bearing of this message upon that situation or
any other definite one is uncertain.

You shall not say "holy" of anything of which this people says
"holy";[33] and what it fears you shall not fear or dread. Yahweh of
hosts is he whom you shall call "holy"; and *he* shall be your fear,
and *he* shall be your dread. And he shall be a sanctuary and a
tripping stone and a stumbling block to both the houses of Israel;
a trap and a snare to the inhabitant of Jerusalem. And many will
stumble on them and fall and be broken and snared and captured.

Perhaps the prophet is here expressing his mind as to
the new type of worship which Ahaz had imported
from Assyria by way of Damascus.

Whatever may have been the occasion of the foregoing oracle, in Isa. 8:16–18 are found some instructions to his disciples and followers given at a time when
he fully intended to close his prophetic career. Perhaps
it was in a period of depression after the discovery that
his counsel in the Syro-Ephraimitish crisis had been
wholly ignored. He here puts his oracles in trust under
the care of his disciples, declares his confidence in Yahweh, and states his conviction that he himself and his
children, whom he has used as peripatetic sermons,
will in course of time be recognized by everybody as
signs and portents from Yahweh, i.e., it will be patent
to all eyes that Isaiah was right and Ahaz was wrong.

[33] The Hebrew has "conspiracy" for "holy"; but the two words are
easily confused in Hebrew, and the use of "holy" for Yahweh in the following clauses makes a strong probability for "holy" in the first verse.
On the other hand, "conspiracy" would give a close connection with
the Syro-Ephraimitish War.

It is especially noteworthy in this connection that Isaiah seems to have given up hope of the deliverance of Judah; he seems to have been convinced that the nation was doomed; yet he holds fast to his faith in Yahweh notwithstanding. He has, consciously or unconsciously, broken away from the national conception of Yahweh as God of the Jewish nation, and is now thinking of him as the God of a small group of the pious— the God of a nonpolitical community of the faithful. The members of the community are still Jews, of course, but their relationship to Yahweh is primarily conditioned by their piety, not by their race. Neither Isaiah nor any of his immediate successors carried this position further. It was pregnant with immense consequences, though; for here is the germ of the later concept of the church. A longer training in the school of suffering was the prime requisite to further progress.

The next crisis in Palestine involved the fall of Samaria and the exile of the people of Israel in 721 B.C. The experiences of 735 had not taught Israel the necessary lesson of submission to and acceptance of the yoke of Assyria. Hoshea, upon the death of the great Tiglath-Pileser in 728 B.C., promptly joined Egypt[34]

[34] The name of the king of Egypt as given in II Kings 17:4 is So. The identification with any known pharaoh is dubious. The least unlikely attempt is that which makes him the same as the Sib'e who in alliance with the Philistines opposed Sargon in 720 B.C. and in 711 B.C., at which latter time he was a general of the pharaoh. The cartouche of a minor dynast bearing the name Sb(y) has been found belonging to the same period as Hoshea. The equivalence of the Hebrew w and the Egyptian and Assyrian b is shown by many cases of interchange (see G. Möller, *Orientalistische Literaturzeitung* for 1919, cols. 145 ff.).

and other western states in an attempt to throw off the
Assyrian yoke; but Shalmaneser V (727–722 B.C.)
quickly quelled this uprising and collected tribute from
Hoshea and his allies.[35] In 725 B.C., however, revolt
broke out again, headed by the same group. Hoshea
seems to have been captured at once by the Assyrians,[36]
but Samaria yielded only in 722–721 B.C., after undergoing the protracted agonies of a three-year siege.[37]
The coup de grâce was given her by Sargon, the new
king of Assyria, Shalmaneser having died while the
siege was in progress.[38]

So great an event as the peril to Samaria could not
fail to stir the mind of Isaiah. It was too near home to
be disregarded. Further, the people of Samaria were
also Hebrews and worshiped the same Yahweh as their
brethren of the south. In Isa. 14:28–32, in its original
form, we probably have an oracle spoken against
Philistia at the time of the death of Tiglath-Pileser
(728 B.C.), when the smoldering longings for freedom
from Assyria were bursting into flame.[39] Isaiah put

[35] II Kings 17:3.

[36] No mention is made of Hoshea in the Assyrian account of the final
capture of Samaria; and II Kings 17:4 states that Hoshea was imprisoned by Shalmaneser, who then proceeded to besiege the capital.

[37] For the reports of Shalmaneser and Sargon upon these events, see
Mercer, *op. cit.*, pp. 40–43; Rogers, *op. cit.*, pp. 323–36; Luckenbill,
op. cit., II, 2–3, 13, 26, 105.

[38] II Kings 17:1–6 apparently credits Shalmaneser with the capture
of Samaria; but the king who captured Samaria is not actually named.

[39] See Gray's *Commentary* for varying views as to the occasion and
meaning of this oracle; also the discussions in *American Journal of Semitic Languages and Literatures*, XLII, 86 ff.; XLIV, 73 ff.

himself on record as convinced that the movement toward revolt was ill advised, and would bring down dire
disaster upon the heads of the participants. The influence of Isaiah may have had much to do with keeping Judah quiescent. Perhaps Isa. 32:9–14 belongs to
this period also. It is an oracle against the rich women
of Jerusalem. They are denounced for their careless
ease and told that their beloved city will be laid waste
and desolate, "a joy of wild asses, a pasture for flocks."
How unreal that must have sounded in the ears of
people who had looked upon the substantial walls of
Jerusalem and its great temple all their lives and had
come to think of them as abiding forever! In the same
period, or at an earlier date, belongs the scathing attack upon the women of Jerusalem in Isa. 3:16—4:1.
Their absorbing interest in the details of their personal
appearance is satirized mercilessly, and with considerable artistic skill. A dreadful fate for Jerusalem similar to that threatened in Isa. 32:9 ff. is here held up
for the contemplation of these sensuous leaders of the
fashions of the city. The only prophecy directed
straight at the people of Samaria themselves in the period just before their final overthrow is Isa. 28:1–4.
This oracle was probably uttered early in the course of
the revolt, before the final three-year siege had set in.
The dissipated people of Samaria are thought of here
as incapable of putting up a stiff resistance and as an
easy and speedy prey to the victorious Assyrians. As a
matter of fact, it took the army of Shalmaneser and

Sargon three years to capture the city.[40] When we realize what a three-year siege by the most efficient war
machine of the ancient world must have meant to the
citizens of Samaria, we may be a bit reluctant to accept
Isaiah's characterization of the people and their leaders
as morally degraded and powerless. A long siege is a
severe test of character. The siege of Samaria, like the
defense of Verdun, is an eloquent testimonial to the
moral soundness of the people involved in those endurance tests.

The downfall of Samaria brought about the end of
the northern kingdom, which now became as Assyrian
province. Natives of other parts of the Assyrian Empire were imported to take the place of the twenty-
seven thousand deported citizens. The result was the
rise of a mixed people in northern Israel, who were
mongrel in religion as well as in blood.[41] With the cessation of the northern kingdom came also the cessation
of its historical tradition. The literature of the north
was preserved only in so far as it fell into the hands of
the southern Jews, with whom it underwent a radical
revision from the point of view of the interests and
needs of Judah. Judah was now brought face to face
with Assyria, who became the nearest neighbor on the
north. There was no longer any windshield for Judah
against the bitter blasts from the north. Egypt, also,

[40] For the Hebrew record see II Kings 17:5, 6, 24 ff. For the accounts of Shalmaneser and Sargon see Mercer, *op. cit.*, p. 43;
Rogers, *op. cit.*, pp. 317–26; Barton, *op. cit.*, pp. 466 f.; and Luckenbill,
op. cit., I, 279–80; II, 2.

[41] See II Kings 17:25 ff.

was now in even more immediate danger from Assyria than ever before. This situation was responsible for the nervousness of Egyptian politicians from this time on; and that in turn was a constant source of trouble for Judah. The prophets are now concerned only with the problems of Judah; but the problems of Judah were henceforth world-problems; and Yahweh's chances for world-recognition are now in Judah's hands.

CHAPTER VI

THE ASSYRIAN PERIL: FROM SARGON
TO SENNACHERIB

THE downfall of Samaria did not bring peace
to western Asia. The thirst for liberty among
the small nations of the Mediterranean coastlands could not be quenched by tyranny. Revolts followed one another in the Assyrian Empire with light-
ning-like rapidity. In 720 B.C., immediately after the
great disaster of 722–721 B.C., Samaria joined with
Hamath, Arpad, Simirra, and Damascus in a desper-
ate struggle for freedom. Egypt, Philistia, and some
Arabian tribes were also involved in this revolt. But
Sargon quickly suppressed this rebellion, destroying
cities, devastating countries, and deporting peoples, as
in the case of Samaria in 721 B.C.[1] Again, in 715 B.C.,
Sargon had dealings with Samaria. After a campaign
against some Arab tribes in that year, he settled some
of his Arab captives in Samaria.[2] Right at the beginning of Sargon's reign, Marduk-apal-iddin, known in
Hebrew as Merodach-baladan, had established the independence of Babylonia, wresting the crown out of

[1] See R. W. Rogers, *Cuneiform Parallels to the Old Testament* (1926),
p. 327.

[2] See Sargon's "Annals," in R. F. Harper, *Assyrian and Babylonian
Literature* (1901), p. 60; D. D. Luckenbill, *Ancient Records of Assyria*
(1926), II, 3; Rogers, *op. cit.*, p. 327.

the grasp of Assyria. Elam also joined with Babylon in the struggle against Assyria. Such a blow to the power of Sargon before he could establish himself firmly on the throne brought new hope and courage to all the foes of Assyria. Among these not the least dangerous were the peoples of Urartu, in the north, who became a constant peril to Assyria. Sargon conducted campaigns against Urartu and its allies in 719, 718, 716, 715, 714, 713, and 711 B.C. To add to Sargon's troubles, Shabaka, the Ethiopian, became master of Egypt in 712 B.C., and at once became active in stirring up difficulties for Sargon in the west. Sargon was thus completely surrounded by enemies. Elam on the east co-operated with Babylonia on the south; on the north, Urartu and its neighbors from the upper Mediterranean coastlands to the eastern shores of Lake Urumia joined hands against him; and, in the west and southwest, Syria, Palestine, Egypt, and Arabian clans completed the circle. But Sargon, like a lion surrounded by jackals, shook them all off and brought them into subjection.

Of immediate interest is the revolt of Ashdod referred to in Isa. 20:1 ff. This was part of a concerted movement against Sargon by Philistia, Egypt, Moab, Edom, and Judah in the years 713–711 B.C. The enterprise was a total failure, for the allies suffered an ignominious defeat at the hands of Sargon's forces.[3] In con-

[3] See Sargon's "Annals" and two other inscriptions for the Assyrian reports; S. A. B. Mercer, *Extra-biblical Sources* (1913), pp. 45 f.; Rogers, *op. cit.*, pp. 328–31; George A. Barton, *Archaeology and the Bible* (1937), pp. 468 f.; Luckenbill, *op. cit.*, II, 13, 26, 27, 105.

nection with this revolt, Isaiah again appeared in action. To this crisis in Judah's fortunes Isa. 20:1–6 is clearly to be attached; perhaps Isa. 28:7–29, 29:1–4, 22:15–18, 1:18–20, and 5:8–24 also belong here. The oracle in Isa. 20:1–6 evidently was spoken early in the course of the conspiracy, and its message was personally and vividly illustrated afresh every time that Isaiah appeared upon the streets of Jerusalem. This exhibition of himself for homiletical purposes extended over a period of "three years." This may mean continuous parts of three years, beginning, for example, in the latter part of 713 B.C., and ending in the beginning of 711 B.C. That Isaiah went about stark naked, there is no sufficient reason to doubt. That is the common meaning of the word used; that is called for by the application of the action in verse 4; and that was a common way of treating captives on the part of the Assyrian conquerors.[4] Through this dramatic procedure Isaiah sought in vain to keep Judah from participating in the revolt. He was convinced that Egypt and Ethiopia would render no adequate assistance against Assyria, but would themselves fall a prey to Sargon's might and suffer deportation of their population. His expectations in this latter respect were not completely fulfilled; Sargon did not set foot in Egypt, but he did

[4] See, e.g., Eduard Meyer, *Sumerier und Semiten in Babylonien* (1906), p. 25; G. Contenau, *La Glyptique Syro-Hittite* (1922), Pl. I; A. T. Olmstead, *History of Assyria* (1923), pp. 112, 115 f., 126, 138; L. W. King, *Bronze Reliefs from the Gates of Shalmaneser* (1915), Pls. IV, X, XV, XLVI, LXXIV.

force the king of Meluchha[5] to surrender to Assyria the fugitive king of Ashdod who had taken refuge with him. Whether or not any unusual punishment was inflicted upon Judah is told us by neither Sargon nor the Hebrew accounts. Certainly, heavy tribute would be levied at the least. Possibly Isa. 10:28–32 is the prophet's anticipation of a direct attack upon Jerusalem at this time. If so, he vividly describes the march as it progresses stage by stage up to the very outskirts of Jerusalem.[6]

Isaiah's judgment upon the lives of the official priests and prophets of his day was very severe. He charged them with drunkenness and mad revelry and with an attitude of scorn toward the truth of God as Isaiah himself preached it. They were putting their confidence in Egypt instead of trusting in Yahweh. That misplaced confidence would betray them into the hands of Assyria. Apparently, the covenant with Egypt was already operative, and just as Ahaz had imported Assyrian practices after his appeal to Tiglath-Pileser, so now with the Egyptian alliance have come in Egyptian religious customs;[7] but it was all to no purpose.[8]

To this same period, perhaps, belongs the denuncia-

[5] Apparently a name for Ethiopia or some part thereof; see Landsberger in *Zeitschrift für Assyrologie*, XXXV (N.F. 1), 271, n. 2; Langdon in *Cambridge Ancient History*, I, 415 f.; Kmosko in *Zeitschrift für Assyrologie*, XXXI, 216.

[6] T. H. Robinson (*History of Israel* [1932], p. 396) and A. T. Olmstead (*History of Palestine and Syria* [1931], p. 475) consider that the passage refers to Sennacherib's advance in 701.

[7] See Isa. 28:15–18.   [8] Isa. 28:7–22; cf. 29:1–4.

tion of Shebna, the king's treasurer.[9] He doubtless was
a leader of the court party opposed to Isaiah's policy,
and so received the doubtful honor of special treatment
at Isaiah's hands. Another oracle that has been much
misunderstood may also belong here, viz., Isa. 1:18–
20:

"Come, now, and let us confer together," says Yahweh,
"If your sins be like crimson, can they be white like snow?
 If they be red like scarlet, can they be like wool?
 If you be willing and listen, you will eat the good of the land.
 But if you refuse and are stubborn, by the sword will you be
    consumed;
 For the mouth of Yahweh has spoken."[10]

The prophet here says that it is preposterous for Israel
to continue in outbreaking sins, and yet expect to reap
the rewards of piety. If they would receive blessings
from Yahweh as a nation they must conform to his
requirements; they will fail to do so on penalty of destruction.

The last oracle belonging to the crisis of 711 B.C. is
Isa. 5:8–24. Here Isaiah denounced the land-grabbing
nobles, who by oppression and extortion were driving
men and their families off their little holdings and
adding them to their great estates. The wealth they
thus obtain by shameful measures they waste upon
riotous living. When the prophet threatens them with
judgment, they jeer at him and challenge him to make
good upon his threats. Judgment will sweep away

[9] Isa. 22:15–19.

[10] The treatment of the two clauses in vs. 18 as interrogative is gram-
matically permissible, and it is demanded by the context (see Gray's
Commentary, ad loc.).

these men from the land, and it will become desolate—
a pasture land for flocks. All this will come to pass because the leaders of Judah have lacked understanding.
Isaiah's panacea for all ills in this crisis, even as at the
time of the Syro-Ephraimitish invasion, was faith in
God. This would keep Judah from entangling alliances
with foreign peoples who could do nothing for her of
any value; and it would lead her to walk in paths of
social justice, and so guarantee to her the blessing of
God. The cornerstone of the true Jerusalem consists
of a great religious principle: "He who has faith will
not be perturbed."[11]

The last great crisis in the history of Judah during
the lifetime of Isaiah was the invasion of Sennacherib,
king of Assyria. When the great conqueror, Sargon,
died in 705 B.C., the subject-states of Assyria seized upon the occasion to strike for freedom. The reports upon
the course of events vary. Sennacherib himself left a
good account of his campaigns in what is now known
as "the Taylor Prism."[12] In the first year of his reign he
overthrew Merodach-baladan, of Babylon, who fled
for his life. His allies the Elamites, certain Arabian
peoples, and some Aramean clans were also conquered
and deported. In the second year, Sennacherib conquered the Kassites and received tribute from the
Medes. Having made things safe at home, he turned
west in his third year. He first drove Luli, king of Sidon, in flight from his throne and put a substitute in

[11] Isa. 26:16. Hebrew is literally "hurry" or "hasten."

[12] For the best translation of this inscription see D. D. Luckenbill,
The Annals of Sennacherib (1924), pp. 23–47 and 128 ff.

his place as vassal. He then worked southward, over-coming everything in his path. Ashdod, Ammon, Moab, and Edom all brought tribute and submitted to his yoke.[13] He dethroned Zidka, king of Askelon, and put a new king in his place, under vassalage to himself. Joppa and three other Philistine towns were besieged and captured. The citizens of Ekron had revolted against their king, Padi, and had handed him over in chains to Hezekiah, who held him in prison. Upon the approach of Sennacherib they appealed to Egypt and Meluchha for help. The Egyptian army was encoun-tered by Sennacherib at Altaku and decisively de-feated. Then Ekron met its fate and was forced to take back Padi as king and become tributary to Assyria.

It was now Hezekiah's turn to be punished. Sen-nacherib declares that he besieged and captured "forty-six of his strong-walled cities and innumerable smaller cities round about them"; that he captured 200,150 people and livestock beyond reckoning; and that he shut up Hezekiah "like a caged bird" in Jerusa-lem, against which he threw up fortifications.[14] He then goes on to say that he turned over the captured cities to the kings of Ekron, Ashdod, and Gaza, and

[13] This stage of the campaign is depicted upon a bas-relief in Sen-nacherib's palace which represents him seated upon his throne at Lachish and receiving tribute and submission from the defeated kings (see C. J. Ball, *Light from the East* [1899], pp. 191, 193; and A. T. Olmstead, *History of Assyria* [1924], p. 308).

[14] Sennacherib's figures are much exaggerated without doubt. There were not forty-six walled towns in all Judah. For the exaggerations of Assyrian records see A. T. Olmstead, *History of Assyria*, pp. 579 f. and 652 f.

that Hezekiah, overcome by fear and by the desertion of certain foreign mercenaries, paid heavy tribute, rendered homage, and suffered the loss of rich booty.[15]

The Hebrew records of the campaign against Jerusalem are preserved in two recensions: (1) Isaiah, chapters 36–38, and (2) II Kings 18:13—20:21. The older of these two recensions is that in II Kings. They are alike in content except that the Kings recension has one episode described in II Kings 18:14–16 that does not appear in the Isaiah-narrative. The older narrative, apart from II Kings 18:14–16, however, is woven of two strands. The first of these includes II Kings 18:17 —19:9a, 36, 37; the second is represented by II Kings 19:9b–35. According to the first, Sennacherib sent his *rabshakeh* with a detachment of troops against Jerusalem. The *rabshakeh* hailed the city and sought to persuade the representatives of Hezekiah and the people at large to surrender, since resistance to the overwhelming might of Assyria was absurd. The generals of Hezekiah carried the message to him; whereupon he besought Yahweh in the Temple and sent word of his trouble to Isaiah. Isaiah assured him that Sennacherib would be called back to Assyria by a rumor of trouble there, and then he would be slain. The *rabshakeh* returned to his master whom he now found attacking Libnah. Sennacherib heard of the approach of Tirhaka, of Egypt, with his army, and so returned to Assyria, where he met death at the hands of his own sons.

[15] For a study of this campaign see *ibid.*, pp. 297–315; cf. Barton, *op. cit.*, pp. 472 f.

The second strand[16] covers the same course of events, but differs in some details. The speech of the *rabshakeh* is now replaced by a royal letter from Sennacherib himself, saying in substance the same thing as the speech. Hezekiah's prayer in the Temple is now given in full. Isaiah sends word to Hezekiah at Yahweh's bidding, that his prayer is answered; and an extended speech of Isaiah's is given in which Hezekiah is assured that no harm will come to him or his city. That very night the angel of Yahweh smote the camp of the Assyrians, leaving 185,000 dead.

In II Kings 18:14–16, we are told that Hezekiah sent to Sennacherib at Lachish proffering his submission and declaring his readiness to pay whatever Sennacherib might demand. The penalty laid upon him was thirty talents of gold and three hundred talents of silver. Hezekiah emptied his treasury and stripped the gold decorations from the Temple of Yahweh and sent the king of Assyria what he demanded.

What are these narratives worth? The last one mentioned at least agrees with the account of Sennacherib himself. Even the amount of gold surrendered by Hezekiah is the same in the Assyrian and the Hebrew narratives. Sennacherib has magnified the silver contribution undoubtedly. It is not at all likely that the Hebrew narrative would have invented such a humiliation of Hezekiah as this account involves. Sennacherib did receive tribute at Lachish from the kings of the region, as shown by his bas-relief. Everything thus sup-

16 II Kings 19:9b–35.

ports the trustworthiness of this record in II Kings 18:14-16.[17]

The account in II Kings 19:9*b*-35 contains serious difficulties. The prophecy of Isaiah in verses 21-31 is evidently an insertion in the story; verse 32 continues verse 20 directly. The purpose of this narrative quite clearly is to magnify the prophet Isaiah, who becomes the central figure in it. The figure "185,000" for the slain of the plague is beyond all possibility of fact. No such rate of mortality in so short a time and on so large a scale was ever known. The army of Sennacherib would hardly have attained such a size as this number involves.[18] Shalmaneser at Karkar claims to have defeated the joint army of twelve kings, numbering in all 71,900 men. The chances are that he magnified his foe to enhance his own glory. The same king says that he crossed the Euphrates with 120,000 troops. The feeding of an army of 185,000 on the scanty resources of Judah would have been a difficult problem for Sennacherib. The great king made no reference whatsoever to any such disaster as is here described. The appalling character of it would have made complete silence impossible; indeed, such a disaster would probably have cost Sennacherib his throne; for he was not without enemies. The story of Herodotus does not furnish

[17] This has been recognized generally since Stade said that II Kings 18:13-16 was the only historical portion in the Sennacherib story of II Kings and Isaiah.

[18] For the size of Assyrian armies see J. Hunger, *Der alte Orient* (1911), No. XII; B. Meissner, *Babylonien und Assyrien* (1920), pp. 101 f.; and Menitius, *Das assyrische Heer und sein Organization.*

much support for this narrative. His horde of mice that gnawed the bowstrings of the Assyrians did not, in any case, kill them; nor did they put the rest of the Assyrian equipment out of commission. The bowmen were not, as far as Assyrian records show, a preponderating element in the Assyrian armies.[19]

The narrative in II Kings 18:17—19:9a is lacking in events, but well supplied with speeches. There is no reason to doubt the sending of an embassy to demand the surrender of Jerusalem. It may seem unlikely that Hezekiah should have depended so much upon the advice of Isaiah, in view of the fact that he had spurned that advice thus far in his international policy. The reference to Tirhaka at the end of the account creates trouble. Tirhaka did not take the throne of Egypt until 688 B.C., thirteen years after the campaign of 701. He may have been in command of this expedition to relieve Jerusalem before he came to the throne, in which case this narrative makes him king prematurely.

To sum up the situation: the difficulties involved in attaching the events of the Hebrew tradition to the campaign of 701 are so many and so great that scholars have shown a tendency to create a second and later campaign of Sennacherib's against Jerusalem and Egypt.[20] But sober criticism finds no sufficient evidence as yet for any such campaign.[21] As far as Jerusalem is

[19] See Olmstead, *History of Assyria*, pp. 83 and 111.

[20] H. Winckler, *Alttestamentliche Untersuchungen* (1892), pp. 32 ff.; Rogers, *op. cit.*, p. 338; Barton, *op. cit.*, pp. 473 f.; I. Benzinger, *Kurzer Hand-Kommentar* (1899), *ad. loc.*

[21] See, e.g., D. D. Luckenbill, *The Annals of Sennacherib*, pp. 12 ff.

concerned, it is difficult to see what need there could be of another expedition from Assyria after the drastic punishment inflicted on Judah in the campaign of 701. Judah must have been completely prostrated if the Assyrian record is at all true to fact. It would seem, indeed, that the disaster to Judah was so overwhelming that the Hebrew tradition felt the need of a corresponding blow to Assyria, and proceeded to create such a counterpoise for the sake of the honor of Yahweh.

It now remains to see what the prophets did in the situation from 705 to 701 B.C. Isaiah did not hide his head at this time. He came to the fore with unflinching courage. When Merodach-baladan was working up his revolt against Sennacherib, he sent an embassy to Hezekiah to persuade him to join the movement.[22] The account of the visit is given in Isaiah, chapter 39 (= II Kings 20:12–19). The visit was made under the guise of solicitude for the health of Hezekiah. But it did not escape Isaiah's eye that the king showed the embassy all his resources. This narrative was written long after Isaiah's day,[23] but it is historical in that it records an actual embassy to Hezekiah and in that it reflects correctly Isaiah's attitude toward political and military attempts to throw off the Assyrian yoke.

Isaiah was equally outspoken in his denunciation of

[22] Merodach-baladan was king of Babylon from 721 to 710 B.C., when Sargon drove him out of Babylonia. But upon the death of Sargon, he again seized the throne of Babylon and held it for nine months, being finally dislodged by Sennacherib in 704. It is not clear at which of these periods the embassy was sent.

[23] See the commentaries of Duhm, Marti, Wade, and Procksch on Isaiah, and cf. Benzinger and Kittel on Kings.

the alliance with Egypt. In his judgment, such expectations of aid are doomed to disappointment. Egypt is powerless to bring relief; she will but increase the punishment from Assyria. In Isa. 30:1–17 and 31:1–3 such sentiments as these are plainly uttered, e.g.,

> The Egyptians will help in vain and to no purpose.
> Therefore have I proclaimed concerning this:
> "Rahab[24] who is brought to an end."[25]

In contrast with the feverish policy of Hezekiah, who is seeking aid in every quarter but the right one, Isaiah reminds him again of the necessity of faith in Yahweh, to which he had previously summoned Ahaz, viz.,

> For thus did the Lord Yahweh, the holy one of Israel, say:
> "Through return and rest you will be delivered;
> Through quietude and confidence will your might be."
> But you were not willing.
> And so you said, "No!
> Upon horses we will flee."
> Therefore you shall flee.
> "And upon racers we will ride"; therefore your pursuers shall
>   be swift.
> You will flee—a thousand at the battle-cry of five,
> Until if any of you survive, you will be like the staff on the
>   top of the mountain,
> And like the banner on the hill."[26]

Apparently, Isaiah's messages in connection with Sennacherib's invasion were purely denunciatory.[27] He saw no other way than submission to Assyria as Yah-

[24] For other references to "Rahab" see Ps. 87:4; 89:10; cf. Isa. 51:9; Job 9:13; 26:12.

[25] Isa. 30:7.   [26] Isa. 30:15–17.

[27] Cf. W. A. Irwin, "The Attitude of Isaiah in the Crisis of 701," *Journal of Religion*, XVI, 406–18.

weh's ordained ruler of the world. All attempts to find
deliverance through alliance with other nations were
doomed to failure. It was Hezekiah's duty to remain
subject to Sennacherib. Any contrary policy would
bring ruin. The sins of Judah were so venal and bla-
tant that deliverance from punishment was out of the
question; repentant endurance of chastisement was the
necessary program for Hezekiah. Isaiah had come to
the conviction by the time of the invasion of Sennacherib that the people of Judah were blinded by
their passion for freedom to the realities of life and were
determined to rush on madly, not knowing that they
were headed for destruction. Their spiritual guides
were blind leaders of the blind.

> Astonish yourselves and be astounded!
> Blind yourselves, and be blind!
> They are drunk; but it is not wine;
> They stagger, but it is not liquor.
> For Yahweh has poured out upon you a spirit of sound sleep;
> And he has closed your eyes—the prophets;
> And your leaders—the seers—he has blindfolded.[28]

When the advance of Egypt seemed to promise relief, in that it distracted Sennacherib's attention and
perhaps necessitated some withdrawal of troops from
Jerusalem, the city went wild with joy. But Isaiah's
opinion of the outcome was not changed. In the midst
of the chorus of joy and praise, he uttered a piercing
and discordant note. In 22:1–4 he portrays the destruction that he sees certainly in store for Jerusalem
and Judah. He describes the vain efforts toward the

[28] Isa. 29:9, 10.

defense of the city, and contrasts these with the failure to turn to the God of hosts in penitence and fear. A spirit of reckless revelry has taken the place that belonged to sorrow for sin.

> "Eat and drink; though tomorrow we die."
> But Yahweh of Hosts has revealed himself in my ears:
> "This guilt of yours will not be expiated until you die,"
> Says the Lord Yahweh of Hosts."[29]

The underlying causes for the chastisement which Judah and Jerusalem were undergoing are listed in Isa. 1:2-17, 21-23. After first charging Judah with base ingratitude and disloyalty toward Yahweh, the prophet proceeds to describe the condition of Jerusalem as it was when Hezekiah was "shut up like a caged bird" in his own capital. He then protests against the elaborate cultus of his day which the people were substituting for the practice of justice and righteousness. Isaiah did not oppose ritual per se; he was but objecting to the exclusive place it occupied in the minds of the people; they were making ritual and religion synonymous terms. He would enrich religion by giving a larger place to justice and righteousness as requirements of Yahweh.

> When you spread forth your hands,
> I will hide my eyes from you.
> Yea, when you multiply prayers,
> I will not hear.
> Your hands are filled with blood.
> Wash yourselves; purify yourselves.
> Put away the wickedness of your deeds
> From before my eyes.
> Cease to do evil;

[29] Isa. 22:13, 14.

> Learn to do good.
> Seek justice;
> Relieve the oppressed,
> Give justice to the fatherless;
> Plead the cause of the widow.[30]

The deflection of Judah and Jerusalem from the right
way and their disloyalty to the high ideals of a true
Yahweh-worship, Isaiah pictures in the following vivid
terms:

> Alas, that she has become a harlot,—the faithful city,
> That was full of justice, righteousness used to dwell in her,
>   But now—murderers!
> Thy silver has become slag;
> Thy liquor is diluted[31] with water.
> Thy rulers are unruly and companions of thieves;
> Everyone loves a bribe and pursues after rewards;
> To the fatherless they do not grant justice,
> Nor does the cause of the widow come before them.[32]

This kind of message was poor comfort in troublous
times. If spoken in connection with the siege of Sennacherib or at any other critical time, the patience of
the populace and the government was in striking contrast to the state of mind in every country during the
World War. We had no patience with criticism; we
called it disloyalty. Hezekiah and his contemporaries
must be given credit for a breadth of mind and tolerance of spirit that arouse wonder. Or was it that the
prophets were privileged characters and had enjoyed
liberty of speech so long that no one dreamed of denying it to them in a time of crisis? They were under

[30] Isa. 1:15–17.

[31] Literally, "circumcised."   [32] Isa. 1:21–23.

the protection of Yahweh, and it was dangerous to do violence to their persons. The condition of the people and country to which Isaiah was preaching such messages is thus pictured by him:

> The whole head is sick,
> And the whole heart faint.
> From the sole of the foot to the head,
> There is no soundness within,—
> But bruises, blows, and bleeding wounds;
> They have not been pressed out, nor bound up,
> Nor have they been softened with oil.
> Your land is laid waste,
> Your cities are burned with fire;
> Your land—aliens are consuming it in your presence,
> And it is a waste, like the overthrow of Sodom,[33]
> And the daughter of Zion is left like a booth in a vineyard,
> Like a lodge in a cucumber patch, like a watchman's tower.
> "If Yahweh of Hosts had not left us a remnant, though small,
> We had been like Sodom, we had resembled Gomorrah."[34]

The only known situation to which these words closely apply was the invasion of 701 B.C. Isaiah's sympathy with his country did not blind his eyes to its moral defects. Indeed, the prophetic theory of life would make him more than ever sure of the sinfulness of his people; for that identified prosperity with piety, and political and military reverses were evidence of sin. No louder testimony to the sinfulness of Judah could be imagined than the fearful devastation wrought by Sennacherib's army. Sennacherib was the agent of Yahweh's wrath against his wicked people,

[33] Hebrew text has "strangers"; probably an error.

[34] Isa. 1:5–9.

and the blows of Assyria were loud calls to national repentance and atonement.

With all his other great emphases, Isaiah is supremely the prophet of faith. His message to Ahaz was one of quiet confidence resting in faith: "If you do not believe, you will not be established." As troubles thickened in the confused political situation, he conceived of Yahweh as laying in Zion a sure cornerstone, "He who has faith will not be perturbed." And when matters reached their worst with the marauding troops of Sennacherib invading Judah and actually laying siege to Jerusalem, he scoffed at the "realist" politicians who sought help from Egypt; for "the Egyptians are men and not gods; and their horses are flesh and not spirit." But, in contrast, "through return and rest you will be delivered; through quietude and confidence will your might be." His age was disturbingly like our own; we have experienced the same growing menace, the same apparent invincibility of brute might, the same fateful approach of disaster, and the same triumphant orgy of brutality. We can understand him now, as we might not have done even ten years ago. And his challenge to his own age re-echoes across the centuries into ours: "He who has faith will not be perturbed." But faith was for him an active and effective principle—a certainty that the intangible things of the human spirit are the most powerful realities of life. His was no pale submission but the vigorous conviction that God is supreme in the affairs of man, that even the brute might of aggressive nationalism will ultimately serve His purposes, and in His destined time He will bring the triumph or righteousness. There is a faith to sustain in days of threat and disaster!

Contemporary with Isaiah and taking the same general attitude toward Jerusalem was the prophet Micah.[35] The general period of Micah's activity is attested by Jer. 26:18 f. as lying within the reign of Hezekiah. It has been claimed that Micah must have prophesied before 721 B.C., because of his prophecy against Samaria in 1:5, 6. But Samaria was not destroyed in 721 B.C., nor did it cease to be a trouble to Assyria from that time on. Indeed, in 720 B.C. Samaria as member of an anti-Assyrian coalition was in revolt against Sargon, and she was an occasion of solicitude to Assyria for years after that.[36] As long as Samaria was standing and was a possible source of trouble to the western states in general and to Judah in particular, it was quite in harmony with the custom of the prophets that Micah should have been prophesying her destruction. Of the seven chapters composing the Book of Micah, only the first three were the product of his own mind and heart. Even in these, there is found some later material, viz., 1:7, 11 and 2:12, 13.[37] In chapters 4–7, some few verses may have originated in Micah's

[35] See J. M. Powis Smith, *Book of Micah* ("International Critical Commentary" [1911]); T. K. Cheyne, Cambridge Bible (1895); S. R. Driver, Century Bible (1906); G. A. Smith, *Book of the Twelve Prophets* (1928), Vol. I; W. Nowack, *Die kleinen Propheten* (3d ed., 1922); Marti, *Dodekapropheton* (1904); E. Sellin, *Das Zwölfprophetenbuch* (1922); T. H. Robinson, *Die zwölf kleinen Propheten* (1936).

[36] See *Micah* ("International Critical Commentary" [1911]), p. 20.

[37] For the considerations weighing against these see J. M. Powis Smith, *Amos, Hosea, and Micah* (1914), *ad loc.*

time, viz., 4:14; 5:9–12; 6:9–16; and 7:1–6.[38] Since
the origin of these passages is wholly uncertain and
since they add little that is new to chapters 1–3, they
will be left out of consideration here.

Micah was a product of the countryside, whereas
Isaiah was a child of the town. Micah's home was at
the edge of the foothills, on the border of the Shephe-
lah, the low-lying maritime plain. He had the clear
vision of the man used to open spaces and to contemplation of the far-reaching sea. His sympathies were
those of the farmer. His soul burned with anger against
the rich oppressors of the great city. He lashed the unscrupulous exploiters of their fellow-men with words
that burned. He felt the sufferings and sorrows of the
poor.

His message, starting with announcement of destruction upon Samaria and chastisement of Jerusalem, pictures the consternation in city after city as
nameless evil draws near (chap. 1).[39] He moves on to
describe the social wrongs that have stirred the wrath
of Yahweh against this people. The rich have expro-
priated the lands of the poor; they have made women
and children homeless; and they have refused to listen
to the words of the true prophets, preferring preachers
likeminded with themselves. Therefore, destruction of
a terrible sort is ordained for them (chap. 2). He then
charges the leaders with gross abuse of their powers for

[38] For the history of the criticism of chaps. 4–7 see *Micah* ("International Critical Commentary" [1911]), pp. 9–16.

[39] See William C. Graham in *American Journal of Semitic Languages
and Literatures*, XLVII, 237 f.

the purpose of their own enrichment, in that they have robbed the poor and treated the weak with violence:

> Hear now, you heads of Jacob,
> And rulers of the house of Israel:
> Is it not your place to know justice,
> You who hate good and love evil?
>
> But they eat the flesh of my people,
> And their skin they strip off from upon them;
> And they lay bare their bones and break them up,
> Like meat in the pot, and flesh within the caldron.
>
> Then will they cry unto Yahweh,
> And he will not answer them;
> But will hide his face from them,
> Inasmuch as they have made evil their deeds.[40]

Another class of influential people then receives Micah's attention, viz., the officially approved prophets. He exposes their methods and motives and sets them in sharp contrast with himself.

> Thus says Yahweh
> Regarding the prophets who lead my people astray,
> Who when they bite with their teeth preach prosperity;
> But as for him who puts not into their mouths—
> Against him they declare war.
>
> Therefore it will be night for you, without vision,
> And darkness for you without divination.
> Verily, the sun will set upon those prophets,
> And the day will become dark over them.
>
> And the seers will be ashamed,
> And the diviners will blush,
> And they will cover the upper lip, all of them,
> Because there is no answer from God.

[40] Mic. 3:1–4.

But I, indeed, am full of power,
And justice and strength,
To declare to Jacob his transgression,
And to Israel his sin.[41]

The closing oracle groups the three great classes of leaders together—the princes, priests, and prophets. It makes them jointly responsible for the coming disaster and foretells the fall of Jerusalem in sledge-hammer phrases.

Hear this, now, you heads of the house of Jacob,
And rulers of the house of Israel;
Who abhor justice,
And pervert all that is right;
Who build Zion with blood,
And Jerusalem with iniquity.

Her chiefs judge for a bribe,
And her priests give oracles for hire,
And her prophets divine for money;
Yet they lean upon Yahweh, saying,
"Is not Yahweh in the midst of us?
No evil can befall us."

Therefore, because of you,
Zion will be ploughed as a field,
And Jerusalem will become ruins,
And the mountain of the house a high place in a forest.[42]

Isaiah and Micah alike seem to have anticipated the downfall of Jerusalem[43] and the consequent end of

---

[41] Mic. 3:5-8.　　　　[42] Mic. 3:9-12.

[43] Budde, in an article on "Isaiah" in the *Zeitschrift für die alttestamentliche Wissenschaft* (XLI [1923], 154-203), makes much of the claim that Isaiah never definitely foretold the fall of Jerusalem. This claim lays undue stress on such fine distinctions as "Jerusalem will *stumble* and

Judah's independent nationality. How could they think of the religion of Yahweh continuing after his nation had ceased to be? It is clear that neither of these prophets ever for a moment thought of Yahweh as passing out of existence along with his nation. But a God with no worshipers was inconceivable to the Hebrew mind. How, then, could Yahweh's worship be continued? Two elements enter into the answer to this question. Micah, as a rustic, evidently did not identify the perpetuity of the nation with the continuous existence of Jerusalem. Indeed, the great city was to him little more than a cesspool of iniquity. He thought of the real Judah as represented by the simple folk of the countryside. The city must be destroyed, but the nation would continue through the solid and substantial people from the country districts. He did not work out the details of a new national organization on such a basis, but his hopes centered in the character of such people as he had learned to know by close observation of the simple home life of the farming class. A second fact familiar to both Micah and Isaiah was the object-lesson constantly before their eyes, across the northern border of Judah. For twenty years Israel had ceased to be an independent government. In 721 B.C. Samaria had been captured by Sargon, and a percentage of the

---

Judah will *fall*" (Isa. 3:8). It exempts Jerusalem from such general statements as "cities be laid waste without an inhabitant" (Isa. 6:11). It fails to do justice to the full force of Isa. 30:15–17. A city as the sole survivor in a deserted and desolate country would be in a sorry state. Micah the Morashtite did not shrink from announcing the fall of the city at the time of Sennacherib's invasion. Was Isaiah less courageous?

population carried into exile. Since that time northern Israel had been an Assyrian province. But the religion of Yahweh had not gone out of existence there along with the government. The great mass of the population had remained at home. They had gone on for two decades worshiping Yahweh at the local shrines in very much the same way as before the fall of the capital. It was a more or less corrupt worship, perhaps, but it had always been so. In any case, it was Yahweh-worship; it remained down to a much later time and kept the books of the Pentateuch as its Scripture. In the light of that experience, Isaiah and Micah could think of Yahweh's worship as going on even after the cessation of Judah's sovereignty. The official religion might be given to some Assyrian god, but the mass of the faithful Jews would remain loyal to Yahweh through all trials. Isaiah seems to have had something of this sort in mind in Isa. 8:16–18.

The Books of Isaiah and Micah contain many glowing messianic prophecies. Are these all later additions? Was there no messianic hope in the eighth century B.C.? The utterance of Amos (5:18) shows that there was such a hope in the air in that age. But Amos took that hope and converted it into a threat of punishment and catastrophe. That hope was a part of the eschatology of the masses during this period. Moreover, we have seen that Isaiah's Immanuel oracle invoked the current popular expectation of the Wonder Child; and it is held that this is in the truest sense a messianic promise.[44] However, Hosea had no sure word of hope

[44] See Procksch, *op. cit.*

for the north (Hos. 2:11–13; 9:12–17; 13:12–16[45]).
And Isaiah's Shear-jesheb prophecy, whether applying to Israel or to Judah, was primarily a message of
punishment. The content of Isaiah's call as recorded
in chapter 6 excludes all possibility of hope. "If there
be even a tenth in it, it shall again be eaten up."
Leaving aside the detailed discussion of the individual
messianic prophecies in Isaiah, attention is called here
to some general considerations on the subject.

The general charge against the many messianic utterances placed upon Isaiah's lips is of threefold character: (1) How are we to explain the sudden rise and
appearance of messianism in Isaiah? The popular
thought was probably full of that sort of hope at all
times; but was Isaiah at all in sympathy with that
popular thought? Was he not an idealist and consequently at all times in a critical and hostile temper toward the conventional attitudes of his time in both the
religious and the social areas? (2) Is not the presence
of this messianic material inexplicable upon the lips of
Isaiah? His message was so clearly dominated by the
thought of disastrous punishment that it is difficult to
imagine him as a spokesman of an opposite type of
thought. It is hard to smile on one side of the face and
at the same time cry upon the other; but Isaiah is in
just that state of mind according to the makeup of the
Book of Isaiah as it now stands. Moreover, there is no

[45] Hos. 13:14 is best rendered interrogatively, viz.:
     "Shall I ransom them from the power of Sheol?
     Shall I redeem them from death?
     O death! Where are thy plagues?
     O grave! Where is thy destruction?
     Repentance is hid from my eyes."

connecting link between the two types of thought. The passage from one to the other is abrupt and unmeditated. Indeed, it has been maintained with force that the present messianic utterances are inserted with regularity after each passage of threat and denunciation to serve as antidotes. These passages lack all formal connection with their contexts, and they are equally defective in agreement with the thought of the undisputed genuine portions of Isaiah. Again, how can we explain the hostility toward Isaiah on the part of the people,[46] if he preached such encouraging messages as are attributed to him in connection with Sennacherib's invasion and in chapters 9, 11, 32, and 35? (3) If Isaiah and Micah preached a message of comfort, it is strange that the contemporaries of Jeremiah should have remembered Micah's threat against Jerusalem[47] and have forgotten everything else. Not only so, but Jeremiah himself in his contest with Hananiah, the prophet in the Temple court,[48] met Hananiah's confident message of deliverance and hope with a challenge to read the history of prophecy and see if it was not true that all the preceding prophets had preached "of war, and of evil, and of pestilence," and not one of them had been a prophet of prosperity. Jeremiah would never have made such a challenge if the prophecies of Isaiah had been known to be largely devoted to messianic hopes; nor would Hananiah have missed such a glorious chance to humiliate and confound him if it had been common knowledge that the great Isaiah was a prophet of good news. Jeremiah's challenge was not taken up, because the facts were on his side.

[46] See, e.g., Isa. 30:9–11.   [47] Jer. 26:18.   [48] Jer. 28:5–9.

If we ask how the messianic oracles came to be placed in these early prophetic books, where they did not originally belong, we may remind ourselves of a similar procedure in the religion of ancient Greece. The Greek oracles at the time of the Persian invasions of Greece were at first quite friendly toward the Persians, anticipating the success of the Persians and preparing for kindly treatment at their hands. But things went badly with the Persians, and they suffered defeat and had to withdraw. Thereupon the oracles changed their attitude and sought in every way to give a new interpretation to their earlier utterances. The same motive, in part, operated here in the minds of later editors. But for the most part the motive of the additions was twofold. There was the desire to stimulate the faith and hope of suffering Judah so that the religious life of Judah might survive the successive shocks it encountered; and perhaps this was the greatest incentive to these additions. There was also the desire to magnify the glory of Yahweh; and this was done by making him reveal to his prophets long in advance the course of events as it actually proceeded. Furthermore, if Yahweh could be shown to have foretold this course of events, then it followed that the promises of glory supposedly made at the same time and renewed in later times would likewise be fulfilled. The messianic prophecies, no matter when made, were the expression of an exuberant faith and an undying hope.[49]

[49] Cf. J. M. Powis Smith, "Isaiah and the Future," *American Journal of Semitic Languages and Literatures*, **XL** (1924), 252–58.

CHAPTER VII

THE PROPHETS AND THE SCYTHIANS

THE reigns of Manasseh and Amon covered a period of reaction. The devastation wrought by Sennacherib had weakened and depressed Judah to a very low level of vitality. Not only so, but under Esarhaddon and Ashurbanipal, the successors of Sennacherib, Assyria's power had been carried down into Egypt, and Thebes had fallen before it (661 B.C.). Judah had continued under the burden of a heavy tribute to Assyria.[1] Esarhaddon made three campaigns into Egypt before his death in 668 B.C., and brought the entire westland into complete subjection. Ashurbanipal also was three times in the west and was equally successful. It goes without saying that these kings saw to it that Judah kept up her payments of tribute regularly.[2]

Ashurbanipal died about 626 B.C. Even before his death there were not wanting signs of deterioration and decrepitude in the Assyrian Empire; and after his death the descent of the great empire into chaos and death was very rapid. Under these circumstances, it is

[1] See R. F. Harper, *Assyrian and Babylonian Literature* (1901), pp. 85 f. and 96 f.; D. D. Luckenbill, *Ancient Records of Assyria* (1926), II, 265–66 and 340–41; for records of payments both to Esarhaddon and Ashurbanipal.

[2] For the political situation in western Asia see J. M. Powis Smith, *Zephaniah* ("International Critical Commentary" [1911]), pp. 156–65.

not surprising to read in Herodotus of a great invasion of Scythians sweeping down from the north over the western portions of the territory of Assyria:

On the death of Phraortes his son Cyaxares ascended the throne. Of him it is reported that he was still more warlike than any of his ancestors, and that he was the first who gave organization to an Asiatic army, dividing the troops into companies, and forming distinct bodies of the spearmen, the archers, and the cavalry, who before his time had been mingled in one mass, and confused together. He it was who fought against the Lydians on the occasion when the day was changed suddenly into night, and who brought under his dominion the whole of Asia beyond the Halys. This prince, collecting together all the nations which owned his sway, marched against Nineveh, resolved to avenge his father, and cherishing a hope that he might succeed in taking the town. A battle was fought, in which the Assyrians suffered a defeat, and Cyaxares had already begun the siege of the place, when a numerous horde of Scyths under their king Madyes, son of Prôtothyes, burst into Asia in pursuit of the Cimmerians, whom they had driven out of Europe, and entered the Median territory. . . . . The Scythians, having thus invaded Media, were opposed by the Medes, who gave them battle, but being defeated, lost their empire. The Scythians became masters of Asia.

After this they marched forward with the design of invading Egypt. When they reached Palestine, however, Psammetichus the Egyptian king met them with gifts and prayers, and prevailed on them to advance no further. On their return, passing through Ascalon, a city of Syria, the greater part of them went their way without doing any damage; but some few who lagged behind pillaged the temple of Celestial Venus. . . . .

The dominion of the Scythians over Asia lasted twenty and eight years, during which time their insolence and oppression spread ruin on every side. For besides the regular tribute, they exacted from the several nations additional imposts, which they fixed at pleasure; and further, they scoured the country and plundered every one of whatever they could.[3]

[3] Herodotus *History* i. 103–6, trans. George Rawlinson.

This flood of destruction sweeping down upon the Mediterranean coastlands naturally spread terror in every direction. The neighboring peoples were panic stricken. To this general state of fear Judah would not be an exception. The tidings of the Scythians would outrun their progress; and for weeks, perhaps months, in advance the population would be living in dread. Under these conditions, two prophets came forward as interpreters of the religious meaning of the situation, viz., Zephaniah and Jeremiah.[4] It was a time of political and spiritual crisis, and they sprang to the task of opening the eyes of the people to its significance; as prophets they could not keep silent. The situation itself constituted their call.

[4] Recently considerable skepticism has been expressed in regard to the story of Herodotus and the bearing of the alleged Scythian invasion upon the preaching of Jeremiah and Zephaniah. Olmstead ignores the episode entirely (*Palestine and Syria*, p. 492); Volz (*Der Prophet Jeremia*, pp. 57 f.) argues against the worth of the story; Lewy ("Der Feldzug der Skythen nach Syrien und Palästina," *Mitteilungen der Vorderasiatisch-aegyptischen Gesellschaft*, XXIX, Part II, 51–55) holds that it can have validity only for events in 592–91 B.C. (hence the episode, whatever it may have been, cannot have occasioned the prophetic calls of Jeremiah and Zephaniah); Wilke ("Das Skythenproblem im Jeremiabuch," *Alttestamentliche Studien für Rudolf Kittel*, pp. 222–54) concludes that, in so far as the relevant prophecies of Jeremiah contain a valid historical reference and are not merely compounded of older phrases, they allude not to the Scythians at all but to the Chaldeans; Horst (*Die zwölf kleinen Propheten*, p. 191) dismisses the matter as untenable; Eissfeldt (*Die zwölf kleinen Propheten*, pp. 184–85), while feeling it necessary to qualify Horst's opinion, yet admits that the arguments of Lewy and Wilke are very cogent, if not actually conclusive. Hogarth (*Cambridge Ancient History*, III, 145 f.) accepts the Scythian invasion as real but doubts its extent and influence through Syria and Palestine. On the other hand, Robinson (*History of Israel*, pp. 412–14) takes the story of Herodotus essentially at face value. For a good discussion cf. also Welch, *Jeremiah: His Time and His Work* (1928), pp. 97–131; Hyatt, "The Peril from the North in Jeremiah," *Journal of Biblical Literature*, LIX, 499–513.

Zephaniah seems to have been a citizen of Jerusalem, if we may so judge from the fact of his knowledge of the topography of that city[5] and of the religious and social situation therein, and the further fact that he seems to speak of himself as living in Jerusalem in 1:4. He may also have been connected with the royal family by blood, as seems to be implied by the superscription when it names Hezekiah as the father of Zephaniah's grandfather. He lacks that sense of intimate fellowship with the poor that belongs naturally to a poor man. His point of view is rather that of the aristocrat.

Zephaniah looked upon the coming Scythian invasion of Palestine as the advance guard of the great Day of Yahweh. This awful Day was to bring destruction sweeping over the entire civilized world from north to south. Assyria, the Canaanitish nations, Judah, Egypt, and Ethiopia were all to meet their doom. The terrors of that great and terrible Day dominated the prophet's mind:

Near at hand is Yahweh's great day, near and speeding fast;
Near at hand is Yahweh's bitter day, hastening faster than a warrior.
A day of wrath is that day; a day of distress and gloom;
A day of clouds and eclipse; a day of the trumpet and battle-cry,
Against the fortified cities and against the high towers.
And I shall press hard upon mankind and they will walk like blind men, because they have sinned against me;
And their blood will be poured out like dust, and their flesh like dung.
Neither their silver nor their gold can deliver them;[6]

[5] Zeph. 1:10, 11.

[6] Vs. 18b is omitted here as a probable gloss; see J. M. Powis Smith, *op. cit.*

For a complete destruction, yea, a fearful one, will Yahweh make
of all the inhabitants of the land.[7]

The sins of Judah denounced by Zephaniah are
made responsible for the coming destruction. At the
forefront of the line of offenses stand sins against Yahweh himself. These include the worship of the Baalim,
sun-worship, idolatry, the worship of foreign gods, and
utter apostasy from Yahweh. The picture here given
of the religious situation accords fully with what we are
told in Kings of the period of reaction under Manasseh
and Amon. This condition, of course, persisted during
the minority of Josiah, and was probably not cleaned
up until the time of the Deuteronomic reform in
Josiah's eighteenth year (621 B.C.). To these sins
against God, Zephaniah adds social injustice of the
rich, perversion of right by the judges, the importation
of foreign styles of dress, the deceit and lying of the
prophets, the irreligion of the priests, and the moral
atheism of those who said that it was of no use to worship Yahweh since he exercised no interest in nor influence upon human affairs.

Zephaniah brought nothing new to the solution of
the problems of his day. He was but echoing the message of his predecessors. He did not put into that message the moral idealism and passion that had characterized Amos and Isaiah. He is principally concerned with the description of a certain fiery form of
judgment that he sees about to descend upon the world
in general and his own nation in particular. He has
nothing constructive to contribute to the upbuilding of

[7] Zeph. 1:14–18.

his nation's life. He is a destructive critic pure and simple. He is not stirred by any profound sympathy for
the peoples about to be destroyed, or even for his own
doomed nation. He does not stress the ethical element
in the coming judgment; it is rather a punishment sent
by Yahweh upon a wicked world that does not recognize his power. The preaching of Zephaniah must
have helped prepare the soil of Judah for the great
change wrought by the Deuteronomic reform. But as
far as any records go, Zephaniah was little more than a
voice crying in the wilderness: "Prepare for the day of
Yahweh."[8]

Called forth apparently by the same crisis in his people's history, the prophet Jeremiah began his work.[9]
This background of the initial period of his preaching
shines through the content of Jeremiah's call to the
prophetic office. Jeremiah felt that he was fore-
ordained to the task of prophet, but he shrank from it.
That he, a mere lad, should presume to rebuke nations
seemed to him unfitting. But he was assured that the
authority of Yahweh's commission and sustaining presence would more than compensate for his youth. If it
seems strange to us that Jeremiah should feel himself
concerned with the fate of nations, let us remember not

[8] For a more detailed treatment of Zephaniah, see J. M. Powis Smith,
op. cit.

[9] See Jer. 1:2. The best English books on Jeremiah are J. Skinner,
Prophecy and Religion (1923); A. S. Peake, *Jeremiah* (New Century Bible,
[1910]); L. E. Binns, *Jeremiah* ("Westminster Commentary" [1919]);
George Adam Smith, *Jeremiah* (1924); Adam C. Welch, *Jeremiah: His
Time and His Work* (1928).

only that Zephaniah, his contemporary, likewise dealt with the fate of Assyria and Ethiopia but also that the affairs of Judah in these closing years of her national history were closely intertwined with the course of affairs in western Asia and Egypt. If Jeremiah knew anything of the recent history of his nation, he must have known of the invasions of the west and of Egypt by Sennacherib, Esarhaddon, and Ashurbanipal. That knowledge would open his eyes to the fact that the future of Judah was part and parcel of the future of western Asia as a whole.

Two visions seem to have been a part of the call experience of Jeremiah. In one, it would appear, he had gone alone, in turmoil of spirit, out over his beloved hills to fight through to some decision on the divine call that he felt almost forcing him into a course from which his diffident soul shrank; and then he chanced to see an almond tree bursting its buds after the long stagnation of the winter season. Doubtless, a score of others had seen that tree the same day, but for them it was just another almond tree. For Jeremiah it was the voice of God; it was the answer his troubled soul craved. As God had watched over the tree all through its seeming sterility and now in his time brought it to life and beauty, so he seemed to say to Jeremiah with audible voice, "I watch over my word to perform it."[10] In that moment of insight and faith the diffident boy

[10] Jer. 1:11, 12. The meaning is brought out through a play on words that escapes the English reader. The words for "almond tree" (*shâked*) and "watch over" (*shôked*) are almost identical in form and sound, so that the Hebrew text furnishes a play on words.

became "a fortified city, and an iron pillar, and brazen walls against the whole land,"[11] against the kings and princes and priests and against the people. They were later to fight against him; but they could not overcome him because of his consciousness that the Lord was with him. The second vision[12] presents to the eye of the prophet a boiling pot, with its "face" turned southward.[13] The meaning is that just as the boiling contents of the pot pour out upon the south, so is Yahweh going to stir up the peoples of the north and send them down south, carrying fire and sword even up to the gates of Jerusalem. This destruction is sent as a punishment for the wickedness of Judah in that people have worshiped other gods than Yahweh and have turned aside from him. Jeremiah is urged to speak this message, harsh though it be, in its entirety to Judah and is assured that Yahweh's support will sustain him against all the hostility of his fellow-countrymen. It would seem that these visions reflect a more or less extended period of hesitation and fear on the part of Jeremiah before he could make up his mind to undertake so terrible a mission. The prophet conceives of his task in much the same terms as his contemporary Zephaniah had done. The present text of verse 10 contains the words "to build and to plant" as a part of the call.

[11] Jer. 1:18.   [12] Jer. 1:13–19.

[13] The Hebrew phrase, "from the north," appears difficult; also, a similar form occurs in vs. 15. However, the affixes to these words must be regarded merely as terminatives of place, not accusatives of motion; see Meek in *Journal of the American Oriental Society*, LX (1940), 229–30, who translates the second of these phrases, "the northern kingdom."

But these words are lacking in the Alexandrine Codex of the Septuagint. They are not in keeping with Jer. 28:8, 9, and they do not easily lend themselves to the situation, when the threatening Scythian flood was likely to sweep everything before it. The probability is that in his initial experience Jeremiah saw nothing but an overwhelming disaster impending upon his world.

The oracles uttered by Jeremiah prior to and under the immediate influence of the Scythian invasion are contained in Jeremiah, chapters 1–6. These chapters were edited later in Jeremiah's career,[14] and also supplemented by later hands. Thus they doubtless lost some of the marks of their earlier origin and were made to apply more closely to the events of the years after the Scythian invasion had passed into history. The content of the early preaching of Jeremiah was very much like that of Zephaniah. The sins of Judah were held responsible by him for the coming of the threatened desolation. Those sins were primarily apostasy from Yahweh and ingratitude for all his blessings. Jeremiah put this in very vivid and forceful terms:

Has a nation changed gods, though they are not gods?
Yet my people has changed its glory for what is useless!
Be amazed, O heavens, at this, and be shocked beyond words!
    It is Yahweh's oracle.
For my people have wrought two evils;
They have forsaken me, a fountain of living waters,
To hew out for themselves cisterns,
Broken cisterns which hold no water.[16]

These gods after whom Judah went astray were, in

14 See Jer. 36:18, 28.   16 Jer. 2:11–13.

part at least, her old loves, the Baalim, with all their disgusting immoralities, of which Jeremiah leaves us in no uncertainty. They were numerous,

For as many in number as your cities are your gods, O Judah![16]

The people doubtless saw no inconsistency in worshiping local gods alongside of Yahweh, the national God. But Jeremiah brought the wide departure from the worship of Yahweh clearly into view by pointing to their worship in the valley,[17] which in all probability was some reactionary cult like the sacrifice of infants or some other pagan practice continuing from the days of Manasseh and Amon. This recognition and cultivation of non-Hebraic religious practices was part and parcel of the political policy denounced by Jeremiah. He protested against any dealings with Assyria or Egypt as worse than futile (Jer. 2:18, 36). The policy of seeking support from one of the great powers against aggression by the other had long been adopted in Judah, and had been obnoxious to all the prophets. The reason for that was twofold. Such a policy grew out of a lack of an adequate faith in Yahweh and reflected unfavorably upon Yahweh. The prophets believed that Yahweh was able to take care of all the interests of his people and needed no extraneous support. Not only so, but policies of alliance with other nations involved more or less formal and official recognition of the gods of the allied peoples. This was naturally offensive in the highest degree to every genuine Yahweh prophet. Jeremiah conceived of the people when dis-

[16] Jer. 2:28.   [17] Jer. 2:23.

aster should befall them as waking up to their iniquity and as making a plea to Yahweh for forgiveness. But with their facile and shallow penitence he contrasted the true penitence that Yahweh desired:

But thus says Yahweh to the men of Judah and to Jerusalem:
"Plough up for yourselves new ground,
And do not sow among thorns.
Circumcise yourselves to Yahweh, and put away the foreskin of your hearts,
O men of Judah and citizens of Jerusalem,
Lest my wrath go forth like fire and burn,
And there be no one to extinguish it, because of the wickedness of your deeds."[18]

In chapters 4–6 of Jeremiah are found the Scythian songs. They were evidently called forth by the close proximity of the peril which Jeremiah foresaw. The preaching of this destruction brought agony to Jeremiah's spirit. This was what he had shrunk from when he felt the urge to become a prophet. Now his whole soul revolted from the burden of woe that he had to put upon his people's hearts.[19] He seems to have left his native place, Anathoth, and to have taken up residence in Jerusalem during the period of the Scythian peril. The fifth and sixth chapters were apparently spoken in the capital city. The danger seems to have come nearer in the course of these songs. In 4:5, 6, the summons goes forth to flee into the strong cities and to take refuge in Jerusalem; in 6:1 f. the inhabitants of Jerusalem itself are called upon to flee. The songs are largely concerned with the description of the approaching

[18] Jer. 3:19—4:4.   [19] Jer. 4:10, 19 f.

enemy and of the destruction which he is to commit on all sides:

> Behold, a people is coming from the north country,
> And a great nation is aroused from the ends of the earth.
> They lay hold of the bow and spear;
> Cruel are they and show no mercy.
> The sound of them is like the roar of the sea and upon horses
>   they ride,
> Arrayed, like a man, for battle against thee, O daughter of Zion.
> We have heard the report of him; our hands relax.
> Pain has seized us, anguish like that of a woman in travail.
> Do not go forth to the field, and do not walk in the road;
> For there is the sword of the foe, terror on every hand.
> O daughter of my people, gird on sackcloth, and bestrew yourself
>   with dust;
> Make you lamentation as for an only son, bitter mourning;
> For suddenly will the destroyer come upon us.[20]

The sins that have brought on this disaster are enumerated in 5:1–8, 23–31, and in 6:13–17. In the prophet's judgment the corruption of the people was widespread and universal; there was not a decent man in Jerusalem. They were all guilty of perversion of justice, false swearing or perjury, the worship of foreign gods, and apparently of gross sensuality. The language of 5:7 and 8 is very strong, and also more than a little disgusting. The question naturally arises why Jeremiah should employ such figures. But our increased knowledge of the popular cults of the time has shown that he is but describing actual religious practices which he and everyone else knew all too well. In the moral revulsion here apparent, and in many similar

[20] Jer. 6:22–26.

utterances by the prophets, we find some understanding of their horror of the cult of fertility carried on by their contemporaries in the name of Baal, and their intense reforming zeal for the worship of Yahweh.

In addition to the cultus irregularities, the rich men are upbraided for the illegal and unrighteous ways in which they have gained their wealth:

> For rascals are found among my people,[21]
> As a cage is full of birds, so their houses are full of graft;
> So they become great and wax rich.
> They are fat; they plan bad things.[22]
> They do not justly judge the case of the fatherless, but they prosper,
> And justice to the needy they do not decree.[23]

The sin of covetousness is charged against all classes, rich and poor. The religious leaders are blamed for double dealing and for a too easy solution of national problems. They are all eager for new and untrodden ways and stubbornly refuse to abide by the old standards. Therefore, their ritual of sacrifice cannot be accepted by Yahweh, and punishment is inevitable.

As a matter of fact, the Scythian invasion passed away and left the world-order essentially unchanged. It was simply a plundering raid by a horde of nomads. It probably inflicted relatively little damage on Judah and Jerusalem, nestling in their protective hills. It certainly did not lay Jerusalem in the dust. The eyes of the Scythians were fixed on bigger game. The terrible

---

[21] The text here is untranslatable.

[22] The text here is bad; see the commentaries.   [23] Jer. 5:26–28.

pictures of destruction imagined by Zephaniah and
Jeremiah were not realized. They were in the eyes of
their contemporaries branded as false prophets. Of
Zephaniah's history after the completion of his prophetic work, nothing is known. But Jeremiah lived to
prophesy another day. The failure of the Scythians to
measure up to Jeremiah's expectations is believed by
some to have cost him the confidence of his people, and
perhaps branded him as a false prophet. They advance this as the reason why he was not consulted in
regard to acceptance of the Deuteronomic law. Instead of him, an otherwise unknown prophetess, named
Huldah, was asked to pass upon the new code.[24] It is
hardly possible that Jeremiah would have been ignored, if he had not been under a cloud. The discovery
of the new law in 621 B.C. was too near the recent
Scythian invasion for either the people or the government to have forgotten Jeremiah's prophecies regarding it. But the effect upon the public was in a real sense
less important than the effect upon Jeremiah himself.
His youth had caused him to shrink from entering upon the task of prophecy. And now his worst fears were
realized! Such a disillusionment must have been a
hard trial for the young prophet's faith. Had he been
mistaken in supposing that he was called of God to
prophesy? Was he properly equipped and qualified to
be an interpreter of the divine will? Dare he ever trust
himself again to speak as a representative of Yahweh?
Had he not been repudiated by his God in the eyes of
all the people? It was a stunning experience for a

[24] II Kings 22:12–20.

young man just entering upon the exercise of his prophetic gifts. That he felt the full force of the blow seems clear from the fact that he lapsed into silence after the Scythian invasion for a period of about fourteen years. The Deuteronomic reform in 621 B.C. did not stir him to utterance,[25] nor did the downfall of Nineveh in 612 B.C. call him forth from his retirement. During this period of quiescence the prophet had ample leisure to indulge in self-examination and in meditation upon the course of events. When he re-emerged into public life, it was as a mature man in possession of all his powers, with his spirit chastened, and with strength and courage renewed, ready to enter upon the hardest of tasks.

The effect of the Scythian invasion and of the preaching of Zephaniah and Jeremiah was not wholly lost upon Judah. It is no more than reasonable to suppose that the Deuteronomic reform of 621 B.C. was, at least in part, due to the influence of recent events. The promoters of the reform recognized that the time was ripe for their movement. The Scythian invasion had, at least, given Judah a good scare. The preaching of the two prophets had forced them to think upon their ways. The invasion of Sennacherib had prepared the way for such a reform movement. The Assyrians had devastated forty-six cities of Judah and the outlying villages and small towns and had desecrated their shrines. The Temple at Jerusalem was the only one that had escaped. The inevitable conclusion in the

[25] A few commentators believe that some passages in the book are Jeremiah's utterances relevant to the reform (cf. G. A. Smith, *op. cit.*, pp. 134 f.; Welch, *op. cit.*, pp. 76 f.; Skinner, *op. cit.*, pp. 89 f.).

minds of the faithful would be that Yahweh had thereby shown his attitude toward the local shrines, on the
one hand, and to Jerusalem, on the other. This experience was recent enough to be familiar to the people's
minds. The reform movement may thus be looked upon as the resultant of the joint influences of the Assyrian and Scythian movements and the interpretation
of the latter by the two leading prophets of the day.
The new elements in the Deuteronomic legislation
were three: (1) the sharp differentiation between the
clergy and the laity made in the limitation of the priesthood to the Levitical group; (2) the centralization of
all lawful worship at the Temple in Jerusalem; (3) the
larger recognition given to humanitarian questions in
the Deuteronomic code. Whether Jeremiah took any
part in or attitude toward this reform is a matter for
debate. The possible allusions to it in the Book of Jeremiah are but two, viz., Jer. 11:1–8 and 8:8.[26]

Certain social consequences of the reform may be
briefly noted. The priesthood at Jerusalem was at once
confronted by the danger involved in an increase of
power and the arrogance accompanying their segre-
gated and exclusive position. They were now the sole
guardians of the sacred ordinances. They became ec-
clesiastical aristocrats. The centralization of all public
worship at Jerusalem involved more or less seculariza-
tion of rural life. In communities far removed from
Jerusalem, it was out of the question to be running up

[26] Welch (*op. cit.*) believes that 3:6–13 relates to the reform, though
not 11:1–8; G. A. Smith (*op. cit.*) sees later allusion to it also in 7:1–15;
11:15–16.

to Jerusalem frequently for religious purposes. Naturally, those functions which had been a matter of common occurrence when the altar was within a few hundred yards of the home fell into disuse when the distance to the shrine extended to mile after mile. The religious side of life must necessarily be less conspicuously in evidence. On the other hand, the deprivation of the opportunity and the facilities for frequent acts of public worship with its official ceremonies became a challenge to the truly religious spirit. It forced upon the people a greater degree of spiritual inwardness, and to those susceptible to such a type of life it opened wide the doors for meditation and prayer. This was a very real preparation for the experiences of exile which were to come upon Judah and force her to dispense with the altar and external ritual for some time. The people of Judah were thus given a chance to accustom themselves to communion with a God who "dwelleth not in houses made with hands."

In other ways the centralization of worship had great influence. The necessity of making all sacrifices at Jerusalem brought with it economic changes. Few men would take a solitary sheep or ox to Jerusalem for sacrificial purposes. A regular business of providing sacrificial animals would grow up. We recall that Jesus drove the money-changers out of the Temple. The regular trips to Jerusalem would tend to break down in some measure the provincialism of the people. Men from different regions of the country would meet and exchange views and information. Such meetings would make the people in general more intelligent as to their own country and their own people and would give them some knowledge of the outside world. But the women of the household would not reap these advantages, directly, at least. They would be the ones to stay at home and look after the children and the livestock. The women in any civilization are the natural conservers of things religious. But these women would have no chance to enlarge their outlook. They would keep on thinking the old thoughts and practicing the old customs. Thus the path of progress would be made difficult, and the work of prophets like Jeremiah become correspondingly harder.

CHAPTER VIII

VENGEANCE AND FAITH

A FEW years ago an Assyrian document came to light in the British Museum which necessitated a revision of current opinions in regard to the fall of Nineveh.[1] Previously that event had been placed at 607 or 606 B.C. The new evidence showed that it took place in 612 B.C. It also appeared that the downfall of Nineveh was not the complete end of the Assyrian Empire, but that the Assyrians retired from Nineveh and set up headquarters in Harran. Furthermore, Pharaoh Necho was not hastening to seize the territory of the fallen Assyrian Empire in 608 B.C. when Josiah met him at Megiddo, but was marching to the support of Assyria against victorious Babylon.[2] It is doubtful whether there was any battle at Megiddo between Josiah's forces and those of Pharaoh Necho; the biblical narrative in II Kings 23:29 simply says that Josiah "went up to meet him, and he killed him as soon as he saw him." It is quite possible that Necho, on his way to the aid of Assyria and desiring to make sure that no foe should arise behind him, sent for Josiah to make sure of his attitude toward Egypt, and, not finding it to his liking, proceeded to make assurance dou-

[1] See C. J. Gadd, *The Fall of Nineveh* (1923).

[2] II Kings 23:29 in the Authorized Version is mistaken in saying that Pharaoh Necho "went up against the king of Assyria."

bly sure by putting Josiah to death. Therefore, the people placed Jehoahaz upon the vacant throne; but Necho dethroned him and held him in captivity at Riblah on the Orontes River, making Jehoiakim king in his stead,[3] and placing him under heavy tribute. But Necho, in turn, reached the end of his rope. In 605 B.C., Nebuchadrezzar, of Babylon, overthrew him at Carchemish and became at once master of all western Asia. These great events were making their impression upon the minds of the prophets, viz., Jeremiah, Nahum, and Habakkuk. The words of the last two of these we shall study in this chapter.

The prophet Nahum spoke apparently just before the downfall of Nineveh in 612 B.C. at the hands of the Babylonians and Medes. Nothing is known of him, his family connections, or his home.[4] He is simply a voice speaking out of the dark. His significance lies in the fact that he is a good representative of what must have

[3] II Kings 23:30-35.

[4] See J. M. Powis Smith, *Nahum* ("International Critical Commentary" [1911]). An attractive view of the origin of Nahum's prophecy is that it recounts, rather than predicts, the fall of Nineveh (see Humbert, "Le Vision de Nahoum, 2:4-11," *Archiv für Orientforschung*, V (1928), 14-19; *Le Problème du livre de Nahoum* (1932); and Ernst Sellin, *Das Zwölfprophetenbuch* (1930), pp. 353-55). The view of these commentators is that Nahum wrote his account of the epochal event to serve as a liturgy in the New Year festival of that year 612. The appropriateness of this lies in the fact that such liturgy regularly celebrated the triumph of Yahweh over his enemies, though commonly the mythological enemies in the cosmic chaos. Apart from this feature, however, the view has great appeal, for the vividness of Nahum's prophecy impresses the reader as the account of an eyewitness. But, on the contrary, see Horst, *Die zwölf kleinen Propheten*, pp. 162-63.

been a fairly common state of mind in Judah when the course of events pointed toward the impending fall of Nineveh. Assyria had long been the taskmaster of the oriental world. The Assyrian kings had enforced their will ruthlessly with fire and sword. They had spoiled one capital after another, and had laid so heavy a tribute upon the peoples as to bleed the vassal countries white. Word of the approaching overthrow of the oppressor would be a gospel of glad tidings at every vassal court.

Nahum exults over the coming disaster, not merely as a good patriot, but also as a loyal follower of Yahweh. The continued dominance of wicked Assyria over the people of Yahweh had been a severe trial of faith to those who were believers in Yahweh's love for Judah. The fall of Nineveh presented itself to many of them as a vindication of the justice of Yahweh and also as a richly deserved fate for the oppressing tyrant. It was much easier to believe in Yahweh with Assyria prostrate in the dust than with the Assyrian lion rampant and destroying on every hand. Out of such feelings of relief and satisfaction as these Nahum sang his paean of exulting joy:

Did not one come forth from you devising evil against Yahweh, counselling wickedness?

Yahweh has commanded regarding you, "There shall be sown of your name no longer;

From the house of your gods, I will cut off the graven and the molten image;

I will make your grave a dishonor."

A shatterer comes up against you; keep the rampart;

Watch the road; brace your loins; strengthen your might to the utmost.

The shield of his warriors is reddened; the mighty men are clothed in scarlet.

They will prepare the chariots on that day; the chargers will tremble.

In the fields chariots rage to and fro; they run about in the open places.

Their appearance resembles torches; they dart about like lightning,

He summons his nobles; they take command of their divisions (?),

They hasten to the wall and the battering-ram (?) is set up.

The gates of the river are opened, and the palace melts away.

And . . . .[5] and her maidens are moaning,

Like the voice of doves, beating upon their breasts.

And Nineveh—like a pool of water are her defenders, and as they flee,

"Stand fast, stand fast," one cries, but no one turns back.

"Plunder silver, plunder gold; for there is no end to the supplies."

There is emptiness and void and waste, and a melting heart and staggering knees.

And anguish is in all loins and the faces of all of them become livid.

Where is the den of lions and the cave of the young lions,

Whither the lion went to enter, the lion's cub, with none to disturb;

Where the lion tore prey sufficient for his cubs and rended for his lionesses,

And filled his dens with prey and his lair with booty?

Behold I am against you; it is the oracle of Yahweh of hosts.

And I will burn up chariots with smoke, and the sword will devour your young lions.

And I will cut off your booty from the land, and the voice of your messengers will be heard no more.[6]

Nothing could be more striking than the contrast

---

[5] Hebrew *Huzzab* is unintelligible.

[6] Nah. 1:11, 14; 2:2, 4–14. Nah. 1:1–10, 12 f. and 2:1, 3 are later additions to the book; see J. M. Powis Smith, *op. cit.*

between Nahum and Jeremiah in their attitudes toward the fall of Nineveh. Jeremiah, brooding over the sins of Israel and mindful of the mistake he had made in regard to the Scythians, had nothing to say upon the subject of Assyria's overthrow. Nineveh's fall started no note of praise or gratitude from his lips. And yet Jeremiah had felt himself called to be a prophet to the nations. But he was crushed for the time being by the burden of his own sorrow. Nahum, on the other hand, bursts into jubilant song at the prospect of the speedy end of his people's foe. This was what he and the masses of the people had longed for ardently. This meant relief for Judah and vindication for Judah's God. Patriotism and religion both found complete satisfaction in the contemplation of such a prospect for the great enemy of God and man. The most vivid and forceful expression of Nahum's joy is found in his picture of the imminent and inevitable end.

Oh city, bloody throughout, full of lies and spoil; plunder ceases not!

The crack of the whip and the noise of the rumbling wheel and the galloping horse,

And the jolting chariot and the rearing horsemen.

And the flash of the sword and the glitter of the spear, and a multitude of slain;

And a mass of bodies, and no end to the carcasses;

Because of the many harlotries of a harlot of goodly favor and mistress of enchantments,

Who betrays nations by her harlotries and clans by her enchantments.

Behold I am against you, it is the oracle of Yahweh of hosts, and I will lay back your skirts upon your face;

And I will show nations your nakedness and kingdoms your shame.
And I will cast loathsome things on you and render you con-
temptible and make you a sight,
So that whosoever may see you will flee from you,
And say, "Nineveh is destroyed; who mourns for her?
Whence shall I seek comforters for her?"

Are you better than No-Amon that sat by the great Nile,
Whose rampart was a sea, whose wall was water?
Ethiopia was her strength; Put and the Libyans were her help.
Yet even she was for exile and went into captivity.
Even her infants were dashed in pieces at the head of every street.
And upon her nobles they cast lots and all her great men were
bound in fetters.[7]
You too will be drunken, you will be faint,
You will seek refuge from the foe.
All your fortresses are fig-trees, your people are first-ripe figs;
If they be shaken, they will fall into the mouth of the eater.
Behold, women are in the midst of you, fire has devoured your bars;
To your enemies the gates of your land are opened wide.

Draw you water for the siege; strengthen your forts.
Enter into the mire, and trample the clay; lay hold of the brick-
mold.
There fire will devour you, the sword will cut you off.
Multiply yourself like the locust; multiply yourself like the locust-
swarm.
Increase your merchants more than the stars of the heavens,
Your sacred officials (?) like the locust-swarm, and your scribes (?)
like the locusts,
That encamp in the walls in the cool of the day.
The sun arises and they flee; their place is not known.

How your shepherds slumber, your nobles sleep!
Your people are scattered upon the mountains, with none to
gather them.

[7] No-Amon, i.e., Thebes, was captured by Ashurbanipal, of Assyria, in 666 B.C.

There is no healing for your wound; your hurt is incurable:
All who hear the report of you will clap their hands.[8]

A little later than the fall of Nineveh, the complete overthrow of Assyria and the rise to supreme power of Babylonia occurred. In 605 B.C., Nebuchadrezzar, of Babylonia, met Pharaoh Necho, Assyria's ally, at Carchemish and put him to rout. From that moment Nebuchadrezzar was master of western Asia. In connection with that event, the prophet Habakkuk freed his mind of a great problem.[9] Nothing is known of the man Habakkuk; it is not clear even whether he was the original prophet or whether he was but the editor of the present book. But we shall attach the content of the original prophecy to his name.

The prophet complains to Yahweh that wickedness

[8] Nah. 3:1–19. The staccato style of Nahum, with its intensity and impelling haste, is difficult to carry over into English. In Hebrew one gains the feeling of actually watching the feverish haste of the mounting horsemen and dashing chariots as the defenders strive frantically to stem the tide of assault.

[9] B. Duhm (*Das Buch Habakuk* [1906]) proposed to place this prophet as a contemporary of Alexander the Great and to regard the entire book as a unit coming from that period. He was followed by Nowack (*Die kleinen Propheten* [3d ed., 1922]) and Sellin (*Das Zwölfprophetenbuch* [1922]), but in his second and third editions (1930) Sellin abandoned this position and reverted to the Chaldean period as the time of Habakkuk. The view of Duhm and Nowack rests upon two wholly conjectural emendations, and presupposes a unity which it is hard to find (cf. G. Hölscher, *Die Propheten* [1914], pp. 442 f.). On the other hand, Horst (*op. cit.*, pp. 167–68) regards the description of the Chaldeans as containing mythological allusions, hence to be ignored. So he concludes that the prophecy antedates the fall of Nineveh and is concerned with Assyrian oppression. How some exegetes love to discount available evidence so that they may indulge in free guessing!

is running riot everywhere in the land. Robbery and violence are prevalent. Law and justice are set at naught. The wicked get the better of the righteous, and the righteous are without recourse. Yahweh has seen and known this state of affairs, and yet fails to take action and deliver the righteous from his troubles. The prophet has long protested to Yahweh regarding this iniquitous state of affairs; but his protest has been unheeded.[10] These conditions are most easily understood as descriptive of the situation within Judah itself. Social injustice in accordance with which the strong plundered the weak was rife in the land. It is the old prophetic message again ringing in our ears.

Yahweh himself now appears as the speaker. He declares that he is about to do an almost incredible thing on the stage of world-history. He is bringing forth the Chaldeans, who will sweep everything before them. These people are thus described in vivid and picturesque language:

For behold I am raising up the Chaldeans, that fierce and hasty nation,
That goes through the broad places of the earth, to seize habitations not its own.
Terrible and frightful is it.
From itself its justice and its dignity proceed.

Swifter than leopards are its horses,
And keener than evening wolves.
And its horsemen come from afar;
They fly, like the vulture hastening to devour.

[10] Hab. 1:2–4.

Wholly for violence does he come.
Yea, he turns not west and east.[11]
And he gathers up captives like the sand.

And he makes sport of kings;
And potentates are a jest to him.
He laughs at every fortress,
And he heaps up earth and takes it.[12]

The ruthless might and unchecked career of the Chaldeans do but complicate the problem of the prophet. It is true that the wicked oppressors in Judah need and deserve punishment. But, after all, the Jews are better than the Chaldeans; and in any case the good Jews are not helped by being made the victims of the violence and plunder of the Chaldeans. How can Yahweh tolerate such proceedings? Is the Chaldean to go on indefinitely defying God and man?[13] Having flung this challenge into the face of God, the prophet represents himself as taking his position upon his watchtower and waiting for the answer that must come.

The answer itself is introduced in the most impressive manner. Yahweh bids the prophet take tablets and write the contents of the vision he is to receive in such large and clear characters that the passer-by may read as he hurries past. Then, with a final assurance that the fulfilment of the vision is not far off and an admonition to the prophet not to become impatient

[11] See George G. V. Stonehouse, *The Book of Habakkuk* (1911), *ad loc.* The Hebrew text here is corrupt.

[12] Hab. 1:6–10.

[13] Hab. 1:13–17. Hab. 1:11, 12 is from the hand of an editor.

for its realization, the content of the vision is revealed to him:

> Behold! swollen, not straight, is his soul in him;
> But the righteous will live by reason of his faithfulness.
> The more so when . . . .
> A haughty man and he will not abide.[14]

The answer that comes to the prophet is not to be thought of as stopping with verse 4. "Tablets," in the plural, would hardly be needed for the writing of two lines of text. The idiom at the opening of verse 5 seems to bind verse 5 closely to verse 4. The text of verse 5 is badly spoiled, so that as it now stands it yields no satisfactory sense.[15] It is clear, however, that the status and fortune of the "righteous" in verse 4 is contrasted with that of the wicked in verses 5 ff. The following verses are filled with denunciations and threats against the wicked oppressor, and they prophesy his complete overthrow. They have been supplemented by later hands at various points where they reflect the ideas of later times.[16]

The first words of this vision are the most important

---

[14] Hab. 2:4, 5.

[15] The "couplet" structure of the passage enhances the conclusion that the answer to Habakkuk carries over into vs. 5. It seems probable, though, that all is lost after "The more so when," and the following words belong with the ensuing series of "Woes." It is an old view that "wine" of our common translations is a corruption of the Hebrew word for "Woe."

[16] See the differing opinions of the commentaries on this question. But there is general recognition of vss. 14 and 18–20 as late. The third chapter, as a whole, is a psalm from later times that has been attached to the text of Habakkuk. Note the superscription and concluding formula.

part of it. They have been made familiar to the Christian world by the use of them in the Epistle to the Hebrews, 10:38; and they were lifted into new life by Luther's use of them as the watchword of his reform movement. But the New Testament rendering and Luther's use of it alike fail to reproduce the exact meaning of the original words. That meaning, of course, grew out of the problem of the prophet as outlined in the previous statement of his difficulty to Yahweh. This prophet, like all his predecessors, believed the formula that piety and prosperity were cause and effect. If a nation or an individual pleased Yahweh by the kind of life lived or policy followed, then that nation or individual would prosper; on the other hand, if the conduct of nation or individual were such as to be displeasing to Yahweh, then misfortune would come upon the transgressor. The prophet is puzzled because this view of life does not seem to be in accordance with the facts as he sees them. He has therefore brought his question to Yahweh, from whom in due course he has received the answer:

> Behold, swollen, not upright, is his soul within him:
> But the righteous shall live because of his faithfulness.

This means simply that the Chaldean power is doomed to downfall, because of its internal weakness. That weakness is suggested by two figures, the one of an inflated bubble or bag that must burst, the other of a crooked wall that must fall or beam that will break. The Chaldean power carries within itself the seeds of its own destruction. But the righteous people, that is, the Jewish nation, will endure and triumph because of its sound character. The word "faithfulness" here is not mere creedal opinion, or even conviction; it is rather faith in action. It means steadfastness of purpose and act; it is almost equivalent to integrity. What, then, has the answer said? Is it not essentially the same old doctrine, piety will prosper and wickedness will come to ruin? Yes, and no!

The difference between this prophet's affirmation that piety pays and that of his predecessors is that he has pondered over this problem and thought it through. He is not now holding a merely inherited faith. It is a faith that he has agonized over in spirit and has reaffirmed for himself after subjecting it to all the light available. It is a reasoned faith rather than one that has been placidly accepted without question at the hands of tradition. It is therefore more likely to stand the strains of the future, for it is firmly founded on personal experience. But Habakkuk differs from his predecessors also in the deeper content he reads into the reward of piety. While it is true that his problem is concerned with objective facts, his answer is in intangible realities; it is in the richness and meaning he finds in the promise that the righteous shall *live*. Over against the swollen, pompous emptiness of the oppressor's career, the righteous finds through his agonized faith a world of life and worth. Just as in some great passages in Jeremiah, there is here a contrast between material benefits and the deep and abiding worth of the things of the spirit, in a personal experience of God.

This contribution from Habakkuk constitutes a new phenomenon in the history of prophecy. Heretofore, the prophets have been content to say, "Thus says Yahweh." They have been nothing if not dogmatic. They have felt assured that they knew the mind of God and were commissioned to interpret it to the nation. But here is something different. This prophet is asking questions. He is daring to call in question a traditional dogma. He is challenging Yahweh to demonstrate the justice of his administration. Previous prophets may have had private questions of this sort which troubled their spirits; but no trace of such doubts had appeared in public expression of their message. This prophet exposes the inner workings of his mind for the benefit of all observers. He has no fears or scruples as to the legitimacy of his own mental and religious processes. He takes for granted the propriety of the interrogative attitude toward his God. He is seeking for light upon a difficult question, and he looks for that light to come from Yahweh, the source of all his light. Thus he furnished to the Scriptures of his race and of the world an illustration and example of the recognition of the right of inquiry and investigation in the field of ethics and religion. Certainly, his search brought him out at the point where he started; but he believed in and exercised the right to question traditional opinions and institutions and to demand of them justification for their existence. He has established for all time the principle that the search for truth is an essentially religious procedure.

This bit of prophecy is an illustration of a familiar truth, viz., that faith is always an achievement, not a mere inheritance. The Hebrews, of the Exilic and post-Exilic periods at least, had to fight for their faith. It was difficult to believe in Yahweh as the supreme God when Yahweh's people were rapidly losing all place and power in the political world. Was Yahweh not able to protect his own people? If so, why continue to worship him? It was hard to believe in the moral order of the universe when a wicked nation was trampling the people of Yahweh into the dust. It is the glory of Judaism that men like Habakkuk kept faith alive in the hearts of the people during a series of national calamities that might well have crushed the life out of it. The faith of Judaism grew richer and stronger the more severely it was tried.

The little book closes with a poem—strictly, with two poems[17]—appropriately in harmony with the theme of the prophet, celebrating the triumph of Yahweh over his enemies and the faith of one who, though all material things fail, yet can rejoice in the Lord and joy in the God of his salvation. Much attention has been given to the problem of whether this chapter is "genuine," that is, whether it is from the prophet Habakkuk. While decisive evidence fails us, yet the nature of the first poem leaves it highly probable that both have been attached here by some reader who saw their fitness for the close of this profound little book. For the first poem is throughout but an adaptation to Yahweh of the incidents of the Babylonian "Creation Epic"; step by step we can follow precisely the movements and adventures ascribed to Marduk in that most famous and most influential liturgy of the ancient

[17] Hab. 3:1–15; 16–19.

world. It is an astonishing fact how completely this pious Hebrew has taken over the most sacred poem of his great pagan contemporaries and used it unblushingly in his worship of the Lord. But not less remarkable is the glimpse we here attain of the bases of that faith which was to sustain the Jewish people through many ages of bitter trying. The enemy of the Lord was the primeval foe, chaos and darkness; but he was also the ever recurring persecutor and oppressor of the Lord's people. Pharaoh, Amalek, Edom, or Nebuchadrezzar, and far down the centuries, Antiochus Epiphanes or even Adolph Hitler—all alike were but the demon of the primeval deep over whom the Lord triumphed at the beginning, over whom he is perennially and eternally triumphant. And as his harried people through the ages and lands have lifted despairing voices, crying, "O Lord, how long?" the answer has come, "A time and times and half a time. . . . . I beheld even till the beast was slain, and its body destroyed, and it was given to be burned with fire . . . . and the kingdom and the dominion, and the greatness of the kingdoms under the whole heaven shall be given to the people of the saints of the Most High."

> Thou wentest forth for the salvation of thy people,
> For the salvation of thine anointed.

CHAPTER IX

JEREMIAH AND THE FALL OF JERUSALEM

AFTER the Scythian menace, whatever it may have signified, and in the years immediately succeeding Jeremiah's "call," great things were happening inside and outside of Judah. In 621 B.C. the Deuteronomic reform swept over the country, backed by the authority of the good king Josiah. In 612 B.C., Nineveh, the capital of the Assyrian Empire, fell at the hands of the Medes and Babylonians. In 608 B.C. Pharaoh Necho came to the assistance of the retreating Assyrians, who had made their last stand in Harran. On his way through Palestine, Pharaoh slew Josiah, king of Judah, at Megiddo. Thereupon, the people of Judah placed Jehoahaz upon the throne in his father's place, only to have Pharaoh Necho put him in prison and set another son of Josiah's upon the vacant throne, changing his name from Eliakim to Jehoiakim. At the same time Judah was taxed to the extent of ten talents of gold and one hundred talents of silver as a war indemnity to Egypt.[1] In 605–604 B.C., Necho was overthrown at Carchemish by Nebuchadrezzar, the Babylonian, with whom the lordship of the world changed hands. The land of Judah received a new overlord and became subject to Babylon for three

[1] II Kings 23:29–35. This tribute was the equivalent, roughly speaking, of about two and a quarter millions of dollars.

years.[2] It is uncertain whether this submission to Babylon followed immediately upon Carchemish or was deferred a few years until Nebuchadrezzar could gather in the fruits of his victory and consolidate his empire. It may well have been that Jehoiakim enjoyed a brief period of independence between the downfall of Necho and the coming of Nebuchadrezzar. In any case, it is safe to say that his final revolt at the end of the three years of submission to Babylon was almost certainly instigated by Egypt.

The death of Josiah in 608 B.C. must have been a terrific shock to Judah. Josiah was a relatively pious king, who zealously carried out the will of Yahweh as made known to him by priests and prophets. Indeed, he is credited with one of the greatest reform movements ever put through in Judah. According to the generally accepted theories and the faith of the times, his reign should have been crowned with success and glory. But, on the contrary, he was cut off suddenly by the sword of the enemy. This situation stirred Jeremiah to utterance. We know his estimate of Josiah to have been favorable. He commended him shortly after his death and contrasted him with his successors[3] in an utterance that showed no lack of courage. Jeremiah confronted Jehoiakim with this message:

> Do not weep for the dead, nor bemoan him;
> Weep sore for the one who goes away;
> For he will not return again,
> Nor see the land of his birth.

This dismisses summarily any lingering hopes that may

[2] II Kings 24:1 [3] Jer. 22:1, 10–19.

have been entertained for the return of Jehoahaz. He has gone to Egypt to stay. But Jeremiah went on to pay his respects to Jehoiakim:

Woe to him who builds his house by unrighteousness,
And his upper rooms by injustice,
Who employs his neighbor without pay,
And does not give him his wages.
The one who says, "I shall build myself a spacious house
And upper rooms that are airy.
And he cuts out windows for it;
And it is paneled with cedar,
And painted in red."

Would you show yourself king in that you excel your father in cedar?
Did he not eat and drink,
And do justice and righteousness?
Then it went well with him.
He judged the cause of the poor and needy.
Then it was well.
"Is not this to know me?" says Yahweh.

For your eyes and heart are on nothing
But unlawful gain,
And upon pouring out innocent blood,
And upon doing oppression and violence.

His final word regarding Jehoiakim, whether spoken at this time or more probably somewhat later, threatens him with disgraceful death. He will die "unwept, unhonored, and unsung." Jeremiah's experience with the Scythians did not teach him caution. He daringly threatened Jehoiakim with violent death and denial of burial.[4] Another version of this prediction given in Jer.

[4] Jer. 22:18 f.

36:30 places it after Jehoiakim had burned the roll of prophecies sent to him by Jeremiah, and adds that Jehoiakim will have no successor of his own blood to sit upon David's throne. But again history failed Jeremiah, for we are told in II Kings 24:6 that Jehoiakim slept with his fathers and was succeeded by his own son Jehoiachin. The Greek translation of II Chron. 36:8 adds that Jehoiakim "was buried in the tomb with his fathers." This is probably a genuine element of the original narrative preserved by the Chronicler.

The same unshrinking courage was in evidence again when Jeremiah appeared in the Temple court one day and foretold the total destruction of that sacred building. The record of this is found in Jer. 7:1– 15 and 26:1–24. We get the content of the message in chapter 7, and its effect upon those who heard it in chapter 26. Jeremiah's message on that occasion was a declaration that the confidence of the people in the protecting power of the Temple in Jerusalem was without any basis in reality. The only guaranty of safety is to be found in true religion, which is not a matter of temple worship but of loyalty to Yahweh and of social justice. Since deeds of real piety are not forthcoming, the Temple at Jerusalem is to suffer the same fate as the temple at Shiloh had undergone in days long past. This announcement aroused great indignation in Jerusalem, and came near costing Jeremiah his life. A mob gathered around him, led by the priests and the prophets, and threatened him with death. The government officials intervened. Jeremiah maintained his position and reminded them that in doing violence to him they would bring innocent blood on themselves, for he had but uttered the words Yahweh had sent him to speak. Thereupon, the people swung over to the side of Jeremiah and supported the officials against the charges of the priests and the conventional prophets. Moreover, some of the elders of the people remembered the prophecy of Micah and cited his immunity in Hezekiah's time as a precedent for toleration in this case. Not only so, but a prominent leader, Ahikam, the son of Shaphan, took Jeremiah's part and saved him from the fury of the hierarchy.[5]

Shortly after this scene, perhaps, Jeremiah was back in Anathoth, his home village, which he had left some time before in order to take up his residence in Jerusalem. While in Anathoth he discovered a plot among his former neighbors to put him to death. The discovery of this treachery stirred him to the depths and aroused in him fierce resentment. They prohibited him from prophesying on pain of death. He retaliated by prophesying the total annihilation of Anathoth and its people as penalty for their impiety.[6] But this experience seems to have brought about a reaction in his own spirit, so that he was confronted by doubts similar to those that had troubled Habakkuk. In this state of mind he expressed himself thus:

Righteous art thou, O Yahweh, though I complain against thee;
Yet of matters of justice would I talk with thee.
Why is it that the way of the wicked prospers,
And all tricksters are at ease?

[5] Jeremiah, chap. 26.   [6] Jer. 11:18–23.

Thou didst plant them, yea, they have taken root;
They bear and indeed yield fruit.
Thou art near in their mouth,
But far from their heart.

O Yahweh, thou hast known me; thou seest me;
And thou hast tested my heart with thee.
Drag them out, like sheep to the slaughter,
And dedicate them for the day of carnage.

How long must the land mourn,
And the herbs of the field wither?
For the wickedness of its inhabitants,
Beasts and birds are consumed.

"Verily, with footmen you have run and they have tried you;
Then how will you compete with horses?
And in a peaceful land you are fleeing,
So how will you do in the jungle of the Jordan?"[7]

In the last stanza Yahweh brings the prophet up short and sharp. What Jeremiah has suffered thus far is not to be compared with what he has still to bear. The passage is an astonishing revelation of the fortitude and unbending courage of this erstwhile diffident boy, whom modern thought has caricatured as the "weeping prophet." Broken with discouragement, he had turned to his God for soft words of soothing and comfort. But the answer that came back in challenge to the strength of his own soul was "Why complain now? You will yet face matters so immeasurably worse that the present will seem a time of peace." It was as if he had heard the challenge of Yahweh hurled at suffering Job, "Gird up now thy loins *like a man!*"[8] Only the

[7] Jer. 12:1–5.   [8] Job 38:3.

strong can endure comfort of this sort; only the brave find its echo within their deepest soul.

Jeremiah spared no pains to make clear to his people and their rulers the fate that he saw awaiting them. He was fertile in the discovery of ways and means by which to impress his message upon his hearers. In 13:1–11, he relates a story of his going to Parah[9] and there burying a soiled loincloth. After the lapse of some time he makes another journey and digs up the cloth, only to find it ruined. All this is to impress upon the mind of Judah that in Yahweh's sight the people are as filthy and useless as the rotten cloth. From an early period in Jehoiakim's reign, perhaps, comes a group of prophecies in which Jeremiah recognizes the futility of his efforts and foresees the downfall of Judah as punishment for the people's lack of faith in Yahweh.[10] Here

[9] So Moffatt; cf. the Jewish translation. The usual rendering, however, is "to the Euphrates." It is true that the word here, *Perath*, is identical with the name of the great river; but, apart from the inherent improbability of Jeremiah's making such a journey of hundreds of miles—it is recorded that he went twice—this rendering is put out of consideration by the fact that in the Old Testament when the Euphrates is meant it is uniformly defined as "the river Euphrates"; the only exceptions are Gen. 2:14, where "river" occurs in the immediate context, and the dubious passage Jer. 51:63. Parah is mentioned in Jos. 18:23 as a locality in the territory of Benjamin. The proximity of this to Jerusalem, as well as its evident familiarity to Jeremiah as a native of Benjamin, renders it highly probable that this is the reference in this passage. The Wadi Farah must also be considered (cf. G. A. Smith, *Jeremiah* [1924], p. 184). While this is not an impossible identification, we have no evidence that this valley bore this or a similar name in antiquity (cf. F. Buhl, *Geographie des alten Palästina* [1896], p. 99).

[10] Jer. 13:15–27; 12:7–12; 11:15–17; 8:4—9:1.

we meet the familiar and striking figure of speech first coined by Jeremiah,

> Can the Ethiopian change his skin,
> Or the leopard his spots?
> Then you also may do good,
> Who are trained to do evil.[11]

Other familiar phrases are found in these oracles, e.g.,

They have healed the hurt of the daughter of my people slightly,
Saying, "Peace, peace," where there is no peace.[12]

and

> The harvest is past, the summer is ended,
> And we are not saved.[13]

and again,

Is there no balm in Gilead; is there no physician there?[14]

When we separate as best we can the genuine utterances of Jeremiah from the mass of later material attached to his name, we are impressed with the freshness and vigor of his style, as well as the vividness of his poetry, even as we are by the courage of his thought.

Jeremiah's oracles against the foreign nations in chapters 25 and 46–51 have given rise to much questioning in recent years. Did Jeremiah concern himself seriously with the fate of the pagan world? Are these oracles characterized by the same spirit, thought, and style as are found elsewhere in Jeremiah's writings?[15] It must be borne in mind that Jeremiah's "call" included

---

[11] Jer. 13:23.   [12] Jer. 8:11.   [13] Jer. 8:20.   [14] Jer. 8:22.

[15] The chief opponents of the genuineness of these chapters have been Schwally, *Zeitschrift für die alttestamentliche Wissenschaft*, VIII (1888), 177 ff.; Smend, *Lehrbuch der alttestamentliche Religionsgeschichte* (1899), pp. 238 f.; Duhm, *Jeremia* (1901), pp. 336 ff.

the non-Israelitish world in its scope.[16] It is also noticeable that the message to the nations in 25:15 ff. is couched in highly figurative terms. Jeremiah there sees himself receiving the cup of Yahweh's wrath from his hands and proffering it to nation after nation that they may drink. It seems reasonable, therefore, to accept the representation of 25:15 ff. in general and to believe that the prophecies in chapters 46 ff. are at least based upon certain materials that originated with Jeremiah himself. No man in the last days of Judah could concern himself with national problems and escape constant contact with international questions. The world of the Fertile Crescent and Egypt was a world of constant intrigue. All politics had to be world-politics. No nation any longer was sufficient unto itself. Jeremiah had very strong convictions upon these matters; and naturally, therefore, his prophecies concerned themselves more or less with foreign peoples.[17]

In 605–604 B.C., the fourth year of Jehoiakim's reign, Jeremiah sent for Baruch, the scribe, and dictated to him the sum and substance of his preaching from the time of his call in 627 B.C., twenty-three years before. Some time afterward, when the roll of sermons was completed, he sent Baruch with the manuscript to read it to the people as they were assembled in the Temple for the celebration of a fast day.[18] One of those who

[16] Jer. 1:10.

[17] The prophecies against foreign nations are defended by Cornill, Giesebrecht, Skinner, Peake, and Sellin; also Bardtke, "Jeremia der Fremdvölkerprophet," *Zeitschrift für die alttestamentliche Wissenschaft*, LIII (1935), 209–39; LIV (1936), 240–62; cf. George Adam Smith, *Jeremiah* (1924), p. 20, n. 3.

[18] Jer. 36:1–10.

heard this reading reported the matter to a group of the nobles assembled in a neighboring house. They sent for Baruch at once and heard the oracles for themselves. They in turn reported to the king, meanwhile giving Jeremiah and Baruch a chance to go into hiding. The king, too, desired to hear the oracles; but, as they were read, he cut the roll in pieces and tossed it into the fire burning in the brazier. Jeremiah, safely hidden from the wrath of the king, thereupon dictated the oracles afresh, and apparently left the new roll in the hands of Baruch. That roll furnished the starting-point for the present Book of Jeremiah.[19] This gave Jeremiah a chance to bring his old oracles against the Scythians up to date by reinterpreting them as applying to the new enemy from the north, viz., the Babylonians. But it also aroused the wrath of Jehoiakim against him and forced him to keep in hiding. About this same time, after the writing of the rolls, Baruch consulted Jeremiah as to his own future. In response to this request, Jeremiah gave Baruch a word of personal assurance to the effect that he need expect no honors or blessings for himself, for destruction was coming upon the whole land; but at least he could count upon saving his own life. Baruch might well have asked: "What is life worth, with nothing to live upon?" But that was not the spirit that actuated Jeremiah's faithful friend.

At this point we may consider certain undated materials in Jeremiah, chapters 14–20. These chapters reflect a great deal of doubt and grief on Jeremiah's part as he contemplated the approaching fate of his beloved

[19] Jer. 36:11-23, 32.

people. They are variously located in Jeremiah's life
by interpreters, there being no agreement as to their
precise date. They may well have occupied Jeremiah's
mind at the time when he was in hiding from the
wrathful Jehoiakim. From chapter 14 it appears that a
severe drought fell upon the land which caused griev-
ous protests against Yahweh on the part of the populace. Jeremiah felt himself debarred from pleading the
cause of Judah with Yahweh, since he knew in his heart
of hearts that such prayers could not be answered because of the faithless and disloyal attitude of the people
toward its God.[20] Jeremiah in the form of a conversation with Yahweh then discussed the work of the
prophets in opposition to himself. These men were
prophets of prosperity and naturally more acceptable to the people than Jeremiah's prophecies of calamity. But Jeremiah was convinced that they were
in the wrong, and did not hesitate to call them liars and
deceivers and to threaten them and the land as a whole
with famine and sword.[21] The picture of death and
desolation is continued in 15:5–9. Jeremiah then gives
us a glimpse into his own inner life. He reveals his grief
that his calling has brought upon him the curses of his
own people. He calls upon Yahweh to avenge him of
his persecutors and declares that he suffers solely because he has spoken Yahweh's word.[22] Yahweh re-

[20] Jer. 14:10–12.   [21] Jer. 14:13–16.

[22] Jer. 15:10, 11, 15–18. This passage (15:15 f.) is supported by
other passages calling down vengeance on Jeremiah's foes, viz., 11:
20 f.; 12:3; 17:18; 18:20 ff.; and 20:12. Of these, Duhm leaves to
Jeremiah only 11:20; 15:15; and 18:20; Cornill accepts only 11:20–

bukes him for his unworthy thoughts and assures him of protection against all his foes.[23] The Jeremiah of this experience is a very human person, subject to the fluctuations of temperament and the gusts of passion that so easily beset us all.[24]

In 18:1–10 is found the famous oracle received in the potter's house. Jeremiah had gone there, for what reason we do not know, though his experience led him later to explain it as divine direction; and as he watched the potter at work, creating new forms, wrestling with refractory material, and shaping the clay to his plans, he recognized, with his remarkable facility for reading religious meaning in commonplace things, a symbol of God at work among the nations molding the course of history to his purposes. Here we come in touch with one of the most persistent, and possibly most important, ideas in the entirety of Old Testament revelation. The prophets and thinkers of Israel saw the course of human life, not as a blind or chance process determined by the casual balance of rival passions or brute force, but as the plan of a God who is righteous and who works far-off, benign purposes; he makes even the wrath of man to praise him. Nor was this a dilettante theory lightly assumed in easy days; it was out of the whirlwind and tempest of

21a; 15:15; Peake 12:3a; 15:15; 17:18a; 20:3 ff., 12; while Giesebrecht, Steuernagel, Skinner, Binns, and G. A. Smith accept them all as genuine.

[23] Jer. 15:10, 11.

[24] Other passages, perhaps from this same period in Jeremiah's life, which reflect his changing moods are Jer. 17:14–17; 18:18–20.

their troublous times the Hebrew thinkers rose to the conviction that the hand of God was shaping the events of their days. So, for Jeremiah, while the world fell in ruins about him, while the crash of Assyrian brutality brought no relief but instead a new master and new aggressions that shook the little Judean kingdom to its very foundations, presently engulfing it in complete ruin, God was the great Potter, shaping out of the refractory materials of the world of that day ends that could be only eternal goodness and beauty.

The passage is interesting, too, as revealing the prophet's attitude to his own predictions; it seems to say that Jeremiah recognized that these were conditional and not absolute. Just as a potter re-works his lump of clay and makes another vessel out of it, if the first attempt is spoiled on the wheel, so Yahweh changes his purpose with reference to his people when they change their conduct either for good or for bad. Looked at in another way, this is equivalent to saying that the purpose of all prediction is to affect the conduct of the people to whom the prophet preaches. If disaster is foretold, it is for the purpose of warning the people from sin; and if blessings are promised, it is to strengthen them in their loyalty to true religion and win them to more faithful service.[25] In this same chapter, Jeremiah's message of destruction as punishment for idolatrous practices stirs up the wrath of his hearers, and they devise evil against him. Of particular interest is the charge they make against him, viz., that he is try-

[25] See J. M. Powis Smith, *The Prophet and His Problems* (1914), chap. iv, "Prophetic Prediction."

ing to overthrow established institutions, which by their nature are of the permanent order of the universe.[26] The three types of religious instruction are cited as the unchangeable, enduring things:

Law will not perish from the priest, nor counsel from the sage, nor word from the prophet.

It is significant that these opponents of Jeremiah did not select more material and tangible institutions of the social and political order as guaranties of permanence, but these pre-eminently spiritual and idealistic and apparently least substantial and enduring elements of the national life. They evidently were not wholly blind.

Jeremiah's repeated, Cassandra-like prophecies were not allowed to go unrebuked. On one occasion when he had dramatically predicted the destruction of Jerusalem,[27] he was arrested by Pashhur, the priestly chief of the Temple police, and was placed in the stocks, in which uncomfortable situation he had to spend the night. When Pashhur released him on the morrow, Jeremiah hurled at him a most terrifying oracle: "Yahweh has not called your name Pashhur, but Magor missabib," i.e., "terror-from-every-side."[28] It may have been as a result of this experience while Jeremiah was naturally low in spirit that he gave utterance to the remarkable soliloquy that we have in 20:7–12. But in any case it is one of a series of revealing personal passages from this most human of prophets. In them

[26] Jer. 18:18.

[27] Jer. 19:1, 2, 10–12a, 14, 15.   [28] Jer. 20:1–3.

we see the deep pain of soul through which the sensitive man went about his calling, persecuted and jeered at until he almost doubted God himself; we see, too, the incomplete revelation of this sixth century B.C., when its finest representative roundly cursed his persecutors and called down the vengeance of God on their callous deeds; but we see also the compulsion of his divine calling, and the fortitude of a gentle soul who could not be turned from his convictions though all might assail: a fortified city, an iron pillar, and brazen walls against which they might fight but could not prevail!

> Thou didst entice me, O Yahweh, and I yielded.
> Thou wast stronger than I and thou didst prevail.
> I have become a laughing-stock all day long;
> Everybody taunts me.
>
> For whenever I speak, I cry out;
> I cry "Violence" and "Destruction."
> For the word of Yahweh has become for me
> A reproach and a jibe all the day long.
>
> So I said to myself, "I will not remember him,
> Nor will I speak any longer in his name."
> But he was in my heart like a burning fire,
> Shut up within my bones.
> And I was tired of enduring,
> And was unable.
>
> For I heard the whispers of many, "Terror from every side";
> "Announce and we will denounce him,"
> All the men of my acquaintance,
> Who keep by my side.
> "Perchance, he will be snared and we may prevail over him,
> And take our vengeance upon him."

But Yahweh is with me like a terrible warrior.
Therefore my pursuers will stumble and will not prevail.
They will be thoroughly ashamed for they will not succeed;
Their perpetual disgrace will not be forgotten.[29]

From that height of assurance, Jeremiah fell again into the depths of despondency, uttering, in 20:14–18, a curse upon the day of his birth which furnished the suggestion for the similar curse in Job, chapter 3.

Somewhere about 600 B.C. Jehoiakim listened to the voice of the siren and joined the movement of revolt against Nebuchadrezzar. At first, Nebuchadrezzar sent only his vassal kings against Judah, but he finally appeared on the scene himself. Meantime, Jehoiakim had died and been succeeded by his son Jehoiachin. He was forced to surrender himself and his capital, after a siege of three months, to the Babylonians in 597 B.C., and was deported with all the leaders of the population to Babylon.[30] From the earlier days of the siege comes the narrative recorded in Jeremiah, chapter 35. A band of Rechabites had taken refuge in Jerusalem from before the advancing army of Babylonians. Jeremiah went down to the Temple court with them, and there in the sight of the onlooking crowd offered them wine to drink. This they declined, alleging that they were obligated to do so by a vow taken by their founder who had bound his followers to the observance of the simple life of the nomads. Jeremiah at once turned this episode to use against his countrymen by contrasting the faithfulness of the Rechabites to the wish of their founder with the faithlessness of the peo-

[29] Jer. 20:7–11. [30] II Kings, chap. 24.

ple of Judah, who pay no heed to their obligations of loyalty to Yahweh. Consequently, all of Yahweh's threats of punishment upon Judah will be fulfilled, while the Rechabites will continue in peace and prosperity forever. What Jeremiah thought of Jehoiachin is plainly stated in Jer. 22:24–30, when he predicted for him permanent exile from his land and the cessation of his dynasty with himself. In fact, Jehoiachin's successor was Zedekiah, his uncle on his father's side.[31]

Shortly after 597 B.C., Jeremiah related another vision that he had received (chap. 24). In this, he likened the people of Judah to two baskets of figs. The exiles in Babylon were like good figs, while the inhabitants of Judah and Jerusalem, left behind by Nebuchadrezzar, were represented by a basket of rotten figs. In this bold fashion, Jeremiah declared that the future of the people of Yahweh was in the hands of the exiles, who in due time would return to their homes, while nothing but ruin and death awaited the people in Jerusalem and Judah. This is noteworthy as Jeremiah's first utterance of hope for a future of his people. It is noteworthy, too, that he conceived of that future as dependent upon the exiles, and not the stay-at-homes. This is a testimony to the practical sense of Jeremiah. He was not prejudiced in favor of the strong and wealthy; he took the part of the poor and helpless when necessary, even as the rest of the prophets had done. But he was keen enough to know that no nation could be built up out of the poorest and weakest of the land.[32] He recognized the necessity of enterprise, abil-

[31] II Kings 24:17.   [32] II Kings 24:14–16.

ity, and character; and he knew that these qualities were more largely represented among the exiles than among the people left behind. Not only so, but the survivors of the land were apparently unduly puffed up by the fact that they had escaped exile. They were rejoicing over the escape of Jerusalem from destruction, and were congratulating themselves that Yahweh could be counted upon to defend his city and people. It is not unlikely that they were even blaming the exiles for their misfortune, saying that they were being thus punished for their gross sins and inferring for themselves great piety since they had not been carried away! To such a state of mind Jeremiah's diagnosis of the situation would come with a great shock.

Out of the same recognition of the importance of the Exilic group came a letter written to them by Jeremiah shortly after their arrival in Babylonia.[33] In this letter Jeremiah urged upon the exiles the necessity of dismissing from their minds any thought of an early return home, assuring them that the captivity would continue for an extended period of time. Therefore the sensible and the loyal thing to be done was to establish for themselves in Babylonia a normal type of life, making homes for themselves, raising families, and entering fully into the commercial life of the land. It is characteristic of Jeremiah's clear mind that he counseled them to co-operate in every way with the native population, and so in furthering the general prosperity they would be contributing most effectively to their own well-being. He declared that Yahweh had not for-

[33] Jeremiah, chap. 29.

saken them, but that even in Babylonia he would hearken unto them if they sincerely sought him. He was also certain that Yahweh would restore his people to their own land in due time, but he denounced those shallow-minded prophets who had gone with the exiles and were buoying them up with false hopes of a speedy return and so preventing them from taking up seriously the responsibilities of their new situation. This letter seems to have brought a vigorous reply from a leader of the exiled community in the form of a protest to the chief priest in Jerusalem to the effect that it was his official duty to silence a man like Jeremiah by putting him in prison. When this letter was read publicly in Jeremiah's hearing, he branded Shemaiah, its writer, as a rebel against Yahweh, and predicted the extermination of his family.[34]

Throughout Judah and the adjacent regions there was manifest at this time a restlessness and unwillingness to accept with docility the condition of continuing vassalage to Babylon. Plots and conspiracies were on foot to strike once more for freedom. In the fourth year of Zedekiah, delegates from Moab, Ammon, Tyre, and Sidon appeared in Jerusalem to arrange for such a joint uprising. Thereupon, Jeremiah felt himself moved to make yokes and bands and to present them to these messengers that they might carry them back to their masters. With these symbols of subjection, he sent also an interpretative message, which was meant quite as much for Zedekiah and his advisers as it was for the conspiring kings, to the effect that the only safe and

<hr>

[34] Jer. 29:32; cf. vss. 21 f.

sane policy for all of western Asia was to accept the
overlordship of Nebuchadrezzar and serve him loyally.
This would insure protection and security; any attempt to defy him would mean exile and captivity for
those who tried it. Furthermore, in accepting the lordship of Nebuchadrezzar they were conforming to the
plan of Yahweh, who had given the peoples of western
Asia into his hands.[35] Jeremiah spared no pains to keep
his country from plunging into a suicidal revolt. He
pressed his views upon king, priests, and people, declaring that submission to Nebuchadrezzar was the
only possible escape from further calamity and destruction.[36]

One of the most powerful groups opposed to Jeremiah at this time consisted of the prophets of his day.
These men were unanimously in support of the spirit of
revolt. Even after the first deportation they were convinced, both in Babylonia and in Judah, that Yahweh
would intervene marvelously, and speedily bring his
people back home. In chapter 28 is recorded Jeremiah's encounter with a representative of this group in
the presence of the priests and the people in the Temple. Jeremiah had gone down to the Temple with a
yoke upon his neck, thus symbolizing the necessity of
Judah's accepting placidly the yoke of Nebuchadrezzar. Hananiah, the prophet, was preaching a message
of hope, declaring that it was Yahweh's plan to restore
Judah within at most two years by bringing back the

[35] Jer. 27:1–11. "Jehoiakim" in 27:1 is an error for "Zedekiah"
(see vs. 3).

[36] Jer. 27:12–22.

exiles and all the furnishings of the Temple. Jeremiah responded to this by saying that he desired such an outcome as much as anybody else did, but that the people would do well to think a little before accepting such a view. Then turning to Hananiah, he said:

Hear, now, this word that I speak in your hearing, and in the hearing of all the people: The prophets who were before you and before me in the past prophesied against many countries and against great kingdoms, of war, and of evil, and of pestilence. But the prophet who prophesies of prosperity—when the word of such a prophet comes to pass, the prophet shall be known, that Yahweh has really sent him.

Thereupon Hananiah countered by taking Jeremiah's yoke and breaking it in the sight of the crowd and saying that in like manner Yahweh would break the yoke imposed by Babylon.

"And the prophet Jeremiah went his way." He could do nothing else effectively. As a wise man he left the scene. What did he think? Did he perhaps question the validity of his own judgment? After all, Hananiah might be in the right? Jeremiah knew too well that he himself was not infallible. Had he really heard the word of Yahweh? But, as thoughts like these succeeded one another in his mind, there came to him again with new power the conviction that he, and not Hananiah, had spoken the truth. Later, on the same day perhaps, he returned to face his opponent and said to him:

You have broken the wooden yokes,
But you will make in their stead iron yokes.

Then he turned upon Hananiah himself and predicted his death within the year as punishment for his false prophecy; and within two months Hananiah died. There is no reason to doubt this statement. Cases of such foreknowledge are not unknown, though they are inexplicable. Such a story is more likely to be true than to have been invented. The fact of Hananiah's death was probably too well known to escape mention.

Two things are of special note in the foregoing episode. First, the fact that Jeremiah's statement that the history of prophecy knew of no prophets of prosperity, but that the unbroken tradition of prophecy was the preaching of disaster. Second, the fact that his test of the validity of a prophecy lay simply in the answer to the question as to whether or not it agreed with the trend of prophetic preaching in the past. The past had known only prophets of woe; there had been no heralds of hope. This statement was unchallenged by Hananiah. Would it not have been a fatal blow to Jeremiah's message if he could have cited such prophecies as Isa. 9:1–17; 11:1–9; Mic. 5:2–6? He and his friends certainly would have known if such prophecies had been extant. Did Jeremiah leave no room for prophecies of hope in the future? He made conformity to the past the test of true prophecy, and his past was a hopeless one. It would almost appear that he meant that only unpleasant prophecies could possibly be true, which carries the desolating implication that nothing happy ever can occur. But Jeremiah was no such pessimist; he prophesied deliverance when such a message was needed. In his letter to the exiles, as we have seen, he held out the certain hope of a return from exile; and we shall see that he looked forward to the revival of happy, peaceful days in Palestine. Apparently we are to understand his words on this present occasion as primarily a protest against the shallow optimism of the time, which, without weighing the moral realities involved, taught glibly that prosperity was just around the corner waiting to be let in. Evidently he had no intention of laying down a hard and fast law for prophecy. He would leave it free to adjust its message to the needs of the changing generations. In any case, that is what the prophets did.

In spite of Jeremiah's warnings and protests, Zedekiah entered into the revolt against Babylon, and soon found the Babylonian army at his front door.[37] Thereupon he sent messengers to Jeremiah to learn what

[37] One of the astonishing results of recent archeological investigation in Palestine has been the discovery, early in 1935, in the ruins of Tell ed-Duweir (now commonly identified as the site of the biblical Lachish) of a group of eighteen inscribed potsherds, clearly dating from the time of Jeremiah and actually mentioning several men known from the biblical records of that period. The documents constitute the literary evidence submitted, so the editor believes, in the court-martial of a certain Hoshaiah. They mention an unnamed "prophet," who, Professor Torczyner holds, is none other than Urijah mentioned in Jer. 26:20-23; still more remarkable, he believes that the episode in which he figures here is the same tragedy that overtook him according to the biblical narrative. In one of the documents the writer mentions that he can no longer see the signal fires of Azekah, apparently the prearranged signals of the advance of Nebuchadrezzar's invading army. It was written, then, at the very moment when the Chaldeans were entering Judah, while the defenders watching in anxious concern from the hills hoped still to ward off the disaster that all too soon was to engulf the nation in ruin (see H. Torczyner, *The Lachish Letters* [1938]; and also the following, who criticize Torczyner's interpretations at several important points: Millar Burrows, in *Journal of Religion*, XIX [1939], 272–76; W. F. Albright, in *Bulletin of the American Schools of Oriental Research*, LXX [1938], 11–17; Cyrus Gordon, in *Bulletin of the American Schools of Oriental Research*, LXX [1938], 17–18; H. L. Ginsberg, in *Bulletin of the American Schools of Oriental Research*, LXXX [1940], 10–13).

Yahweh was purposing to do for his people.[38] Jeremiah's answer was to the effect that the city and the king would fall into the hands of Nebuchadrezzar, and that the only salvation for the people was to desert to the Babylonians. At this same time Jeremiah is represented as having assured Zedekiah that he would die in peace and receive honorable burial.[39] As a matter of fact, Zedekiah was blinded by Nebuchadrezzar and carried captive to Babylon.[40] The last sight upon which his eyes rested was the execution of his two sons. Was Jeremiah again mistaken? It is more probable that the narrator of Jeremiah's words failed to give his statement the conditional form in which Jeremiah almost certainly made it. It is incredible that Jeremiah should have made such an unconditional promise of safety to Zedekiah after all that Zedekiah had done in violation of the prophet's advice and warning.[41]

In the early course of the siege, an army from Egypt approached to relieve Jerusalem from the Babylonian pressure. Thereupon, the Babylonian army withdrew in order to meet the new foe.[42] Some time earlier in the course of the siege, apparently as a pious gesture intended to invoke Yahweh's assistance in the crisis, Zedekiah had issued a decree, with the consent of the slaveowners, granting liberty to all Hebrew slaves. But when the siege was raised, the slaveowners made haste to repossess them.[43] At this the anger of Jere-

[38] Jeremiah, chap. 21.   [39] Jer. 34:1–5.

[40] II Kings 25:7; Ezek. 12:13.

[41] See Cornill's discussion of this oracle, where this point is strongly presented.

[42] Jer. 37:5.   [43] Jer. 34:8–11.

miah blazed forth against these rich and unscrupulous oppressors. He cited the law to them and told them that they and their king would all fall into the hands of the Babylonians who would burn their city with fire.[44] After the departure of the Babylonians, Jeremiah was visited by an embassy from Zedekiah, who wished to know whether or not the Babylonians would return. Jeremiah in the strongest possible terms declared that the Egyptians would retreat in flight and that the Babylonians would renew the siege and retake the city.[45]

It was during this interval, while the siege of the city was interrupted, that Jeremiah sought to leave Jerusalem in order to visit some landed property which he possessed in Benjamin. But he was arrested at the city gate and charged with an attempt to desert to the Babylonians. This he flatly denied, but in vain; for he was cast into prison by order of the government.[46] There he remained for some time, until Zedekiah sent for him privately and asked once more for a word from Yahweh. Jeremiah told him again that he would be captured by Nebuchadrezzar. Then Jeremiah besought the king for relief from the hard conditions of his imprisonment and obtained permission to be placed in a more airy and spacious prison, where an order was given for his daily food as long as food was left in the city.[47]

About a year before the fall of the city, Jeremiah's faith in the future of his country was put to a severe

[44] Jer. 34:12–22.   [46] Jer. 37:11–15.

[45] Jer. 37:3–10.   [47] Jer. 37:16–21.

test. A message was brought to him in prison by his nephew that he was desirous of selling a piece of land in Anathoth and that, since the right of redemption belonged to Jeremiah as nearest of kin, he was giving Jeremiah the first chance to buy the field. Jeremiah recognized the significance of this occasion and treated it as a word of God to himself. He at once accepted the offer and had the deed prepared in duplicate, properly signed, witnessed, sealed, and filed away. After doing this, Jeremiah seems to have had some doubts about the wisdom of the action. He presented his doubts and fears to Yahweh, and was encouraged by the renewed assurance that after the Exile there would be a return and restoration, so that once more fields would be bought and sold in Judah as of old.[48] Had Jeremiah refused this opportunity to demonstrate in a practical way his faith in Yahweh and in the future value of real estate in Judah, his preaching of hope and promises of restoration would have been worse than useless.

Worse treatment yet was in store for Jeremiah. The princes and officers strenuously engaged in the defense of the city were of course not pleased by his outspoken advice to the men of the city to desert to the Babylonians. So they protested to Zedekiah against such liberty of speech, and obtained authority from the king to do with Jeremiah as they would. Thereupon they cast him into a dungeon in the prison yard in which the mud was deep and where he was without food. When this was reported to Zedekiah by Ebed-melech, an Ethiopian eunuch, the king ordered the Ethiopian to take a guard, pull Jeremiah out of the mire, and let

[48] Jeremiah, chap. 32.

him loose in the prison yard.[49] Soon after, Zedekiah
again sent for Jeremiah and held a secret interview
with him, in which he asked his advice, guaranteeing
him immunity from attack by the princes of the court.
Jeremiah urged upon Zedekiah absolute surrender to
Babylon, which would bring him escape from death,
and warned him that continuance in resistance would
mean utter ruin for himself, the city, and the people.
Then the king pledged Jeremiah to silence regarding
the real content of the interview, and arranged that he
should tell the princes that he had sought an interview
with the king in order to plead for better treatment for
himself. Jeremiah assented to this, and so reported
when the princes questioned him on the matter.[50]
Here it is necessary to admit that Jeremiah told a
downright lie. The excuse for it, if not the justification,
is quite obvious. If Jeremiah had told the truth, he
would in all probability have lost his life, and so have
been denied the privilege of any further service to his
country. Not only so, but the princes, who were the
real masters of the situation, Zedekiah being a weak-
ling in their hands, would undoubtedly have proceeded to further violent measures and would have
done away with or at least dethroned Zedekiah, and
have put one of their own party on the throne in his
place. This might have added the horrors of civil war
to the terrors of the siege. In view of the dread possi-

[49] Jeremiah did not forget the kindness of Ebed-melech (see Jer. 39:
15-18).

[50] Jer. 38:1-27.

bilities of telling the truth and the likelihood that the people as a whole would suffer still more than they would under Zedekiah, it is no wonder that Jeremiah concealed the facts.

Finally the city fell. Not until starvation had done its deadly work did its heroic defenders give way. There was no weak surrender, but a stubborn resistance to the bitter end. The Babylonians broke through the wall, seized the city, and caught the fleeing king in the vicinity of Jericho. The fate of city and king is described in Jeremiah, chapter 39. The Babylonians at once released Jeremiah from his prison and put him under the charge of "Gedaliah the son of Ahikam, the son of Shaphan; so he dwelt among the people."[51] Here he remained in peace for a few months, while many Jews who had fled from their country during the campaign returned home and gathered around Gedaliah, the new governor. Perhaps during this period of relative peace and quiet, Jeremiah produced the greatest utterance accredited to him—the prophecy of the new covenant.[52] Herein Jeremiah penetrated deeply into the nature of religion, declaring that no external law would control the lives of the children of the coming Kingdom of God, but that Yahweh would write

[51] Jer. 39:11–14. Another story, of later origin, represents the Babylonians as carrying Jeremiah in chains with the rest of the captives as far as Ramah, where he was released and given the choice of going to Babylon under royal favor or of staying in Judah with the stricken people. Jeremiah chose the latter course, and was sent away with a supply of provisions and a present of money to join Gedaliah, the governor of Judah, appointed by Babylon (Jer. 40:1–6).

[52] Jer. 31:31–34.

his laws upon the tablets of the hearts of his people, so that they would find themselves under an inner compulsion to walk in the ways of Yahweh. This is the nearest that the Old Testament writers come to the idea of the new birth, or regeneration. It is noteworthy, however, that Jeremiah did not contemplate this as a part of the existing order, but as characteristic of the new Golden Age or Kingdom of God to which he looked forward.

The peace after the surrender was soon broken by partisan strife, murder, and civil war.[53] The survivors of this internecine strife set out to flee into Egypt, being afraid of the vengeance of the Babylonians. But before taking the final step, they consulted Jeremiah and assured him that they would do whatsoever Yahweh should command. After ten days of meditation, Jeremiah reported that it was Yahweh's will that they should stay in Judah where his blessing would rest upon them, but that if they should fly to Egypt they would die by sword, famine, and pestilence.[54] They replied to this that Jeremiah was not speaking Yahweh's word but was serving merely as the mouthpiece of Baruch. Consequently, they defied Jeremiah and fled into Egypt, taking the people with them and forcing Jeremiah to accompany them. Jeremiah, upon arrival in Egypt, prophesied dramatically that Nebuchadrezzar would conquer Egypt, thus rendering their flight thither utterly futile;[55] and he proceeded to reiterate

[53] Jeremiah, chap. 41.

[54] Jeremiah, chap. 42.   [55] Jeremiah, chap. 43.

against the Jews in Egypt the type of denunciation and
threat they had been used to hear from him in Jerusalem.[56]

The last appearance of Jeremiah, of which we have
record, is related in Jer. 44:15–30. Jeremiah's chief
charge against his people from the beginning of his
career had been that they were disloyal to Yahweh in
that they were worshiping other gods. Indeed, on one
occasion he is represented as having said: "According
to the number of your cities are your gods, O Israel."[57]
One of these many deities was the occasion of this episode. The people protested against Jeremiah's message
in denunciation of their worship of other gods, and the
women told him that as a matter of fact the country
had prospered as long as they had worshiped the
"queen of the heavens," but that since they had ceased
doing so all manner of misfortune had befallen Judah
and its people. Therefore they proposed to continue
the worship of the "queen of the heavens" in spite of
all he might say.[58] This implies clearly that the Jews
had worshiped this goddess of old, probably prior to
the Deuteronomic reform, and that the cessation of
that worship was a relatively recent thing. What a
depth of spiritual darkness in the minds of the masses is
revealed by this controversy! To what a high level the
prophets were striving to elevate their people! A contemplation of the ignorance, sensuousness, and superstition of the people might well have plunged the

[56] Jer. 44:1–14.   [57] Jer. 2:28.   [58] Jer. 44:15–19.

prophets into despair. But they were incurably hopeful in the best sense. They never ceased their efforts to educate and free their people from their enthralment to the traditions of the past and to point out to them the better way. Jeremiah responded to this defiant attitude of his people by threatening Jewry in Egypt with the same kind of disaster that had befallen Judah and Jerusalem.[59]

So we leave Jeremiah, an exile in a strange land, surrounded by his own people, who have refused to learn anything from their tragic experiences and resent all efforts on his part to teach them. He is a homeless, helpless, solitary soul—an idealist in the midst of a materialistic generation. He has lost everything, property, home, country, and hope—everything but his own soul. He was misunderstood, unappreciated, persecuted, and imprisoned by his contemporaries, only to be taken up by history and given the place of honor in the goodly fellowship of the prophets, who "died not having received the promise." But we have entered into their heritage. The long course of the ages has been enriched through their travail of soul; and slowly in the working-out of the Divine plan there has come nearer that day of truth and right which they saw from afar, and to which they dedicated their life's endeavor. Jeremiah did not fail. Even while his days were closing

[59] Jer. 44:24–26. The end of chap. 44 predicts the return of a few Jews from Egypt to Judah and the death of Pharaoh-Hophra as a captive in the hands of his foes. Pharaoh's death in 564 B.C. is shrouded in mystery; but these words were written after that event by later editors (see commentaries, *ad loc.*).

in gloom, afar among the homesick exiles in Babylonia or the miserable remnant in Judah—we do not know— a younger prophet, Ezekiel, who must have known him in Jerusalem and have learned from him, was continuing his work of leading his recalcitrant people in better thoughts of God and man. And not he alone; there came others, still greater, through the unceasing progress of the ages; and the knowledge of God has been a light that even yet "shineth more and more unto the perfect day."

CHAPTER X

THE FATHER OF JUDAISM?

THE prophet Ezekiel is one of the enigmas of Old Testament history and interpretation. No one at this moment knows with certainty either himself or his work; and this not for lack of materials about him but because of our inability to use them. The entire Book of Ezekiel purports to come from him; and it contains ostensibly considerable information of the sort we wish. Besides it is coherent and unified, presenting a convincing picture of the prophet. It can well be summed up in a brief statement, thus:

The Book of Ezekiel records the activity of Ezekiel between July, 593 B.C., and April, 571 B.C. The materials constituting the book are for the most part arranged in chronological order, though the latest date given in the book is found in 29:17. The book falls naturally into four parts: (1) the prophecies against Judah uttered before 586 B.C., viz., chapters 1–24; (2) the oracles against the foreign nations, viz., chapters 25–32, spoken for the most part between 588 and 586 B.C.; (3) mainly promises for the future, which are undated but presumably were uttered after 586; and (4) a description of the restored temple and city and, in a measure, the land of Palestine (chaps. 40–48), dated in 573 B.C. Ezekiel himself was a priest who was carried captive in 597 B.C. In Babylonia his priestly occupation was gone, but, being a profoundly religious man, he could not cease thinking about religion and the problem of the Exile; and so he soon found himself functioning as a prophet. But when he became a prophet he did not cease to be a priest in spirit, with the natural result that his prophecy is to a great extent couched in priestly terms and dominated by priestly interests. With all this, there went also a deeply mystical temperament. He was subject to sudden attacks of "the hand of Yahweh."[1] The common expression for a revelation from Yahweh in Ezekiel is "the word of Yahweh came unto me," but in 1:3 it is significant that this expression is supplemented or interpreted by the phrase, "the hand of Yahweh was there upon him." The interpretation of some episodes in Ezekiel's experience is greatly facilitated by an adequate recognition of the place of ecstasy and trance or vision in Ezekiel's prophetic activity.[2]

But in recent years we have grown uneasy about this too facile interpretation. We are now so keenly aware of many divergent facts in the Book of Ezekiel that no one may proceed calmly to expound it at face value as the genuine work of the prophet. Indeed, for those who feel an interest in the history of biblical criticism it is relevant to point out that this Book carries down into our own times the sort of problem and uncertainty that centered in the Pentateuch about a hundred years ago, and evoked acute popular reactions about the turn of

[1] Ezek. 1:3; 3:14, 22; 8:1; 33:22; 37:1; 40:1.
[2] See the first edition of this work, pp. 161–62.

the century, when the famous "Documentary Theory" was attracting general attention. It is a remarkable aspect of biblical study that this is so. One may well be astonished that through a period of intense critical activity, which subjected every other book of the Old Testament to minute examination and, in cases, to seemingly radical analysis, only this one remained immune. But whatever may be the explanation, even within the last twenty years scholars were insisting or quietly assuming that the Book of Ezekiel alone of the prophetic books has come down to us practically intact from the hands of its first author. There were exceptions to this complacency; and critical theories were advanced which can now be seen as the true prelude to our present dilemma. But the prevalent mood of scholarship was that the critical problem of the Book of Ezekiel was minor, and had little bearing on the interpreter's task. The steps by which we have moved away from this position to the more healthy perplexity of today it is scarcely in place to trace here.[3] Only some of the more notable incidents in the process we may delay to mention briefly. In 1900 Kraetschmar presented the view that our present book is a combination of two

[3] A good account with incisive criticism is to be found in J. Battersby Harford, *Studies in the Book of Ezekiel* (1935), pp. 9–53. It is sketched more briefly by I. G. Matthews in his *Ezekiel* (1939), pp. viii–xii. In addition to these, more important literature of recent developments has been: Hermann, *Ezechiel* (1924); Hölscher, *Hesekiel: Der Dichter und das Buch* (1924); Torrey, *Pseudo-Ezekiel and the Original Prophecy* (1930); James Smith, *The Book of the Prophet Ezekiel: A New Interpretation* (1931); Herntrich, *Ezechielprobleme* (1932); G. A. Cooke, *Ezekiel* (1938); Bertholet and Galling, *Ezechiel* (1938)

original recensions of the prophet's work. Hölscher in 1924 made the revolutionary discovery that Ezekiel was a poet, but that our book is so overlaid with later accretions that its basic poetic form is generally obscured; by a process of criticism he isolated some 160 verses, in whole or in part, as the genuine work of the prophet in a book said now to total 1,272 verses. C. C. Torrey excited keen interest by his theory that the book is a pseudepigraph written in the third century B.C. but purporting to come from the reign of Manasseh. James Smith likewise, though independently, associated the book with the reign of Manasseh, but believed it was written by a citizen of the northern kingdom of Israel and was concerned with the fall of Samaria in 722 B.C. Herntrich's work in 1932 went far to convince scholars that Ezekiel's prophetic ministry was exercised, in part at least, in Jerusalem. Galling, treating part of 40–48 in his joint work with Bertholet, undertook to demonstrate the genuineness of this disputed section; in this he was supported by Cooke.

The certain results of this lengthy period of discussion are as yet meager. It is generally conceded[4] that our book is highly composite and that the spurious material comes in part from a Babylonian editor, but also in some undetermined measure from "scribal" activity that continued through a considerable time. Ezekiel himself is now believed to have begun his work in Jerusalem, apparently some time before the disaster of 586 B.C. This shift of opinion has come about, not through disputing the traditional explanation that in

---

[4] Except by Professor Torrey and his following.

addressing his oracles to the inhabitants of Jerusalem Ezekiel was really aiming to edify his fellow-captives in Babylonia, but rather through such facts as Herntrich so well emphasized: e.g., that the kernel of chapter 7 is genuine beyond question and exhibits a feeling and realism that can be understood only on the basis of the author's presence in the doomed city as matters drew on to the final crisis. Still more conclusive, waiving for the moment the complicated question of analysis of the passage, is 6:12, in which the author distinguishes the exiles from the inhabitants of the city as the "far" and the "near." Some commentators confess an ignorance of the prophet's fate when the city fell; whether or not he was ever in Babylonia remains an open question. There is a tendency to accept the date in 29:17 as valid,[5] and hence to recognize that he continued his ministry as late as 571 B.C. Most other dates in the book are regarded with suspicion as probably the work of some systematizing editor. Further, the prevailing mood, in spite of Galling and Cooke, is to regard chapters 40–48 as coming from another hand and another time.

And there we reach the modest limits of our present advance! Some scholars claim to have found the final answer, but unfortunately they do not convince their fellow-workers; others more wisely put forth their conclusions as tentative. The nature of the problem and

[5] The validity is beyond question (see Olmstead, *History of Palestine and Syria* [1931], p. 535). The only question that may be entertained is whether the date is editorial. But the case for genuineness is stronger here than for many other of the dates in the book.

the direction of our further progress will be apparent even from this very cursory sketch. All depends upon a sound critical analysis of the book, more specifically of chapters 1–39, that will separate the original utterances of Ezekiel from the pious accretions of later ages. Only when this is done can we accurately delineate the prophet and his message, or understand the purport of the additions with which subsequent religious thinkers sought to make the book relevant to the problems of their times. If we may judge by the commentaries of Cooke, Bertholet and Galling, and Matthews, which together provide certainly the best treatment of the book as yet in existence, the present mood is to accept as genuine a large part of chapters 1–39. As a result, the prophet and his message emerge not essentially altered from traditional concepts, except for the points already noted. But this is a position that will not long endure examination. On one side, it has failed to take adequate account of a wealth of critical data that the book provides; on the other, it is determined too largely by subjective criteria that remind one of the worst phases of Pentateuchal analysis. A sentence from Matthews' commentary—a really excellent work—will exemplify the point. He says: "The familiar phrases, *rebellious house*, *my net*, *the prince*, and *may know that I am Yahweh*, and the symbolic enactment of coming captivity, resembling chapters 4 and 5, all remind us of Ezekiel."[6] His conclusion, then, is that of the entire chapter 12, only verse 16 is spurious. But on what grounds are the quoted phrases identified as of the

[6] *Op. cit.*, p. xxxviii.

genuine Ezekiel? Search through the book reveals little more basis for the view than provided here. It is an
arbitrary assumption; and then such phrases are used
as criteria of genuineness in other passages.[7] Actually,
evidence of the sort just now intimated is available to
show that every one of these expressions comes from
one or another of the later supplementers of the book.
But too, even though "the symbolic enactment of coming captivity" is reminiscent of chapters 4 and 5, it is
surely, then, far too undiscerning a criticism that
would thus authenticate the entirety of a chapter;
rather the passage demands meticulous analysis to determine how much of this "symbolic enactment" is
actually some other person's reminiscence of chapters
4 and 5.

This estimate of the present mood in the study of
Ezekiel will be seen to call for a more severe criticism
of the book with results perhaps closer to Hölscher's
drastic conclusions; or rather, let us say, the available
facts indicate that such results would be more in accord
with its history. Unfortunately, in a brief study such
as the limits of this chapter permit, one cannot present
and discuss adequately these facts; that is the task for
an entire monograph. Here we can but indicate some
of the evidence, and then go on to such summary interpretation of the book as may be possible.

It is convenient to turn first to 36:24–38. The allusion here to the dispersion of the Jews through nations
and countries at once rouses suspicion. Can this really

[7] Another example would be Cooke's concession to an ill-considered
theory of prophetic inspiration (*op. cit.*, p. vi).

come from the days of Ezekiel? Then the major fact of
Jewish expatriation was the Exile in Babylonia, though,
indeed, there were also Jews in Egypt; and some would
hold that economic conditions were already functioning to scatter them more widely. Nonetheless, the real
Diaspora came later. But against such dating of this
passage is the hope expressed in verses 33 f. of a rebuilding of the ruined cities and the repopulation of
Palestine. This would seem to indicate a time prior to
Nehemiah, though the consideration is not final, for
Nehemiah's work was confined in the main to Jerusalem, and the restoration of the land came slowly.
Further, the passage may be merely a pious reminiscence. But fortunately we are not left thus weighing
divergent considerations. We possess objective evidence of a striking sort. The Greek papyrus of Ezekiel,
No. 967—a manuscript conceded to be of the third
century A.D.[8]—does not contain these verses.[9] They
were not, then, in the Hebrew Book of Ezekiel at the
time the Greek translation was made, possibly not even
when the manuscript was copied. The passage originated at some unknown date after, say, 200 B.C., perhaps even in Christian times.[10]

But this same promise of bringing the scattered Jews

[8] F. C. Kenyon, *The Chester Beatty Biblical Papyri: Ezekiel, Daniel,
and Esther* (*1937*); A. C. Johnson, H. S. Gehman, and E. H. Kase,
The John H. Scheide Biblical Papyri: Ezekiel (1938).

[9] See F. C. Beare in *Chronique d'Egypte*, XIII (1938), 388 f.

[10] Actually, Thackeray had reached this conclusion long before the
discovery of 967; he suggested that the passage was copied into our
Book of Ezekiel from a Jewish-Christian lectionary (*Grammar of the Old
Testament in Greek* [1909], pp. 11–12).

from the nations and gathering them from the countries occurs elsewhere in the Book of Ezekiel in 11:17–20; 20:33–38, 40–42; 34:13–16; 39:27–29. It is a striking fact that 11:17–20 voices further the identical hope of a new heart that is found in 36:26; and the other passages are in the same idyllic mood of tender promise and solicitude. There can be no reasonable doubt that here we have uncovered the hand of a gentle and pious Jew[11] of the Greek period or later, who encouraged his contemporaries with glowing promises of restoration of the dispersed of Israel and a miracle of grace whereby they should be worthy of their high calling as the Lord's people.

But we do not stop with this. Allusions to the Diaspora occur also in 4:13; 5:10, 12; 6:8–9; 12:15–16; 22:15; 38:8. All these except the last are stern in mood. Their author is not the winsome soul whom we have just now discovered; instead, he considered that his day and age called for rebuke. And he employed the oracles of Ezekiel, already sanctified by age, as a text from which to expound his homily. But here again we note a further connecting idea; 20:43 introduces the notion of the shame for their wicked deeds felt by the restored Jews. But a similar thought is in 12:15–16.[12] And then we observe an interesting fact. This sense of shame obtrudes itself into the idyllic passage with which we began; it is in 36:31. And, further, several of the passages in our first class are supplemented

[11] It is open to discussion whether all these passages are from the one hand—39:27–29, for example, is in a similar, rather than the same, mood.

[12] It is also in 5:14–15; 6:8–10; 14:22–23; 16:63; 39:26.

with notes of rebuke that are clearly foreign to their context.[13] This is quite remarkable. Late as we are compelled to consider the date of the gentle commentator, there was another still later, whose mood was stern, who felt that the conduct of his associates compelled him to correct even the other's views. When and where did he live?

But now let us try another approach to our problem. Recent scholarly opinion seems tending to indorse Hölscher's analysis of chapters 4 and 5. Herntrich, Cooke, and Matthews show but minor deviation from one another or from Hölscher, thus giving a consensus of opinion that is impressive.[14] May one add that for those who approach the question from the Hebrew text and see the cogency of Hölscher's poetic arrangement, the position is conclusive? There is left, then, as a genuine oracle of Ezekiel little if any but 4:1-2, 9-11, and 5:1-2. Most, if not all the rest, of the two chapters, which total thirty-four verses, is commentary and expansion of this original nucleus. But it is not a unit. We have here the comments of numerous men, as will be seen from the divergent interpretations given in 4:12-15 and 16-17, as also from the successive interpretations that follow one another in chapter 5. And the division between the oracle and the interpretations is clear to the observant student. Matthews rightly says of 5:5-17 that it is "prolix and theological."

We have then discovered a clue for the identifica-

---

[13] See 11:21; 20:39, 43-44; 39:26; perhaps, too, 34:16b, 17-18.

[14] On the other hand, Bertholet takes another line; and Torrey and his following apparently accept the chapters entire. Matthews' support, too, is more complete in chap. 5 than in chap. 4.

tion of Ezekiel's oracles. Let it be repeated that we are not in the least attempting to present with any fulness the evidence for such analysis, but only indicating some considerations and following them to conclusions that can readily be supported with much more cogent argument than is here appropriate. However—to go on to chapter 6—there is no good reason for the extreme view of Hölscher who dismisses the entire chapter as "rhetorische Prosa"; on the contrary, it has all the marks of genuineness. But, coming to it from the analysis of chapters 4-5, we soon detect the hands of commentators; verses 6-10 have a tone that is already familiar. However, verses 1-5 are certainly genuine (except for a few expansive comments), and verses 11-12. Whether these two sections originally belonged together as the two strophes of a single poem, or whether their present juxtaposition is the work of an editor, is a problem we may evade.

But it would still be premature to generalize as to the nature of these first thirty-nine chapters of Ezekiel; they have various critical features. Chapter 7, for example, confronts us primarily with problems of text rather than of analysis. There is no doubt of the genuineness of the chapter, in the large; but its transmission has been extremely bad. Verses 1-12 contain a duplicate, or in parts triplicate, recension of a single poetic strophe warning of the immediate end of the city; verse 11 is corrupt to the point of utter nonsense. Verses 13 ff. continue the theme of the approaching destruction of Jerusalem in a poem of great intensity and vividness. Much of it is well preserved, but there are a number of glosses, chiefly about verses 21-25.

Chapter 12 introduces another type. It is seen to fall into four sections: (*a*) verses 1–16, (*b*) 17–20, (*c*) 21–25, and (*d*) 26–28. The last of these is to be ignored, first on the grounds of its close similarity to (*c*), but then more cogently because of its omission by the Greek papyrus 967, already mentioned. But the other three are in essence genuine, though again considerably expanded. The worst is (*a*), which is also the most important part of the chapter. It will be seen to consist of three parts: instructions, obedience, and interpretation. The first of these gives, as in 7:1–12, a conflate text; the second may be considerably enlarged by an interpreter through citations from the first; and the third has suffered in the fashion characteristic of this book as a whole: it has been made the basis of a later homily. It is of importance to note that the "prince" had nothing to do with Ezekiel's oracle; he is dragged into the interpretation through a strange textual error. As stated clearly in verse 10, the oracle concerns Jerusalem and "all the house of Israel."

But Ezekiel certainly wrote in prose on occasion. No one may dispute the vision of the valley of dry bones (37:1–15), for example. That chapter 18 is also prose is obvious. It is so strange to all else in this perplexing book, however, that one may be pardoned for entertaining serious doubts of its source. But for lack of conclusive evidence to the contrary we have no recourse except bow to tradition.[15]

Chapters 1–3 and 8–11 present still another problem. Matthews may be essentially right (following

---

[15] It is a legitimate and appealing guess that the entire chapter is nothing but a typical commentator's expansion of 33:12.

Hölscher) in seeing in chapter 1 a union of two sources: one the description of the cherubim and the other an idealized account of a storm at sunset, which for the writer was a revelation of God. The latter, made up of verses 4–5, 22, and 26–28, he takes to be the original—a poetic passage from Ezekiel himself. Chapters 2 and 3 then follow with the prose record of his call, but they are greatly expanded in the style familiar to students of this book. A similar conflation, Matthews believes, occurred in chapters 8–11.

The oracles against the nations (in the main, chaps. 26–32) contain some genuine nucleus. This is most evident in the denunciations of Egypt (chaps. 29–32), though Ezekiel seems also to have made unfavorable comments on Tyre: a part of chapter 28 appears to have come from him.

It would not be fair to the reader to undertake a detailed exegesis of the prophet's work on the grounds of an analysis that is here scarce more than suggested, and that must seem, for lack of supporting argument, merely ex cathedra and a priori. We may only sketch Ezekiel's message in the same broad outlines. Indeed, as already pointed out, no one is yet competent to give a careful exposition of the book: we still know far too little about it.

In spite of the unsolved problem of "the thirtieth year" (1:1), a question that still is relevant although it, like most all the dates in the book, is of doubtful genuineness, it seems probable that in chapters 1–3 we have Ezekiel's account of his mystic musing on a luminous storm that became for him a call to a lifework of prophecy. The nature of this task was revealed to him through the subjective experience of eating a roll, which is described as written with "lamentations and mourning and woe." He came to realize also his responsibility to his people as like that of a watchman guarding a threatened city. When this experience occurred and where we do not know; but the course of his work shows that it must have been in or near Jerusalem, and it cannot have been subsequent to the early years of Zedekiah's reign, for clearly that is the period of his oracle in chapter 15. This little poem (vss. 1–5, with characteristic introduction) deals with the shallow and chauvinistic pride of the inferior folk who found themselves elevated to unexpected importance by the deportation of the better elements of the population in 597. Ezekiel tells them that the nation at its best was never great: it was as unimportant among the great powers as a vine among the trees of the forest; how much more now when it is ruined! The oracle is reminiscent of Jeremiah's famous comparison of the good and bad figs (Jeremiah, chap. 24). In similar mood is the genuine nucleus of chapter 16, reminding Ezekiel's fellow-citizens in Jerusalem of their commonplace ancestry; they were, he says, a mongrel race of Amorite and Hittite stock. It seems to have been a favorite theme of the prophet's at this period, for again the poem on the cedar of Lebanon (31:1 f.), which Cooke rightly suspects was not at all a threat against Egypt, portrays the arrogance of the Jewish nation.[16]

[16] The figure of the cedar of Lebanon always refers to Israel or Judah, not to foreign peoples. Further, "Pharaoh" is omitted by papyrus No. 967. The commentary in vss. 10 ff. is in characteristic style; it was written not earlier than Exilic times (vs. 11) and apparently in Palestine (vs. 12).

The genuine elements of 8:1—11:13 present the prophet's horror of the pagan practices carried on right in the Temple—an iniquity fully indorsed and shared by even the responsible members of the community. And 6:1–5 expresses similar reprehension and solemn warning against immoral fertility rites performed outside the city, in the valleys and on the hilltops. The denunciation of the magic-mongering of the "prophets" and "prophetesses" in chapter 13 may also come from this period, for it contains no allusion to immediate national crisis and its atmosphere seems Palestinian.

But we have a considerable number of oracles from the time of the final siege of Jerusalem; some of these lend themselves to a relative dating within those tragic years. The genuine parts of chapters 4 and 5 are somewhat early; the deprivations that became so horrible as 586 drew on to its terrible denouement are as yet but a matter of prophetic warning. The defeat of Hophra in 588 seems to be the occasion of 30:20–22.[17] A little later was presented the symbolized captivity of the forlorn garrison found in chapter 12. But at the very end, when matters had reached a hopeless crisis, though Zedekiah had not yet made his ill-starred attempt at escape, is to be placed chapter 7.

The fate of the prophet in the sack of the city is a question on which information is meager. The crucial passage is 11:14–15, in which Ezekiel is identified with some group whom the men of Jerusalem repudiate,

[17] The dating assigned in vs. 20 is of no authority (see Matthews, *op. cit.*, pp. xii ff.).

claiming the land for themselves. The Hebrew text identifies the group as Ezekiel's "kinsmen," but the Septuagint apparently read a closely similar word meaning "captivity." If this latter is correct, we have a priceless scrap of information on the prophet's fortunes. Matthews says confidently that the oracle was composed after the fall of the city in 586.[18] This, if correct, would be strong corroboration for the view suggested by the Septuagint reading. But in any case, the fact that the prophet with his group was somehow separated from the inhabitants of Jerusalem, who denounced them and gloated over their own possession of the land, is most readily intelligible on the grounds that Ezekiel was numbered among the captives of 586[19] and here, in the brief interval before actually setting out on the arduous march to far Babylonia, replied to the taunting sneers of the pitiful remnant who were to remain. Some little support for this view is afforded by 33:23–29; reference to Judah as "waste places in the land of Israel" would seem most appropriate after 586. But the passage is uncertain; the threefold destruction (vs. 27) is in the mood of 5:1–2, just as the false confidence of the people here threatened is like that revealed by chapter 15. On the other hand, if Matthews is correct[20] in his view that "the dry

[18] *Ibid.*, p. 39; but this view is based on the commentary rather than on the original oracle.

[19] If Matthews' theory that Ezekiel's family were priests from north Israel attracted to Jerusalem by the privileges of the Deuteronomic reform had better support, it would be relevant here.

[20] *Op. cit.*, p. xlvi.

bones were factual" (37:1 f.) and the valley was near Jerusalem, then Ezekiel must have been in Palestine long after 586, for the bones were "very dry." The matter, then, is very uncertain. The evidence of 11: 14–15 is the strongest we possess; it is attractive to see in it a corroboration of the tradition that Ezekiel prophesied in Babylonia, but admittedly it is not conclusive.

The further course of Ezekiel's career it is impossible to trace. The oracle in 29:17–20 has every mark of genuineness; and, quite apart from the vexed problem of the dates given in this book, it carries the prophet's activity down beyond the failure of Nebuchadrezzar's attack on Tyre, and apparently into the period when relations with Egypt had become strained.

Though a considerable part of the so-called prophecies of comfort is spurious, yet there is a nucleus which shows that Ezekiel could and did build and encourage, as well as denounce and threaten. The most famous of these is the vision of the valley of dry bones, just now mentioned. The oracle on the shepherds of Israel (chap. 34) appears also to contain a genuine element, though it may have been uttered during the reign of Zedekiah; it is the late additions that have given it the appearance of a prophecy of restoration.

We see, then, that the oracles of Ezekiel are in the main, though not exclusively, poetic. A notable feature of them is their use of allusion, one might almost say of innuendo. In a style typical of the Orient, they sketch a situation with light, quick strokes, then leave the implication to the perception and intelligence of the audience. Yet the meaning and application is quite clear, notwithstanding ancient interpreters who have commonly distorted it, purposely or otherwise. Occasionally, though, it would seem that the prophet has himself anticipated his expositors, just as Jesus often explained his parables. The remarkable fact is that even so he has not precluded misinterpretation.

Ezekiel's themes concerned the empty pride and false confidence of his compatriots in the reign of Zedekiah, their immoralities practiced as part of the popular pagan cults, and the oppression (24:6 f.) and exploitation (34:2 f.) that flourished in Jerusalem. For these, ruin would come. Like Jeremiah he saw no hope for the rebellion of 588, but incessantly warned of impending ruin to the city and the nation. He derided the collapse of Hophra's attempt to raise the siege; and later he gave some little attention to international politics, though the major part of the foreign prophecies now in his book is from other hands. After the destruction of the state he encouraged belief in a restoration through the powerful intervention of Yahweh. He was throughout sensitive to his high responsibility as a religious leader: he was a "watchman" for his people in a time of danger. One of his great contributions to his people's religious development was his teaching of the responsibility of the individual.

This is a bare and bald sketch of a great career; it makes no attempt to carry over the fire and earnestness that motivated the living prophet, or to portray the faith that sustained him through long discouraging years. The demands of the critical problem at present crucial in an approach to his book have left no space for this more congenial task. But the very baldness of our summary will serve a purpose in projecting into relief the question: What of the ritualistic interest for which Ezekiel is traditionally famed? For we have found none except that he denounced the immoral and pagan rites assiduously followed by his compatriots, which is surely a very modest basis for his reputation. Actually, the other prophets had more to say on ritual than he. But his fame in this regard rests primarily on the spurious section (chaps. 40–48) and then on the immense bulk of commentary in which his brief oracles have come to be imbedded through centuries of pious study and teaching.

It is an interesting question why his book came to be so treated; for it is unique among the prophetic books of the Old Testament. The others have all a greater or less amount of "post-Exilic" additions, but these are not to any notable extent made up of homiletic commentary, which in true sermonic style cites a text and then expounds and applies it. But such is in large measure our book of Ezekiel. And why? Unfortunately, the answer can be only of the speculative character that too often in Old Testament study has passed for established results. The history of the Old Testament text through many centuries, notably through the period when the Book of Ezekiel was assuming final form, is completely obscured. To make the matter worse, we know very little of the history of the Jewish people through this time. We can, then, speculate only that the timeliness of Ezekiel's oracles, living as he did through the national disaster and into the new conditions of the Exilic period, made them peculiarly suitable as a basis for teaching and exhortation. We have seen the late date to which this process went on; it is regrettable that we lack similar objective testimony as to the point at which it began. There is nothing unreasonable, though, in the view that some of the spurious material in the book dates from a time soon after Ezekiel's activity. We possess, then, in the book a cross-section of Jewish piety and teaching through the last five centuries B.C. or perhaps longer.

Valuable as the book was thought to be as the work of the great formative figure of early Exilic times, it becomes well-nigh priceless as the deposit of Jewish piety through those little-known centuries when Jewish institutions were taking shape and when the leadership of the rabbis, destined to be of incalculable importance to the development of Judeo-Christian thought, was evolving from the chaos which the national calamity of 586 B.C. entailed. One of the fruitful tasks of the immediate future of Old Testament study is an investigation of the work of these men as we have it preserved in the Book of Ezekiel. We may not pursue it here. We have noted the diverse moods they express. Some are as stern as the prophets of the eighth century; others as gentle and winsome as the great unknown thinker of Isa. 40–55. A few of them are poets in their own right. But all alike are impelled by the moral earnestness and conquering faith that characterized the true prophets throughout. For all alike the supreme fact of human life is the reality of God and His righteousness. For some it is an awesome righteousness that must vindicate itself in judgment and in blood; others saw it as a supreme goodness, the love of God that was one of the great discoveries of Israel's religious pilgrimage. Where they lived, and what Jewish communities they found it necessary to warn or encourage, we do not know. It is a safe presumption that most of them were Palestinian; but it is not impossible that some of those who dreamed of the gathering of Israel were themselves children of the Diaspora, whether in Egypt or Babylonia, or in the pregnant spread of Jewish life westward, we cannot say. But all alike were heirs of the treasures of Abraham's children, and all lived in those formative centuries when Jewish life was taking determinative shape and preparing to make yet nobler contribution to the onward march of man. The Book of Ezekiel is not the father, but the child, of Judaism.

CHAPTER XI

THE RISE OF PERSIA AND THE UNKNOWN VOICE

THE reign of Nebuchadrezzar, under whom Ezekiel had lived and worked, was long (605–562 B.C.) and prosperous. He concentrated his energies upon Babylonia itself, in rebuilding cities, in erecting and repairing temples, and in dredging out old canals and digging new ones. He neglected the outer provinces of the empire and aroused jealousy especially by the favor he showed toward the city of Babylon. Upon his death political anarchy set in, and internal strife from that time on made it impossible to present a united front against an effective foreign invader. His successor was his son Amel-Marduk (= Evil-Merodach of II Kings 25:27 f.), who reigned for two years (562–560 B.C.), and was then murdered by his own brother-in-law, Nergal-shar-usur (560–556 B.C.), better known to us as Neriglissar. He handed the throne down to his son, Labashi-Marduk, who had reigned only nine months when he was murdered by a band of conspirators who placed a Babylonian ruler on the throne that had been occupied for seventy years by Chaldeans. At the end of the reign of this ruler (555–538 B.C.), Nabuna'id by name (otherwise known as Nabonidus), the land of Babylonia changed hands.

The Medes had received all the eastern and northern provinces of the deceased Assyrian Empire, while
the Babylonians had taken the western provinces. In
585 B.C., Cyaxares, the Mede, had pushed his frontier
far to the west, after defeating the kingdom of Urartu
in battle, and had established the boundary between
himself and the Lydians at the river Halys. His son,
Astyages, reigned after him until 553 B.C. At that time
there arose Cyrus the Persian, Prince of Anshan, in
Elam. He attained power in his own country and proceeded at once to attack Astyages, whom he overthrew, thus becoming lord of all the territory dominated by the Medes. The spectacular rise of Cyrus to
power startled the surrounding peoples, who became
alarmed. Consequently, about 547 B.C. Croesus, of
Lydia, Amasis, of Egypt, and Nabuna'id, of Babylonia, joined with Sparta in an alliance against Cyrus,
whose growing power menaced them all. But Cyrus
learned of their plans and thwarted them by prompt
action. He attacked Croesus, of Lydia, and brought
him to subjection before his allies could rally to his aid.
He followed up this success by conquering the Greek
states of Caria and Lydia within the next three years.

Immediately after his victory over Croesus, Cyrus
intrusted his western operations to one of his generals
and hastened in person to attack Babylonia. By 546
B.C. southern Babylonia was invaded from Elam and a
Persian governor was installed in Erech. After a brief
lull in the hostilities, Gobryas, who was governing Assyria for Cyrus, inflicted a severe defeat on the Babylonians at Opis (539 B.C.). Bel-shar-usur (=Bel-shaz-

zar), the son of Nabuna'id, was in command of the Babylonian troops in that battle. His father, the king, was then at Sippar, far to the south of Opis; but he at once, upon hearing of the defeat at Opis, fled to Borsippa, still farther to the south. Two days after the victory at Opis, Gobryas entered the city of Babylon, without the necessity of striking a single blow. The citadel at Babylon, however, seems to have held out in resistance and not to have yielded to the Persians until March, 538 B.C., at which time Cyrus himself was probably present.[1]

During the closing years of the Babylonian rule, the prophet whose sermons are contained in Isaiah, chapters 40–55, was observing the course of events and interpreting their meaning to the exiles in Babylonia.[2] All scholars of today agree that these prophecies were not written by Isaiah in the eighth century B.C.; and the great majority likewise are convinced that the author was a contemporary of the Exile and wrote out of

[1] For the stories of these events as told by both Nabuna'id and Cyrus see the "Annals of Nabonidus" and the Cyrus cylinder in R. F. Harper, *Assyrian and Babylonian Literature* (1901), pp. 168–74. Cf. R. W. Rogers, *Cuneiform Parallels to the Old Testament* (1926), pp. 371–84; R. P. Dougherty, *Nabonidus and Belshazzar* (1929), pp. 167–85; see, too, G. G. Cameron, *History of Early Iran* (1936), chap. xii.

[2] For introductions to these chapters see the list of commentaries on Isaiah given on p. 86; also Volz, *Jesaja II* (1932); and Torrey, *Second Isaiah* (1928). A considerable number of scholars now hold that the work of "Second Isaiah" does not terminate at chap. 55, but includes chaps. 56–66 as well. However, against this see Volz, *op. cit.* It is generally agreed that chap. 35 is "Second Isaiah's"; some would say chap. 34 also.

the midst of Exilic conditions.[3] He was stirred up to prophesy by the rapid rise of Cyrus to power. He saw in this new world-ruler the one chosen of Yahweh to give his people their freedom. The prophet's task was to prepare the people to take advantage of their freedom when the opportunity should come. This meant the creation of a new state of mind among the exiles. The people had lost the hope of a return; they had made up their minds to accept the inevitable, and to make the best of the situation in which they found themselves. It was the same mood as had compelled Ezekiel to undertake to rouse in them a new faith and to stir within them new longings and hopes.

Out of that situation grew the prophet's message. And at once we realize we are in an atmosphere very different from that of the pre-Exilic prophets. Instead of their stern rebukes and threats of impending doom, we find a prevailing hope and encouragement. True, Second Isaiah knows how to rebuke his contemporaries; he knows well their blindness and their long dark past. But his face is toward a future glorious with promise soon to be fulfilled. It is in a characteristic mood that the united body of his prophecies begins with words of comfort and moves on through a remarkable argument demonstrating the power of God as seen in the mighty works of nature, and his supremacy over all the world. Nowhere is the omnipotence of Yahweh more eloquently or powerfully presented than

[3] Scholars vary in opinion as to the region in which this prophet lived; but here we shall assume his residence in Babylonia. This supposition becomes doubly strong if we assign Isaiah, chap. 35, to the same writer, as there is good reason for doing.

by this unknown prophet. It was inevitable that many exiles should doubt Yahweh's ability to help them, since in their thinking he had been worsted by the gods of Babylon. But this writer tells in glowing words of his greatness and his tender care and solicitude for his homeless people who had already "received of the Lord's hands double for all their sins." We can still feel the eager wonder and thrill with which he an nounced the dawn of the long-hoped-for day:

On a high mountain get you up,
O heralds of good news to Zion!
Lift up your voice with strength
O heralds of good news to Jerusalem!
Lift it up, fear not:
Say to the cities of Judah,
"Behold your God!"
See! the Lord God is coming with might,
His own arm having won him the kingdom;
See his reward is with him.
And his recompense before him.
Like a shepherd he tends his flock,
With his arm he gathers them;
The lambs he carries in his bosom.
And gently leads those who give suck.

Do you not know? Do you not hear?
Has it not been told you from the beginning?
Have you not understood from the foundations of the earth?
It is he who sits above the circle of the earth,
So that its inhabitants are like grasshoppers;
Who stretches out the heavens like a curtain,
And spreads them out like a tent to dwell in;
Who brings nobles to nothing,
And makes judges of the land like the chaos.[4]

[4] Isa. 40:9–11, 21–23; see also Isa. 40:12–20.

But it was not alone the military might of Babylon that created a problem for exiled Jewish faith. These deported folk had come from a mere country town to the heart of a great empire and to the vicinity of the greatest city of the time; and they were compelled to realize the pettiness of their Palestinian life. The Babylonian culture overwhelmed them. In particular the age-old study of the heavens was just at this time evolving into a real science, which through the medium of the Greeks was to become the ancestor of modern astronomy. It opened to these bewildered Jews a vista of heavenly majesty and wonder such as to mock their claims that their god had in the beginning created the heavens and the earth. It was an ancient instance of the problem that seems ever to beset the popular mind—the apparent conflict between science and religion. But Second Isaiah met it with a triumphant faith that, far from bafflement, found in this fresh flood of knowledge a better revelation of the nature of God. "Enlarge your thought of the Lord," he seems to say, "his greatness is far beyond anything you have dreamed."

> Lift up your eyes on high,
> And see: who created these?
> He who brings out their host by number,
> He calls all of them by name;
> Because of the abundance of his resources and since he is
>   of irresistible strength,
> Not a single one is missing.[5]

And this transcendant might and tender love was

[5] Isa. 40:26.

now to exercise itself in the restoration of his people to the land of their fathers, but not by the weary road along which they had tramped their desolate way into exile, for God would open for them a highway right through the blazing expanse of the desert and provide it with abundant water and trees by the roadside. It is one of the prophet's favorite themes, probably most familiar in the words of this same great fortieth chapter,[6] from which we have already quoted at length, but it is as well the inspiration of chapter 35, that may well be considered one of the most beautiful lyrics in the entirety of the remarkable poetry coming to us from ancient Israel. The poem moves on in fervent account of the miraculous road to which

> The glory of Lebanon shall be given
> The splendor of Carmel and Sharon.

Its wonders shall be such that

> The lame man shall leap like a hart
> And the tongue of the dumb shall sing.
> For waters shall break out in the wilderness
> And streams in the desert.

There will be no lion on it, nor any of the grotesque demons figured on the Procession Street of Babylon, but

> The ransomed of the Lord shall return by it;
> They shall come to Zion with singing,
> And with everlasting joy upon their heads;
> They shall attain to joy and gladness,
> And sorrow and sighing shall flee away.

The obverse of the supreme power of Yahweh is, of

[6] Vss. 3–4.

course, the utter powerlessness of other gods in general, and of idols in particular. No finer exposure of the futility of idols had then been written than that furnished by this prophet:

Those who form idols are all a desolation,
And their objects of desire are of no use;
Their witnesses do not see,
Nor do they know, that they may be ashamed.

Who has formed a god,
And molded an idol to be of no use?
Surely, all his associates will be ashamed;
For workmen are but human beings!

They will all assemble together; they will all take their stand;
They will be terrified; they will also be ashamed.
The iron worker works in the coals,
And with hammers he shapes it,
And works it with his strong arm.
But he becomes hungry and strength fails;
He drinks no water, and he faints.

The woodworker stretches a line,
He circumscribes it with the pencil,
He works it with planes and circumscribes it with the compass;
And he makes it after the pattern of a man,
Like the beauty of a human being—to sit in the house!

He cuts down cedars for it;
And he takes a fir or an oak,
And he braces it with wood from the forest.
He plants a cedar and the rain makes it grow.
Then a man uses it for fuel;
And he takes thereof and warms himself.

Indeed, he kindles a fire and bakes his bread.
Then he makes a god and worships;
He makes an idol and prostrates himself before it.

The half of it he has burned up in the fire;
Over half of it he eats meat,
He roasts a roast and is satiated.

Indeed, he warms himself and says,
"Ah! I am warm, I have seen fire!"
And the rest of it he makes into a god, his idol.
He prostrates himself before it and worships,
And prays to it, and says,
"Deliver me, for thou art my god!"

They do not know; nor do they understand;
For their eyes are beclouded, so they cannot see,
Their minds so that they have no wisdom.
So it does not occur to his mind,
Nor is their knowledge or discernment to say,
"Half of it I have burned in the fire,
And I have baked bread on its coals,
I am roasting meat and eating;
And shall I make the rest of it into an abomination?
Shall I prostrate myself to the product of a tree?"[7]

To reinforce his argument for Yahweh's sole right to recognition as God, he has recourse to a new argument. He calls attention to the predictions made by the prophets of Yahweh in the past which have already been fulfilled. This sort of material occupies his attention a great deal.[8] He challenges the worshipers of other gods to show anything like this in support of their claims. There is none like Yahweh that can tell the end from the beginning.[9] In this connection he speaks of Cyrus,

[7] Isa. 44:9–19. For similar utterances see Isa. 40:18–20; 41:6 f.; 46:1–7.

[8] Isa. 41:21–29; 42:9; 43:9, 10, 12; 44:6–8; 48:14.

[9] Isa. 46:9, 10.

king of Persia. He is the great outstanding figure of the times, and he is the one through whom the prophecies of the past are to find complete fulfilment.[10] Cyrus, indeed, is so much the servant and agent of Yahweh that he ventures to apply to him the title of Messiah (45:1), and to call him Yahweh's "shepherd" (44:28).[11]

If Yahweh was to be credited with so much power, indeed, with supreme power, then how could it be that his people had been allowed to endure so many reverses? If Yahweh did not exert his strength in defense of his people, could it be that he really loved them? To this problem, our prophet addressed himself directly. He assured his people that the love of Yahweh for his people was beyond comparison with the most devoted and enduring human love:

> But Zion says, "Yahweh has deserted me and the Lord has forgotten me."
> Can a woman forget her baby,
> And not have pity upon the child of her womb?
> Even if these shall forget,
> Yet I will not forget thee.

[10] Isa. 41:2–4, 25; 44:28; 45:1; 46:11; 48:14, 15.

[11] Torrey argues cogently (*op. cit.*) against the genuineness of this mention of Cyrus. It seems probable that 44:28 is spurious; but it is by no means as certain as Torrey believes that "Cyrus" is to be deleted from 45:1 on metrical grounds. It is true the inclusion of the word makes the line 3:3, while the prevailing measure in the context is 3:2. But one does not go far in the study of Hebrew metrics without realizing that this interchange is a frequent stylistic device of Old Testament poets. However, the important consideration is that, even if we concede the point fully to Torrey, the description of the figure in this and related passages leaves it extremely difficult to understand how any other than Cyrus can have been meant by the author. In other words, if "Cyrus" is a gloss, it is, none the less, a true interpretation.

> See, I have engraved thee on my palms,
> Thy walls are constantly before me.[12]

And again:

> For like a wife deserted and grieved
> In spirit has Yahweh called thee,
> And like a wife from youth when she is rejected, says thy God.
> For a brief moment I forsook thee,
> But with great mercies will I gather thee.
> In quick anger I hid my face from thee for a moment.
> But with enduring love will I have compassion on thee;
> Says thy vindicator, Yahweh.
> For like the days of Noah is this to me;
> In that I swore that the waters of Noah
> Should not again pass over the earth;
> So have I sworn not to be angry with thee,
> Nor to rebuke thee.
> For the mountains may remove,
> And the hills may totter,
> But my love will not leave thee,
> Nor will my covenant of peace waver;
> Says Yahweh who has compassion on thee.[13]

It is noticeable that the prophet did not seek to prove the love of Yahweh for Judah by a process of argument. No love can be demonstrated by argument, least of all the love of God. He simply poured out his own convictions in glowing certainty, and sought to kindle a similar flame in the minds and hearts of his hearers. He believed with all his heart in the love of Yahweh, and he sought to make that faith of his own a contagion laying hold of the lives of his fellow-Jews.

However, one of the most famous features of these chapters, and certainly one of the greatest in all their

[12] Isa. 49:14–16.   [13] Isa. 54:6–10.

greatness, is the presence of the so-called "Servant of Yahweh Songs." These are four in number, viz., (1) Isa. 42:1–4; (2) Isa. 49:1–6; (3) Isa. 50:4–9; and (4) Isa. 52:13—53:12. In these four "Songs" a different rhythm is employed from that in their contexts, and the theme is constantly that of the experience and the mission of the Servant. Opinions differ somewhat as to the authorship of these "Songs," some holding that they were written by a different hand from that of the author of Isaiah, chapters 40–55, as a whole;[14] but the arguments for that view are hardly convincing. They seem rather to be an essential element in Isaiah, chapters 40–55, without which its argument would be incomplete.

A further variety of opinion exists as to the identity of the Servant of Yahweh.[15] Is the Servant to be identified with some individual in the course of history, or yet to come, or with some part within the Hebrew nation, or with the Jewish people as a whole? A brief survey of the main facts involved will make our position here perfectly clear. The term "Servant of Yahweh," or "my Servant," occurs outside of the "Servant of Yahweh Songs" themselves in the following places: Isa. 41:8 ff.; 42:18–22; 44:1, 2, 21, 26; 45:4; 50:10. In Isa. 41:8 ff.; 44:1, 2, 21; and 45:4 the term "Servant" is definitely identified with or explained by the word "Israel." In the remaining passages, there is nothing that calls for a different meaning for "Serv-

[14] See for this point of view the commentary of Duhm (3d ed., 1914); cf. the brief history of interpretation in F. C. Eiselen, *The Prophetic Books of the Old Testament*, I (1923), 224–34; also Eissfeldt, *Der Gottsknecht bei Deuterojesaja* (1933).

[15] See n. 14.

ant."[16] Now, if the term "Servant" everywhere in this prophecy means "Israel" outside of the "Songs," it certainly is to be supposed that the meaning of the term will be the same inside of the "Songs," if the "Songs" and the other prophecies are by the same writer, as we have supposed. Only if the facts or usage within the "Songs" themselves compel some other interpretation ought we to think of changing the meaning.

In Isa. 42:1–5 the Greek version of Isaiah inserts "Jacob" before "my Servant" and "Israel" before "my chosen," thus showing that the identification with the nation goes back into pre-Christian times. The phrase "I uphold" in 42:1 is used of Israel in 41:10; "my chosen" appears also in 41:8; 43:20; and 45:4, where it is applied to Israel; and the pouring out of Yahweh's spirit (42:1) is promised upon the Israelites in general in 44:3. In the following context at 42:6, the term "the people" is used of the nations at large, as in 42:5 and 40:7. So in the first song there is nothing forcing us here to find a different sense for the word "Servant."

The second song[17] presents more difficulty. The terms of verse 1 are very intimate and personal; but "Israel" is "called" in 41:9 and 48:12, "formed from the womb" in 46:3. Not only so, but the identification with "Israel" occurs in this very song itself (49:3).[18]

---

[16] In Isa. 42:18–22, the description of the Servant and the reference to the "people" in vs. 22 make the identity of the "Servant" as Israel clear. In 44:26, the word "Servant" should be pluralized, as it is by the Septuagint (cf. "his messengers").

[17] Isa. 49:1–6.

[18] "Israel" is present in all the versions, and lacking in only one Hebrew manuscript.

This would seem to settle the matter. But difficulty
arises in verses 5 and 6, where the Servant is represented by the common translation as doing something
for Israel and therefore as an agent separate and apart
from Israel. If, however, the passage can be so translated as to make the point of view here regarding the
Servant accord with the standpoint elsewhere, we certainly ought to accept such a rendering. To that end,
we translate 49:5, 6 as follows:

> And now, Yahweh,
> Who formed me from the womb to be his Servant,
> Says that he will bring Jacob unto himself,
> And that Israel will be gathered unto him—
> For I am honorable in the eyes of Yahweh,
> And my God has become my strength—
> Yea, he says, "It is too light a thing,
> Since thou art my Servant,
> That I should raise up the tribes of Jacob
> And restore the preserved of Israel;
> And so I will give thee for a light of the nations,
> That my deliverance may be unto the end of the earth."

This translation employs a usage of the Hebrew language, too little recognized, for expressing the equivalent of indirect narration,[19] and it removes our difficulty without any need of textual change. There is
now no reason for seeking for a new meaning for
"Servant" here.

In the third song,[20] when we keep in mind the highly
figurative and personal style of these "Servant Songs,"
there is nothing compelling us or even inviting us to
change the identity of the Servant. The same quality

[19] See J. A. Bewer, *Studies in Memory of G. A. Kohut* (1935), pp. 88–90.
[20] Isa. 50:4–9.

of style must be remembered in the most famous and familiar of the "Songs," viz., Isa. 52:13—53:12. In the common rendering of 53:8, the Servant again seems to be distinguished from Israel. The text there, however, is apparently corrupt, as is shown by the Septuagint, and when corrected, reads:

By an oppressive judgment he was taken;
And who considered his generation?
For he was cut off from the land of the living;
Because of the transgression of the peoples he was stricken to the death.

New translation is also called for in 53:10, 11, where a slight change of text is required, which in no way affects the identity of the Servant.

Yet it pleased Yahweh to crush him by disease;
To see if he would offer himself in atonement,
That he might see his seed and prolong his days,
And that the purpose of Yahweh might prosper through his hand;
That he should see of the tribulation of himself to his satisfaction,
That through knowledge of him my Servant should fully justify many,
And should bear their sins.

It seems, then, that there is no need to see in the term "Servant" in the "Songs" any other meaning than that which is found elsewhere. The Servant is Israel, sometimes spoken of in terms of reality, recognition being made of Israel's failings and sins; at other times, spoken of in idealistic terms, a significance being given to the conduct of Israel in the past that none but an enthusiastic idealist could ever have used.

Nonetheless there is today a strong tendency to return to the identification of the Servant as an individual. The favorite view is that he was a contemporary of the prophet, a man of great gentleness and beauty of character who, however, was persecuted and done to death; in these "Songs" the prophet interprets his passion and confidently asserts his vindication.[21] Others would take the "Songs" to be autobiographical; the Servant is Deutero-Isaiah himself.[22] More strangely the suggestion is actually advanced that all this glorious poetry and religious idealism concerns no other than the petty political figure of King Jehoiachin, who languished for thirty-seven years in a Babylonian prison.[23] And the traditional interpretation that identified the Servant with the expected Messiah does not lack scholarly advocates,[24] even to the length of claiming that this real prediction thus looks forward to a true savior, who, though the prophet did not realize it, could be none other than Jesus of Nazareth.[25] Closely related to this, notwithstanding its seeming remote-

[21] Oesterley and Robinson, *Hebrew Religion* (1930), pp. 264–70; Kittel, *Great Men and Movements in Israel* (1929), pp. 393–401; Rudolph, "Der exilische Messiah: Ein Beitrag zur Ebed Yahweh Frage," *Zeitschrift für alttestamentliche Wissenschaft* (1925), pp. 90–114.

[22] Mowinckel, *Der Knecht Jahwäs* (1921); Gunkel, *Ein Vorlaufer Jesu* (1921); Haller, *Das Judentum* (1925), p. 66.

[23] II Kings 25:27; so Sellin, *Introduction to the Old Testament* (1923), pp. 143. Yet more strange is the view of J. L. Palache (*The Ebed Yahweh in Deutero-Isaiah* [1934]) that identifies the Servant with an obscure scion of the Davidic line, and finds this man mentioned by name in 42:19.

[24] Fischer, *Wer ist der Ebed?* (1922). Rudolph (see n. 21 above) holds that the prophet saw in the pious individual, whom his theory postulates, the Messiah (cf., too, Torrey, *op. cit.*, p. 141).

[25] So Fischer, *op. cit.*

ness, is the view that we have here an influence of the popular beliefs of the ancient East with the Servant taking the part of the dying god of the fertility mythology.[26]

It will be seen thus that the problem of these four poems is still an acute issue in Old Testament study. It is too much to suppose, then, that the final word can be spoken here. The best to be hoped is that certain considerations may be advanced which will be of value as investigation yet moves on.

Most, if not all, these views are cogent in their recognition of the vivid personal realism[27] of the "Songs," which seems to indicate that the poet had in mind some definite individual. And those who advocate the messianic interpretation possess the strong ground that ever since the beginning of the Christian era it has been recognized in the church that the depth and religious idealism here so wonderfully set forth find their actual historic "fulfilment" in Jesus. But this is a very different matter from holding that such, then, is the correct interpretation of the "Songs." What is wanted is an understanding of the prophet's actual thought; the sequel of that thought is not our concern for the moment. But all alike these proposed interpretations run afoul of the considerations advanced above;[28] the argu-

[26] Haller, *op. cit.;* Gressmann, *Der Ursprung der israelitische-jüdischen Eschatologie* (1905), pp. 326–27; but in *Der Messias* (1929) he makes him an idealized messianic figure (see pp. 323–39).

[27] Cf. Torrey's comment (*op. cit.,* p. 140): "An *individual* portrait, once or twice so sharply outlined as to be startling."

[28] Pp. 228–31. Cf., too, W. F. Albright (*From the Stone Age to Christianity* [1940], p. 255), who, while repudiating national and individua

ments for the national interpretation may not be lightly set aside.

However, the suggestion of Gressmann mentioned just now deserves more consideration than it has received. In the form in which it is sometimes understood the theory is open to all the objections that have been urged against it;[29] certainly, the great fifty-third chapter of Isaiah is not a Babylonian cult song of the death of Tammuz, nor is it based on one. The Babylonians at their best never remotely approached the profound depth of this passage, which has well been called the greatest religious poem ever written.[30] But we have come to realize with the passing years the immense influence upon Israel's religious life of the pagan cults of the dying and rising god, which were so prevalent in the ancient world that we may describe them as Israel's religious native air. In particular, the discovery at Ras Shamra on the north Syrian coast of a remarkable series of documents which, when deciphered, were found to be epic poems of this cult as practiced there in the ancient city of Ugarit, and, possessing astonishing parallels to Old Testament literature and ritual,[31] have provided proof for those who

interpretations alike and demanding rather an eclectic view, formulates a position that is little more than a new statement of the national interpretation. For the relation of the cults of the dying and rising gods to the concept of the Servant, cf. *ibid.*, p. 252.

[29] See Fischer, *op. cit.*   [30] Torrey, *op. cit.*, p. 409.

[31] See J. W. Jack, *The Ras Shamra Tablets: Their Bearing on the Old Testament* (1935); R. Dussaud, *Les Découvertes de Ras Shamra et l'Ancien Testament* (1937); C. F. A. Schaeffer, *The Cuneiform Texts of Ras Shamra-Ugarit* (1939). Interpretation of the texts, and in some measure their reading, is still beset with great difficulty and uncertainty. An extensive literature of discussion has arisen. A detailed bibliography is given by Schaeffer in *Ugaritica* (1939), pp. 147–207.

needed it that Israel's basic religious thought, in common with her neighbors, was faith in the efficacy of the
death and resurrection of a god as the means of grace
and welfare. From and with this viewpoint she went
forward on her remarkable religious development.
Her pagan concepts were in considerable part not so
much sloughed off as transmuted and sublimated
through her advance in the purity and exaltation of
the thought of God. There is, then, no a priori objection to finding influences and deposits of the pagan
Tammuz-Adonis-Osiris cycle of mythology and cults
in even the greatest of Old Testament literature. And
the facts are such as to lead cogently to this view,
whatever theological bias one may entertain. We have
already spoken of these matters in connection with the
interpretation of Hosea's work. But one further feature
is relevant here, that is the fact that the ritual of this
ancient Passion Play demanded that the part of the
god be taken by someone who actually or in symbol
should enact his death and resurrection. Various devices were employed throughout the immense expanse
of the history of all these oriental lands to effect this
purpose. But because of their concept of corporate personality,[32] through which the king *was* the state in a
deep sense, gathering up in his person its weal or woe,
he was indicated as the logical individual to perform
this honorable but painful task. It was as an aspect of
this that in Babylon the king held office for only one
year at a time, and each New Year's Feast must present himself in the temple of Marduk there to be tried

[32] See H. W. Robinson, *The People and the Book* (1925), pp. 375–78.

with contempt at the hands of the priest before he might again receive the throne from the god.[33] We do not know how far Israel followed her great neighbors in the details of this ritual; the direct evidence is less than conclusive.[34] But some hold that a central feature of the autumn feast in Jerusalem was the enactment of this drama, with the ceremonial enthronement of Yahweh, more specifically of his anointed representative.[35]

However this may be, of one thing we may rest assured, that Second Isaiah was quite familiar with this ritual, whether he observed it as part of the religious practice of his own people or as a foreign rite of their Babylonian captors. Elsewhere he refers pointedly to aspects of the New Year's festival in Babylon. In 46:1–2 he pours contempt on the solemn procession of Marduk and Nabu being carried forth to their appointed place of meeting, where in day-long conclave they decided the fates of the incoming year. But in 35:9–10, to which reference has already been made, he clearly takes a cue from features of the Babylonian Procession Street along which the gods went forth, claiming that the great religious way of the Jews will be so much better that it will have no terrifying lions and griffins on its walls,[36] nor be desecrated with pagan idols; it will be for

[33] See Langdon, *The Babylonian Epic of Creation* (1923), pp. 25–26.

[34] See Snaith, *Studies in the Psalter* (1934); Pap, *Das israelitische Neujahrfest* (1933); but also A. Causse in *Revue d'histoire et de philosophie religieuse*, III (1923), 262–68; A. Lods in *Revue de l'histoire des religions* (1925), pp. 15–34.

[35] See Mowinckel, *Psalmstudien*, II: *Das Thronbesteigugsfest Jahwes und der Ursprung der Eschatologie* (1922), and Schmidt, *Die Psalmen* (1934).

[36] Olmstead, *History of Palestine and Syria* (1931), p. 549.

the redeemed, the ransomed of the Lord will walk there.

That in this divine passion of ancient myth and cultus, through which there came life and healing to the nations, we are to recognize the basic motif of the Servant "Songs," in particular of chapter 53, cannot be finally proved. But the a priori considerations are so strong, and the parallels if not allusions to the ritual drama are so numerous and so close as the Servant's experience moves on through contempt, persecution, and death apparently to resurrection and final triumph, that the view commends itself as the most probable of the many which our present uncertainty has spawned so prolifically. In addition, it pre-empts all the arguments advanced by the exponents of the individual interpretations; for it was a single individual each year who enacted this painful exposition of the divine life-giving suffering and death. The personal realism of the "Songs" is a reflex of personal experience, through which, however, our author saw with the clarity of inspiration the meaning of his people's hard fate: they together, not some petty monarch, were the Servant of the Lord, enacting in their tragic history the divine cycle of death and resurrection, through which life and healing should come to all the world. This nameless prophet of the Babylonian captivity, whom we call Second Isaiah, was one of the great creative thinkers of Israel's history. He, in a measure far transcending Hosea's insight, perceived the eternal realities in this profound sacrament of the ancient world, and, stripping them of their pagan forms and expression, set forth

here in words of matchless beauty and depth the great
truth that suffering is divine, that through pain and
loss and death the Kingdom of God comes in power.
It is the same thought that Israel's greatest son in a
later day expressed, saying, "Except a grain of wheat
fall into the ground and die it abideth alone; but if it
die, it bringeth forth much fruit."[37]

This is a solution of the problem of its national history for Israel that challenges wonder. What a generous evaluation of the peoples of the non-Hebraic world
this was that conceived them worthy of Israel's pain!
What large-heartedness is here attributed to Israel
when it is claimed that this suffering was borne uncom-
plainingly, if not, indeed, willingly, for the sake of the
good of the rest of the world! How could a Hebrew
ever have arrived at the thought of Israel suffering for
the sins of mankind as a whole? Two things must be
reckoned with in answering this question. First, whatever Israel may have endured in the past, the suffering
is all over now, and the misery of the past is to be more
than compensated for by the glories of the future. Second, this singer was but widening the scope of a very
old conception. The dominating thought in the Hebrew family and national groups was that of social
solidarity. The individual existed for the family, the
family for the clan or tribe, and that in turn for the
nation as a whole. What this poet did was to take this
thought of social solidarity and make it applicable to
the world at large. The whole world was looked upon
by him as a huge human family. Every nation in it

[37] John 12:24.

existed for the benefit of all. All were, potentially at least, children of one God and Father. Israel, then, as one member of this great family, had been suffering for the good of the entire family. Israel's sufferings, therefore, had not been in vain. Not only were they in satisfaction of the demands of the divine justice, paying the penalty for the sins of all mankind, but they were also to be effective in the redemption of the human race and in its regeneration to a new life as worshipers of the one and only God. This singer was a voice crying in the wilderness. He was the first to utter the thought of one nation's responsibility for any other nation's interests than its own. He laid the sins and sorrows of the world upon Israel's shoulders. Israel refused to accept the responsibility or the burden. Here and there in later history the call of this great Unknown found an echo in the bosom of a Hebrew idealist. But the grandeur of this conception of national life has not yet found realization upon the earth. Our 100 per cent Americanism shudders in terror before such an ideal as this.[38]

It at once appears, upon consideration of such an interpretation of the Servant's person and work as this, that the problem of Israel's sufferings is met much more directly by this message than it could possibly be by any interpretation of the Servant as a person. Some aspects of the figurative description of the Servant and

[38] For a more detailed presentation of this aspect of the Servant's function see J. M. Powis Smith, "The Ethical Significance of Isaiah, Chapter 53," *Journal of Religion*, III (1923), 132–40; and *The Moral Life of the Hebrews* (1923), pp. 149–64.

his work coincide closely with some elements and episodes in the records of the life and work of Jesus. But
the conception of the Servant's work as a whole is
couched in wholly different terms from those that fit
the person and work of Jesus. This is an attempt to
furnish a solution of an international problem and to
bring consolation and inspiration to the Jewish nation
as a whole. The spirit that breathes throughout these
"songs" is a spirit of intense devotion to the Jewish
program of life and of longing to see the whole world
accept Jewish leadership and Jewish ideals. The whole
purpose and work of this prophet was in a very real
sense part of a messianic program. He was urging his
people to prepare themselves for the coming messianic
opportunity. His great fear was lest the opportunity
should come and his people not be ready for it. He
would stimulate and encourage them to believe in a
great future and to expect its dawn at any moment.
He looks confidently for the coming of the opportunity
for the exiles to return to Judah. He paints glowing
pictures of the joys of that journey and of the way in
which all natural difficulties and hardships will be
overcome; see, for example, Isa. 40:3–11; 41:18–20;
and chapter 55. Hard-headed and practical as the
Jews of Babylonia doubtless were, they treasured the
words of this great idealist, even though they did not
wholly surrender themselves to the power of his ideals.
His admirers then, as now, were probably many; his
followers few.

CHAPTER XII

PREMATURE MESSIANIC HOPES

THE prophets Haggai and Zechariah lived and worked in Jerusalem. Their period of activity extended from 520 to 518 B.C. In 538 B.C. Cyrus, of Persia, had issued an edict permitting the return home of all captive peoples, including the Jewish exiles.[1] The writer of Isaiah, chapters 40–55, had looked upon Cyrus as the one who would usher in the messianic age for the world. He had done his best to arouse interest in and enthusiasm for the return movement, but with slight success. Very few took advantage of the opportunity to go back to Judah when it presented itself. There was no rush home in 538 B.C. The process of return was gradual and slow. As a matter of fact, Haggai and Zechariah, speaking only eighteen years after this date, make no allusion to the return of exiles on a large scale. No reader of their books would ever suspect that they were written for a community made up largely of returned captives. There was little

[1] See Ezra 1:1–4; II Chron. 36:22, 23. For Cyrus' generous treatment of his enemies reference may be had to Herodotus i. 86 ff., and Xenophon's *Cyropaedia* iii. 1 ff.; iv. 4 f.; vii. 2; viii. 1 ff. Cyrus tells us in his own words that he collected all the captives from the west and restored them to their homes (see the "Cylinder of Cyrus" as translated in R. F. Harper, *Assyrian and Babylonian Literature* [1901], p. 173; and R. W. Rogers, *Cuneiform Parallels to the Old Testament* (1926), pp. 380–84.

in Jerusalem, aside from sentiment, to make it inviting to the exiles. The city was left desolate. The Temple was desecrated and destroyed. All business was at a standstill. Instead of a thriving mart, the city had become a defenseless ruin, where a broken and discouraged people eked out a precarious existence. On the other hand, there is good reason to think that the Jews in Babylonia had prospered. They had acted upon the advice given them in Jeremiah's letter (Jeremiah, chap. 29), and built themselves into the economic and industrial life of the Babylonian community as a whole. They had all their investments and business interests in Babylonia. The proposition to pull up stakes, sell out, and start all over again in a new and far-off location would not appeal with great force to successful Jewish merchants or farmers in Babylonia.

Another difficulty in the way of the creation of great enthusiasm for the return movement lay in the fact that most of the original exiles of 597 and 586 B.C. must have died before 538 B.C. Very few of the exiles of 538 B.C. had ever seen Jerusalem or Judah. Those who had once lived there had left it so early in life as to have forgotten practically all about it. They had lived in Babylonia practically all their lives and in no real sense ever thought of Judah as "home." They were content where they were; or, if not wholly satisfied, probably thought it "better to bear the ills they had than to fly to ills they knew not of." It is not probable that there was any great degree of homesickness among the Jewish population of 538 B.C. A still further element working against the creation of a general desire to return to

Palestine was the length of the arduous journey. The shortest practicable route for a great company of people was to the north and west, along the banks of the Euphrates; west through Palmyra to Damascus, then south to Judah and Jerusalem. But this was a journey of weeks, and also was so difficult that the more usual route was the longer one up the Tigris, across northern Mesopotamia to Syria, and thence southward to Palestine. The seriousness of this obstacle is attested by the fact, which we have noted, that the writer of Isaiah, chapters 40–55, promised the exiles a royal road straight across the intervening desert, with all the natural difficulties removed by divine intervention.[2] It would appear, then, that there was no concerted return in large numbers, but that the movement was confined to small groups of enthusiasts or malcontents who trickled back to Judah from time to time as occasion served.[3] These made no marked impress upon the life of the Jerusalem community, for they were too few in number, and probably also too insignificant in char-

[2] Isa. 40:3–5; 41:17–19; 43:19–21; 48:21; 49:9–11.

[3] The movement was very like the Zionist restoration of our own days, and receives vivid illumination from a study of the latter. It will be recalled that prior to the beginning of Nazi persecution of Jews in Germany the immigration into Palestine was relatively insignificant; indeed, in one year more Jews emigrated than came in (see *Palestine Royal Commission Report* [1937], pp. 62, 279). And we are given to understand that a considerable proportion of the earlier *halutsim*, as these Jewish pioneers are called, were young and unattached or possessed of some compelling enthusiasm. The large number of Jews the world over had business or professional bonds detaining them in the lands that had become home to them, as also in many cases to their fathers for ages past.

acter and ability, to count for much in the group as a whole.

Thus eighteen years passed away with no great change in conditions among the Jews either in Jerusalem and Judah or in Babylonia. But about 520 B.C. things began to take place in the Persian Empire that attracted the attention of alert patriots among the Jews. Cambyses, the Persian monarch, was in Egypt in 521 B.C. Gaumata seized the opportunity afforded by the absence of Cambyses to head a revolt against him in Persia. Gaumata put up the claim that he was Bardes, son of Cyrus. As a matter of fact, Cambyses had assassinated Bardes. Cambyses hastened to return to Persia; but on the way thither he called his councilors together, confessed to them the murder of Bardes, and thereupon committed suicide.[4] Gaumata was thus left in possession of the empire. But he was slain by Darius Hystaspes in October, 521 B.C. Revolt thereupon broke out all over the Persian Empire. Babylonia revolted twice, as did also Susiania. Media, Sagartia, Margiana, and Persia each organized a movement of rebellion, and in the last-mentioned country a new Bardes presented himself as entitled to the throne. Darius set himself the task of crushing these revolts, and overthrew his foes one after another in succession. But he did not succeed in restoring peace

[4] So G. Buchanan Gray in *Cambridge Ancient History*, IV (1926), 23. But the sources for the death of Cambyses are not clear; for a presentation of this uncertainty see W. R. Rogers, *History of Ancient Persia* (1929), p. 84; and H. R. Hall, *Ancient History of the Near East* (1932), p. 569.

and order until 520–519 B.C. His report of his victories is proof of his gratitude to Ahuramazda, his god:

Thus speaks Darius the king: That which I did came to pass solely through the grace of Ahura Mazda. Since I have been king I have fought nineteen battles, by the will of Ahura Mazda I smote them! Nine of their kings I took as prisoners. One, Gaumata by name, the Magian, lied and spoke as follows: "I am Bardiya the son of Cyrus." This one made Persia rebellious. One, by the name of Atrina, the Susian, lied and spoke as follows: "I am the king of Susa." This one made Elam rebellious. One, Nidintu-Bel by name, a Babylonian, lied and spoke as follows: "I am Nebuchadrezzar, the son of Nabonidus." This one made Babylon rebellious. One, by the name of Martiya, a Persian, lied and spoke as follows: "I am Ummanish, king of Susa." This one made Susa rebellious. One, Parumartish by name, a Median, lied and spoke as follows: "I am Hashatriti of the seed of Umaku-Ishtar." This one made Media rebellious. One, Citrantakhma by name, a Sagartian, lied and spoke as follows: "I am king of Sagartia, of the seed of Umaku-Ishtar." This one made Sagartia rebellious. One, Parada by name, a Margianian, lied and spoke as follows: "I am king in Margiana." This one made Margiana rebellious. One, Vahyazdata by name, a Persian, lied and spoke as follows; "I am Bardiya, the son of Cyrus." This one made Persia rebellious. One, Arahu by name, an Armenian, lied and spoke as follows: "I am Nebuchadrezzar, the son of Nabonidus." This one made Babylon rebellious.

Thus speaks Darius the king: These nine kings the hands of my army seized within these battles. Thus speaks Darius the king: As for these provinces which became rebellious, a lie made them rebellious, so that they deceived the people. Thereupon Ahura Mazda gave them into my hands; according to my desire I treated them.[5]

[5] See the full text of this inscription from Behistun in Harper, *op. cit.*, pp. 174–87; also F. H. Weissbach, *Die Keilinschriften des Achämeniden* (1911), pp. 8 ff.

During the progress of these movements of revolt, the two prophets, Haggai and Zechariah, both began their activity. They were partners in a common enterprise—that of getting slumbering Judah wide awake and ready for the messianic dispensation that they thought was close at hand.[6] Haggai's sermons were all preached in the year 520 B.C.;[7] Zechariah began in 520 B.C., perhaps two months later than Haggai's first appearance, and continued until the end of 518 B.C.[8] The unsettled state of the Persian Empire was the immediate occasion of their appearance as prophets. To their eager eyes the widespread movements of revolt looked like the breaking-up of the organized world, which promised for them the appearance of the Messiah. With this general situation in mind, let us see what message and program these prophets had to present.

Haggai's little book contains four discourses. The first of these is 1:2–11. Haggai urged his people to begin at once the rebuilding of the ruined Temple of Yahweh in Jerusalem. They said that they were not ready, that it was no time to be starting a building enterprise. Haggai replied that they seemed to be able to build homes for themselves; and assured them that the poor crops and hard times from which they were suffering were caused by the fact that Yahweh's displeas-

[6] For introductions to Haggai and Zechariah see the commentaries on these prophets by H. G. Mitchell in the "International Critical Commentary" (1912), W. Emery Barnes in the Cambridge Bible (1917), and Friedrich Horst in *Handbuch zum Alten Testament* (1938).

[7] See Hag. 1:1; 1:15; 2:1; 2:10; 2:20.

[8] See Zech. 1:1, 7; 7:1.

ure was resting upon them because they had so shamefully neglected the rebuilding of his house. Therefore, let them begin building operations at once, and so secure for themselves the restoration of the divine favor in the form of national prosperity.

About three weeks after this challenge, the people, led by their governor, Zerubbabel, and the high priest, Joshua, entered upon the assigned task, with Haggai's assurance that Yahweh was with them.[9] But after the work of building had gone on for about a month and the scope and plan of the building began to emerge, Haggai found it necessary to furnish new encouragement. Some were comparing the present Temple with what they had seen or heard of the Temple of Solomon, and the comparison was not favorable to the present enterprise. The first enthusiasm of the people was wearing away under the strain of the heavy and continuous work. Haggai therefore assured them again that Yahweh was with them and would bless them. To that end Yahweh would overturn the nations, and the wealth of the nations would come pouring into the new Temple, so that its glory and splendor would far transcend that of Solomon's Temple.[10]

Two months later, Haggai preached another message of reproof and encouragement. He called their attention to the difference between the infectious quality of "holy" flesh, on the one hand, and that of a dead body, on the other, and pointed out that holiness was not anything like so penetrating or "catching" as "uncleanness." Even so, the people were forgetting that

[9] Hag. 1:12–15.   [10] Hag. 2:1–8.

the few weeks or months in which they had been doing
the will of Yahweh in the rebuilding of his house could
hardly be expected to counteract or annul the influence of the long generations during which they had
gone the way of wickedness.[11] It is evident that they
were beginning to complain because as yet they had
seen nothing of the prosperity and glory so generously
promised by the prophet. But having pointed out the
unreasonableness of this attitude, Haggai at once renewed his promises and assured them of immediate fulfilment. He reminded them of the fact that the crops
had been poor up to the time of the beginning of the
temple-building, and that since they had begun building there had not been time for a new harvest; but the
coming harvest would be bounteous, indicating the be-
stowal of the divine blessing which had rested on the
community since the building was undertaken.[12]

The last recorded oracle of Haggai was spoken on
the same day as the foregoing. In it he predicted a
great world-upheaval on the coming Day of Yahweh.
Amid the ruin of the nations, Zerubbabel is to be
singled out as Yahweh's servant, whom he has chosen
for special honor. The full significance of this reference
to Zerubbabel does not appear until we come to the
message of Zechariah.

Zechariah's first sermon was preached two months
after the first appearance of Haggai. The people had

[11] But Rothstein in *Juden and Samaritaner* (1908), suggested that the
reference is to the Samaritans. In this he is followed by L. E. Browne,
Early Judaism (1920), pp. 55 f., and Horst, *op. cit.*

[12] Hag. 2:10–19.

been building for a little over a month. In his first sermon Zechariah warned his hearers of the seriousness of
their responsibility in listening to him, the prophet of
Yahweh. He reminded them that the prophets of old
had preached to unwilling hearers and had failed to
secure from them the acceptance of their message. But
the predictions of those great prophets had been fulfilled, and the nation had good cause to regret that the
words of the former prophets had not been heeded. In
view of this sad history, it would be well for the contemporaries of Zechariah to heed his message as the
word of Yahweh and to conform to his demands.[13]

The second of Zechariah's discourses was given more
than three months later. Through this vision of the
heavenly horsemen, the divine assurance is again given
the people that the Temple will be completed and the
capital and cities in general will again overflow with
population and prosperity[14] There followed upon this
first vision a series of six more visions, extending from
Zech. 2:1 to 6:8. The first of these simply assures
Zechariah that the nations that have oppressed Judah
are all to be overthrown.[15] The second impresses it upon the mind of Zechariah, and through him upon the
people, that the Jerusalem of the future will need no
walls, for Yahweh will be its sufficient protection. The
population will also be so numerous that it will overflow the countryside.[16] To this is now appended a summons to the exiles to flee from Babylon, and an as-

[13] Zech. 1:1–6.

[14] Zech. 1:7–17.

[15] Zech. 1:18–21.

[16] Zech. 2:1–5.

surance that Yahweh's people are as immune from danger at the hands of their foes as is the apple of Yahweh's eye. The day is coming when many nations will serve Yahweh and be numbered as his people, while Jerusalem will once more become the chosen city of Yahweh.[17]

The visions continue with the picture of Joshua, the high priest, clothed in dirty garments and standing before the angel of Yahweh, with the Satan close at hand as his accuser.[18] But the Satan is rebuked by the angel, and the attendants are ordered to clothe Joshua in proper clothing and to put a priestly miter upon his head. Joshua is bidden to keep the law of Yahweh and to guard the sacred Temple against profanation. Further, the assurance is given to Joshua that Yahweh is about to bring forth his servant, the "Branch" (or "Sprout"). We recall that Zerubbabel was called the "servant of Yahweh" by Haggai (2:23); and that in Jer. 23:5 and 33:15 the title "Branch" is applied to the coming Messiah. The coming-forth of the Branch is to be the opening of a period of peace and prosperity.[19]

The visions continue in chapter 4. The vision of the golden candlestick and the two "sons-of-oil" was intended to present impressively the thought that Yah-

[17] Zech. 2:6–13.

[18] This is the first appearance of "the Satan" in the history of Hebrew literature. The term here is not a proper name, for it has the definite article prefixed; so also in Job, chaps. 1 and 2; the only other appearance of this agent is in I Chron. 21:1, where it is a proper name

[19] Zech. 3:1–10.

weh was in close touch with and in immediate control
of the course of human events. The two "sons-of-oil"
or "anointed ones" were in all probability meant to
symbolize Joshua, the high priest, and Zerubbabel, the
servant of Yahweh and the Branch. These two are the
earthly representatives of Yahweh on high. In study-
ing this vision, it becomes apparent at once that verses
6b–10a are intrusive elements in the vision and of right
belong somewhere else. The best place for them is before 2:6 ff. They present very forcefully the proposition that the vindication of Judah and its glorification
are not to be thought of as coming about through
human power, but rather as caused by the spirit of the
all-powerful Yahweh. All difficulties will melt away
before Zerubbabel, and he will carry through the rebuilding of the Temple to triumphant conclusion. The
beginnings may look small, but the end will be
glorious.

The vision of the flying roll and the bushel measure
portrays vividly the cleansing process that is to remove
all wickedness from the holy land and to transport it to
Babylonia, where wickedness will be at home, "in her
own place."[20] The series of visions closes with the representation of the four chariots, each with its team of a
separate color.[21] The bearing of the vision upon the
situation is not very obvious. Perhaps the prophet
thought discretion the better part of valor here, and
therefore did not wish to make his meaning too plain
to the Persians. Apparently, the vision was meant to
convey the comforting assurance that Yahweh was

[20] Zech. 5:1–11.   [21] Zech. 6:1–8.

about to reduce Babylonia, the center of the Persian Empire, to acquiescence in his great plans for the coming messianic age and the glorification of Judah.

The series of visions is followed by the record of a very significant action in 6:9–15. The record as it stands in the Hebrew text is not quite clear. Why should more than one crown be placed on the head of the high priest? And why should "crowns" in verse 14 be followed by a verb in the singular, as "shall be" is in its Hebrew form? Further, the "Branch" of verse 12 can be none other than Zerubbabel, who is so designated in Zech. 3:8; he is also credited with the expected completion of the Temple in Zech. 4:7, 9, even as the "Branch" is here in verse 13. Not only so, but the Septuagint offers a variation in verse 13, reading "and the priest shall be at his right hand." These facts seem to point to some tampering with the original text. We are fairly safe in reconstructing the episode somewhat as follows. Just after a small company of exiles had returned to Jerusalem, Zechariah felt called upon to lead the way in inducting Zerubbabel into his office as the promised Messiah. Consequently, he had two crowns made, and in a small private group he proceeded to place these crowns upon the heads of Zerubbabel, the governor, and of Joshua, the high priest. The crowning of Zerubbabel was a deliberate attempt to launch the messianic movement in full force; Joshua, the priest, was crowned in order to give recognition to the priestly order in the messianic program. That Zerubbabel was actually regarded by his contemporaries as the Messiah is clear from this incident, from the references to him as the "Branch," and from the allusion to him in Hag. 2:23. It may seem strange that the figure of the Messiah, which for us is so idealized, should ever have been identified with a mere petty politician such as Zerubbabel; but it must be recalled that the basic idea was that of the "anointed of the Lord," hence originally some human leader. And long after Zerubbabel, messiahs continued to arise, making trouble for Greek or Roman overlords of Judah. This particular attempt to introduce the messianic age proved abortive, of course. What happened to its promoters and to its central figure we do not know, but can readily imagine. The Persian government was tolerant and liberal; but no government would look with equanimity upon a movement to set up a crowned king over one of its subject provinces. The tragic ending of the movement is sunk in oblivion. Later hands took the narrative of this episode and eliminated from it the name of Zerubbabel, but left that of Joshua standing, since the supremacy of the priestly order became more and more conspicuous as time went on. The collapse of this messianic movement was a heavy blow to Jewish expectations. Its full results we are unable to trace because of the scantiness of our records from this and the subsequent period.

Chapters 7 and 8 of Zechariah contain the record of the inquiry made in 518 B.C. by a delegation sent to the priests as to whether or not the custom of observing fasts in the fourth, fifth, seventh, and tenth months should be any longer continued. Zechariah took it upon himself to offer an answer. He declared that the fasts were of no value in and of themselves; but that obedience to the requirements of Yahweh was the all-important thing. Because the prophets of old had not been heeded when they issued a call to follow after justice and to practice mercy and kindness to the poor and helpless, the punishments of the past had been severe and long continued. But those days are over. The future is full of hope and promise. Fasts will be turned into feasts; and peoples from every nation will come pouring into Judah to seek Yahweh in Jerusalem. The nations will be crowding around the Jews, pleading to be permitted to join their number because they have heard that God is with the Jews. Jerusalem will be called "the city of truth," and Zion will be named "the holy mountain." The scattered exiles will all be brought back home, and the streets of Jerusalem be filled with old men and women whose hearts shall be lightened by the merry laughter of the boys and girls who fill all the open spaces. These oracles of encouragement in all probability were spoken before or during the brief period of messianic activity recorded in 6:9–15. The hopes they reflect were all dashed to the earth by the unwritten calamity that brought that movement to an untimely end.

It may well be that some of the messianic oracles now incorporated in Isaiah, chapters 1–39, were called forth by the emergence of Zerubbabel as Messiah. If that situation called forth two prophets, Haggai and Zechariah, with messianic interpretations, it is not at all improbable that other zealots should also have seen in Zerubbabel the promised Messiah ushering in the dawn of the Golden Age. We cannot date these messianic chapters in Isaiah with any certainty, and placing them here is, at best, but a conjecture. But some of the characteristics of the messianic hope that centered around Zerubbabel recur in some of these messianic pictures also. Zerubbabel actually was a descendant of the great King David, and to that extent, at least, he was a promising candidate for the vacant messianic throne.

One of the most famous prophecies is found in Isa. 9:1–6:

The people who have been walking in darkness will see a great light;

They who have dwelt in a land of densest darkness—upon them will the light shine.

Thou wilt multiply the nation, thou wilt magnify its mirth;

They will make merriness before thee like the merriness at harvest-time,

Just as men exult when they share spoil;

Because the yoke of his burden and the staff of his shoulder,

The stick of his driver, thou wilt break as in the day of Midian.

For every boot worn in the tumult of battle,

And every mantle rolled in blood,

Will be for burning, as fuel for the fire.

For a child has been born to us, a son has been given to us.

And the government will be upon his shoulder, and his name will be called,

Wonderful Counsellor, Mighty God, Father forever, Prince of Peace.

Of the increase of dominion and of prosperity there will be no end

Upon the throne of David and upon his kingdom

To establish it and to support it in justice and righteousness,

From henceforth, even for ever.

The zeal of Yahweh of hosts will do this.[22]

[22] A considerable number of scholars today, however, believe that no adequate reason exists for denying the authorship of this passage by the prophet Isaiah (see Budde, *Jesajas Erleben* [1928], pp. 1 f., 105 f.; Procksch, *Jesaja I übersetzt und erklärt* [1930]. pp. 144 f., 150).

The picture contemplates a world in which the Jewish nation will be free from all oppression and under the rule of the Messiah. War is to be a thing of the past, and justice and righteousness are to be in supreme control of all human affairs. The Messiah is to be a paragon of power, wisdom, and love—a very God. This is all very much like what Haggai and Zechariah promised their people.

Isa. 11:1–9 may also belong to this general period. Its hopes are very much of the same order as the foregoing:

There will come forth a shoot from the stump of Jesse,
And a branch from his roots will bear fruit.
The spirit of Yahweh will rest upon him,
A spirit of wisdom and discernment,
A spirit of counsel and power,
A spirit of the knowledge and fear of Yahweh.
He will not give judgment according to what his eyes see;
Nor will he reprove according to what his ears hear;
But he will judge the poor in righteousness,
And he will reprove with equity the meek of the earth;
He will smite the violent with the rod of his mouth,
And with the breath of his lips he will slay the wicked.
Righteousness will be the girdle of his loins,
And fidelity the girdle of his waist.

The wolf will dwell with the lamb,
The leopard will lie down with the kid,
The calf, the young lion, and the fatling also,
And a little child will drive them.
The heifer and the bear will be friends,
Their young ones will lie down together,
And the lion will eat straw like an ox.
The suckling will play upon the whole of the adder,

And the child just weaned will put his hand on the serpent's lair.
They will not hurt nor destroy in all my holy mountain;
For the earth will be filled with the knowledge of Yahweh,
As the waters cover the sea.

The same unlimited idealism appears here as in the Book of Ezekiel and in Isaiah, chapters 40–55—an idealism that was carried to its logical conclusion in the work of Haggai, Zechariah, and such writers as the author of this beautiful dream. Similar visions of a blessed future are presented in Isa. 32:1–8 and 33:17–24. Hopes like these gave Israel courage in days of darkness. It would almost seem that the darker the outlook, as seen by the eye of the ordinary man, the brighter and more glorious were the visions seen by the eye of faith.

CHAPTER XIII

THE CRY FOR VENGEANCE

IN THIS chapter we bring together three pieces of prophetic literature, viz., Isaiah, chapters 56–66; the Book of Obadiah; and the Book of Malachi. The considerations for dating these writings are not so clear and definite as we should like. Their post-Exilic character is beyond question; but as to the specific portion of the post-Exilic period to which they belong there is room for considerable difference of opinion. Here we shall treat them as coming from the close of the long period of silence that came after the collapse of the boom for Zerubbabel as Messiah. They represent, in part, the spirit that found its outlet in the work of Nehemiah and Ezra, and probably belong in close proximity to the reform movement.

The chapters closing the Book of Isaiah are not easily handled as a unit. They rather represent the work of more than one prophet, being a collection of anonymous prophetic writings.[1] There is a noticeable lack of unity in the standpoints of the various chapters. But, in general, the situation which they all reflect is that of a people profoundly discouraged and in need of great stimulation. Consequently, much of the content of these chapters concerns itself with the task of inspiring

[1] For a discussion of the date of this material see the commentaries on Isaiah, cited on pp. 86 and 219.

a disheartened people. To that end were the prophecies uttered that promise disaster and destruction to
the foes of Yahweh and of Judah. See, for example,
Isa. 61:5 and 66:16–19. The most terrible and vindic-
tive of these utterances is that in Isa. 63:1–6. This is a
picture of Yahweh or his destroying angel coming up
from Edom with his clothing reddened with the blood
of those whom he has trampled to death. Such words
as these show how the wrongs inflicted upon Judah in
the time of its weakness by her neighbors, especially the
Edomites, rankled in the bosom of the Jewish people.
Nothing less than a bloody retribution would satisfy
their lust for vengeance. On the other hand, in 56:3–7
we find a contrary attitude toward the pagan world,
which would open the doors of Yahweh's house to all
nations:

> My house will be called a house of prayer for all peoples.

Certainly, those who would avail themselves of this
hospitality must become proselytes to the Jewish faith.
The two requirements made of them are that they shall
observe the Jewish Sabbath and keep the covenant of
Yahweh. This last item is apparently vague, but it
probably implied compliance with the entire Jewish
ritual and law. But the ritualistic interest did not eliminate the old ethical interest and passion of prophecy.
Ritual is made of subordinate value as compared with
ethics, in Isa. 58:3–7, 9 f.; 59:3, 4, 7, 12, 15; and 61:8.
That an incorrect ritual was fraught with much evil is
clear from the denunciations of idolatry and superstition in Isa. 57:1–9 and 65:1–7.

The people for whom these chapters were written were sunk deep in a slough of despond.

Wherefore have we fasted, and thou seest not?
Wherefore have we afflicted ourselves, and thou takest no heed?[2]

That is the way in which they were thinking. Religion ought to pay good dividends; but the more religious they were, the less they seemed to get. Why were they permitted to go on suffering oppression and wrong at the hands of their enemies? To such questions an answer was readily forthcoming from the prophets:

Yahweh's hand is not shortened so that it cannot save,
Nor is his ear heavy, so that it cannot hear.
But your iniquities have separated between you and your God.[3]

Therefore is justice far from us,
And justification does not overtake us.
We look for light, but behold darkness.
For brightness, but we walk in gloom.
We grope for the wall like the blind;
Yea, as they who have no eyes, do we grope;
We stumble at noonday as in the twilight;
We are in dark places like the dead.
We all growl like bears,
And mourn sore like doves;
We look for right, but there is none;
For deliverance, but it is far from us.[4]

One of the most touching expressions of plaintive protest in all literature is placed upon the lips of the Jewish community in the form of a prayer to Yahweh:

Look forth from the heavens and see,
From thy holy and beauteous dwelling;
Where are thy zeal and thy deeds of might?
The compassion of thy heart and thy mercies have been restrained
    for us.

[2] Isa. 58:3.   [3] Isa. 59:1, 2.   [4] Isa. 59:9–11.

For thou art our father!
Abraham has not known us,
Nor Israel recognized us.
Thou, O Yahweh, art our father,
"Our vindicator from of old" is thy name.

Why hast thou made us to wander from thy ways, O Yahweh?
Why dost thou harden our heart against the fear of thee?
Return, for the sake of thy servants,
The tribes of thine inheritance.

Wherefore did the wicked decimate thy saints?
Wherefore did our enemies trample upon thy sanctuary?
Why have we been as those over whom thou hast not ruled from
    of old,
And over whom thy name has not been called?

O that thou wouldst rend the heavens and come down!
That at thy presence the mountains might quake,
As when fire makes the water boil,
So as to make known thy name to thine enemies,
That the nations might tremble at thy presence.

When thou didst do terrible things which we did not expect,
Thou didst come down, the mountains quaked.
From of old they had not heard, nor given ear;
No eye has seen a god except thee,
Who works for him who waits for him.

Thou dost look with favor on those who do righteousness,
And remember thy ways;
But now thou art angry, for we have sinned,
And we have been wicked from of old.
And we are all of us like one unclean;
And all our righteousness is like a defiled garment;
And we do all fade like a leaf;
And our guilt carries us away like the wind.

There is no one calling upon thy name,
Or arousing himself to take hold of thee.

For thou hast hidden thy face from us;
And hast delivered us into the power of our guilt.

Now, O Yahweh, thou art our father;
We are the clay and thou art our potter;
And all of us are the work of thy hands.
Do not be angry with us, O Yahweh, exceedingly,
And do not remember our guilt forever.

But look now, we are all thy people!
Thy holy cities have been a wilderness;
Zion has been a wilderness; Jerusalem a desolation.
Our holy and beautiful house
Wherein our fathers praised thee
Was burned with fire;
And all our treasures were destroyed.
Wilt thou restrain thyself for these things, O Yahweh?
Wilt thou be silent, and afflict us exceedingly?[5]

This state of deep depression needs to be offset by words of correspondingly high anticipation. Such words are found in Isaiah, chapters 56–66, in abundance. There is no section of Hebrew literature in which the spirit of hopeful faith expresses itself more exultantly and beautifully than here. The darker the immediate situation was, the brighter did the skies of the prophetic future shine. The pictures of the Golden Age painted in this period of gloom are familiar to all readers of the Bible. They are a challenge to the faint-hearted of any age. Such words are found all through the chapters, but are especially noteworthy in chapter 62; 65:8–25; and 66:20–23. The most beautiful vision of the future is found in chapter 60, of which a new rendering may be given:

[5] Isa. 63:15—64:11.

Arise, shine, for thy light is come,
And the glory of Yahweh is risen upon thee!
For, behold, darkness covers the earth,
And dense darkness the peoples;
But upon thee Yahweh will arise,
And his glory will be seen upon thee;
And nations will come to thy light,
And kings to the brightness of thy rising.

Lift up thine eyes round about and see!
They are all assembling, they come to thee!
Thy sons will come from far,
And thy daughters will be carried on the side.

Then thou wilt see and beam with joy;
Thy heart will be stirred and be enlarged.
For the riches of the sea will be turned unto thee;
The wealth of nations will come to thee.

A flood of camels will cover thee,
The young camels of Midian and Ephah;
They will all come from Sheba.
Gold and incense will they carry,
And the praises of Yahweh will they proclaim.

All the flocks of Kedar will be gathered unto thee,
The rams of Nebaioth will minister to thee;
They will come up with acceptance on mine altar,
And I will glorify my glorious house.

Who are these that fly as a cloud,
And as the doves to their cotes?
For the isles will wait for me,
With the ships of Tarshish in the lead,
To bring thy sons from far,
Their silver and their gold with them,
For the name of Yahweh, thy God,
And for the Holy One of Israel; for he has glorified thee.

And aliens will build thy walls,
And their kings will minister to thee;
For in my anger I smote thee,
And in my favor will I have mercy on thee.

And thy gates will be open continually,
Neither by day, nor by night will they be closed,
That the wealth of the nations may come to thee,
And their kings leading on.

For the nation or the kingdom that will not serve thee will perish;
The nations will be utterly destroyed.
The glory of Lebanon will come to thee,
The cypress, the cedar, and also the elm,
To glorify the place of my sanctuary,
That I may make the place of my feet glorious.

The sons of thy oppressors will come cringing unto thee,
And those who despised thee will prostrate themselves at the soles
    of thy feet.
And they will call thee the city of Yahweh,
The Zion of the Holy One of Israel.

Instead of thy being deserted and hated with no one passing by
I will make thee an everlasting majesty,
A joy to generations to come.
Thou shalt suck the milk of the nations;
And at the breast of kings thou shalt suck.
Thou shalt know that I Yahweh am thy deliverer,
And that thy vindicator is the mighty one of Jacob.

Instead of bronze, I will bring gold;
Instead of iron, I will bring silver;
Instead of wood, I will bring bronze,
And instead of stones, iron.
I will make thy government peace,
And thy taskmasters righteousness.
There will not be heard any longer in thy land violence,
Destruction, nor devastation in thy boundaries;

But thou wilt call thy walls, "Deliverance,"
And thy gates, "Praise."

The sun will be no more thy light by day,
Nor will the moon give thee light for brightness;
But Yahweh will be thy everlasting light,
And thy God thy glory.

Thy sun will no more set,
Nor will thy moon be gathered up;
But Yahweh will be thy everlasting light,
And the days of thy mourning will be completed.

Thy people will be all of them righteous,
Forever will they possess the land,
The branch of my planting, the work of my hands to be·glorified.
The little one will become a thousand;
And the small one, a strong people;
If Yahweh will hasten it in its time.

The little Book of Obadiah is in its original elements a product of this same general period. It reflects bitter hatred against Edom and a burning desire for vengeance upon that land and people. The first five verses of Obadiah appear also in Jer. 49:9, 14–16. It is pretty generally granted now that they were original with Obadiah, and were therefore borrowed by the editors who produced the present Book of Jeremiah. The Book of Obadiah is itself the product of editorial activity. The original prophecy seems to have consisted of verses 1–7e and 10–14, 15b. The remaining verses also deal with Edom, but seem to reflect a later eschatological point of view.[6]

---

[6] For an introduction to Obadiah see J. A. Bewer, *Introduction to the Literature of the Old Testament* (1933), pp. 251 f.; F. C. Eiselen, *The Prophetic Books of the Old Testament* (1923), II, 430–39; T. H. Robinson, *Die zwölf kleinen Propheten: Hosea bis Micha* (1936), pp. 109–11

The acts of Edom that called forth the spirit of vengeance seen in Isaiah, chapter 63, Obadiah, and Malachi are also spoken of in Ezekiel, chapter 35, Ps. 137:7, and Lam. 4:21 f. The writer of Obadiah seems to be aware of a movement that is on foot having for its end an attack upon Edom. He contemplates this outlook with undisguised satisfaction. He sees in the coming onslaught the divine purpose to punish Edom for its share in the humiliation and robbery of Judah at the time of the overthrow by the Babylonians in 586 B.C. In verses 10–14 he chides Edom for its reprehensible conduct on that occasion, and in verse 15*b* he threatens her with a fate similar to that which she helped inflict upon Judah; she will reap what she has sown. This portion of the book seems to reflect an actual historical situation; the remainder of the book deals with eschatological pictures rather than with historical realities. Both parts alike look upon an adequate revenge upon Edom as an indispensable part of the divine program. This is practically the sole interest of the book; the later writer does take a brief glimpse at the nations at large whom he would subject to the same fate as Edom, but Edom is his first and last concern. The spirit of such writings is easily understood, and is not wholly without warrant; but it is unworthy of the best standards of the great prophets.

The Book of Malachi reflects the same attitude toward Edom, but differs from Obadiah in two main particulars. Malachi does not look forward to a punishment upon Edom, but regards it as already accomplished. Further, Edom's fate is not his supreme concern; he passes on, after a brief allusion to Edom, to other matters that are closer at hand and of more immediate importance.[7] The Book of Malachi is thus a bit later in origin than Obadiah, but still belongs in the period of gloom and discouragement, prior to the reform movement under Nehemiah and Ezra.

The author of Malachi sets himself to the task of encouraging his people and of quickening their faith. He recognizes clearly the state of mind of his contemporaries, and meets them on their own level. He himself is full of courage and enthusiasm, and is dominated by an invincible faith. These attitudes he seeks to awaken in the minds and hearts of his people.

The prophet's generation was skeptically minded. They were saying that Yahweh evidently had no love for his people, their sad situation was demonstration enough of that proposition. In the opening section of the book, the prophet gives a proof that Yahweh does love Judah. He finds that proof in a recent disaster that has befallen the people of Edom. How can Judah say that Yahweh does not love her when she has before her eyes the devastation of Edom? Is not punishment of Edom irrefutable proof that Yahweh loves his people? It is quite evident that the attitude of the Jews was essentially this: "Anybody who injures Edom is our friend."[8] This is exactly the attitude of hatred toward Edom that we have seen in Isaiah, chapter 63, and in Obadiah.

[7] For an introduction to and detailed interpretation of the Book of Malachi see J. M. Powis Smith, *Malachi* ("International Critical Commentary" [1912]), also Horst, *Die zwölf kleinen Propheten: Nahum bis Maleachi* (1938), pp. 253–67.

[8] Mal. 1:2–5.

In the next section of this prophecy[9] one of the reasons why Judah has not enjoyed prosperity is clearly pointed out. It lies in the fact that the performance of the ritual has been grossly neglected. How can Judah expect to be favored by Yahweh when she has failed to give Yahweh his due? They have been careless and indifferent in the arrangements and provisions for sacrifice. The exiled communities in Egypt and elsewhere have organized a worship in the heart of the pagan world that puts the worship of the mother-Temple in Jerusalem to shame. The priests themselves who ought to be the guardians of the purity of the altar have winked at irregularities and said: "What is the difference?"

A second reason for the absence of Yahweh's favor is formulated by the prophet in 2:10–16. This, to our modern minds, is much more serious, but was not necessarily so to the contemporaries of the prophet himself. The men of Judah have been perpetrating a great social wrong. They have been indulging in the practice of heartless divorce. They are in the habit of discarding the wives they married in their youth and filling their places with alien women who are addicted to idolatry.[10] These marriages were probably dictated by ambition for wealth or influence, and were in absolute defiance of every feeling of justice or fair play, not to speak of love. How can the Jews expect Yahweh

[9] Mal. 1:6—2:9.

[10] The passage is very difficult to interpret, and some of its phrases are peculiarly obscure; but it seems probable that these women were officially attached to pagan shrines; that they were hierodules. Such practices were rampant in Judah until the reforms of Nehemiah and **Ezra**; indeed, there is evidence that they persisted to a much later date.

to accept their sacrifices, carelessly offered at the best, when the cries of the expelled wives are continually sounding in his ears?

A third difficulty in the way of the free outpouring of the grace of Yahweh is stated in 2:17—3:6. It is found in the skeptical state of mind prevalent among the Jews. They have been thinking and saying that God has no interest in the execution of justice, that he does not discriminate in his treatment between the righteous and the wicked. To that charge the prophet replies that the Day of Yahweh is near at hand. In that great and awful Day, Yahweh will come with cleansing fire and clean out the wicked from the priesthood so that the sacrifices may once more be acceptable, as in days gone by. But the cleansing process will not stop at the Temple, but will go forth throughout the land doing away with all social wrongs, personal sins, and all doers of injustice. Only the unchanging goodness of Yahweh will keep the Jews from total destruction.

Another obstacle in the way of the manifestation of Yahweh's love is presented in 3:7–12. The Jewish people are wholly unreasonable in expecting Yahweh to bless them when they have robbed him of his natural rights. Tithes and offerings belong to Yahweh but they have been withheld. The indispensable prerequisite to the granting of the divine blessing is that they shall bring the whole tithe into the storehouse. Then will blessings be poured out so abundantly that there will be no room to store them away. The forces of nature will work unhindered to fill the coffers of Jewry, and the nations of the earth will look with envy upon Judah as the beloved of Yahweh.

The last difficulty encountered by Yahweh in his desire to bless his people appears in 3:13—4:3. It is a part of the skepticism already dealt with. The people are saying that religion does not pay; for those who flout it are in enjoyment of prosperity, while the pious are poor and wretched. To these complaints, the response is that conditions are about to change. The Day of Yahweh is near at hand, when the destructive wrath of Yahweh will fall upon the wicked, utterly destroying them; while prosperity and power will be granted the pious. They will hold sway over the godless, and will enjoy intimate fellowship with Yahweh himself.

The closing section of the Book of Malachi is a later editorial addition. It presupposes the authority of the Mosaic Law and promises a preliminary work of reconciliation between parents and children to be carried through by the prophet Elijah, who will return to the earth before the coming of the great and terrible Day of Yahweh. This work must be done lest Yahweh should on his great Day "smite the earth with a curse."

We might very well have called this chapter "The Decline of Prophecy." There are some great conceptions expressed by these writers. But the range is narrow and the air is heavy. We are dealing, not with realities, but with the "stuff that dreams are made of." The stir and energy of the great prophets are gone. The existence of independent nationality was vital to the well-being of prophecy. When the nation as such died, prophecy received its death sentence. The post-Exilic prophets were but feeble echoes of the great voices of the past.

CHAPTER XIV

A CALL TO WORLD-WIDE SERVICE

THE reform effected by Nehemiah and Ezra was not carried out by the support of all the people. It involved an exclusive, nationalistic, Jewish spirit that did not commend it to some of the more generous minds. A powerful protest against the particularistic spirit of the movement, with its opposition to the entrance of any foreigner into the Jewish circle, was voiced in a campaign document which has reached us as the Book of Jonah. This writing was called forth by the movement toward exclusion of foreigners, and is to be thought of as having arisen in close connection with the reform, either before it was actually adopted, or after its effects were beginning to be evident.[1]

The book was not written by Jonah, but about Jonah. There actually was a prophet by the name of Jonah (see II Kings 14:25). This prophet lived in the days of Jeroboam II, or just before his reign, and was credited with having foretold the conquests of that king. He, therefore, belonged not in the class of men like Amos and Hosea, who criticized the government,

[1] For an introduction to the Book of Jonah see J. A. Bewer, *Jonah* ("International Critical Commentary" [1912]); F. C. Eiselen, *The Prophetic Books of the Old Testament* (1923), II, 439–71; T. H. Robinson, *Die zwölf kleinen Propheten: Hosea bis Micha* (1936), pp. 117–19; and G. A. Smith, *The Book of the Twelve* (1928), pp. 483–528.

but is rather to be thought of as a popular prophet who supported the policies of the king and promised him success and prosperity. Such a prophet, therefore, would have been an opponent of men like Amos and Hosea.

The Book of Jonah was written long after the death of Jonah. It is clear from the way in which Nineveh is mentioned that the city was no longer standing. Nineveh was destroyed in 612 B.C. The writer of the book was not acquainted with the size of the city, or with the extent of its population. The ruins of the place as laid bare by modern excavators show that the circumference of the town was not more than $7\frac{1}{2}$, or at most, 8 miles. Yet the book speaks of Jonah as going into the city a day's journey before he began to preach. That would have taken him clear through Nineveh as it actually was. Similarly, it is clear that the population of Jonah's Nineveh cannot have been less than 500,000. But the total area of the real Nineveh was about 1,800 acres.[2] When we recall that the modern skyscraper was not known and that the houses of the ancient world were prevailingly one-story buildings, we recognize the difficulty of housing a half-million people on 1,800 acres. Furthermore, the language of Jonah is that characteristic of the late period of Hebrew history, and the thought is likewise too generous and all inclusive to belong to the intensely nationalistic pre-Exilic pe-

[2] There may well have been a considerable area occupied by populous suburbs—a consideration that somewhat weakens both these objections. Yet, after all allowance is made, the case for a late dating is unshaken.

riod. These things all combine to place the book in the middle of the fifth century B.C., or thereabouts.

The Book of Jonah is a story told to convey to the reader a great idea. The pedagogic value of the story-telling method is clearly recognized today. The parables of Jesus are the best-known elements of his message. Those parables are not plain, prosaic records of actual episodes in the life of Jesus. They are the product of his imagination. They were illuminated and energized by going through the mind of Jesus. He did not tell his hearers a definite and specific incident that he or they had just seen. He created a typical episode or incident that gathered up into itself all that was vital and essential in the kind of experience that he was employing for the purpose of his message. The parables, therefore, were not true transcripts of actual deeds and words; they were true to the truth of common experience, but were not verbatim reports or photographic plates of reality. Indeed, it is not at all necessary that a story should be literally true in order to have great value for moral and spiritual ends. Charles Dickens did much to reform the iniquitous private schools of England in his day by writing a novel, *Nicholas Nickleby*, in which he caricatured and thus made vivid to the minds of many readers the pettiness, stupidity, and brutality of those places of torment. Harriet Beecher Stowe did not give actual history in her novel, *Uncle Tom's Cabin*, but her story stirred to indignation the minds of thousands of northerners who actually knew next to nothing about the real condition of the slave. Mrs. Stowe's book was an exaggeration, but was no less effective on that account. So, likewise, the Book of Jonah sought to teach a great truth, and the value of the story it tells is not in any sense dependent upon the dimensions of a whale's gullet.

We shall follow the story through, noting the progress of the thought. Jonah, the prophet, living at Gathhepher, on the border of the territory of Zebulon, felt himself called to prophesy at Nineveh in the name of Yahweh. At once he turned in the opposite direction, went down to Joppa, and took ship there for Tarshish, the farthest possible port from Nineveh. No sooner had the ship set sail than Yahweh hurled a violent wind upon the sea and the waves were wrought to a great fury, so that "the ship thought that it was going to be broken to pieces." The sailors cried out to their various gods in terror, and set to work to lighten ship by casting overboard everything that was loose. Meantime, Jonah had gone down into the hold, where he was lying fast asleep, worn out by the fatigue of his hasty flight from his duty. The captain hunted him out and reproached him for not being awake and engaged in praying to his God that they all might be saved. Not knowing what else to do, the sailors began to cast lots, that they might learn who was responsible for their sad plight. The lot fell upon Jonah, who then proceeded to tell them what he had done to cause the great storm. This account made the sailors terrified, and they besought Jonah to tell them how they might placate his angry God. Jonah, stricken with remorse, urged them to put him over the side and let the ocean swallow him up. This is the only decent thing that Jonah did in the entire story. But the sailors, pagans as they were, were unwilling to toss away a man's life in that fashion; so they rowed hard to bring the ship to land but all to no avail. Thereupon, the reluctant sailors, breathing a prayer to Jonah's God for forgiveness for what he had compelled them to do, tossed Jonah to the angry waves, which at once subsided from their fury, so that the sea became once more calm. The sailors were amazed and at once offered a sacrifice to Yahweh and made vows to be performed when they reached shore. This is the first stage of the story, and it ends with the fact that the idolatrous heathen sailors recognized the power of Yahweh, the Hebrew God, and vowed service to him. It may be noticed at this point that the story so far has seen the performance of three miracles, viz., (1) the sending of the strong wind at the requisite time and place; (2) the direction of the lot so that it fell upon Jonah, the guilty man; and (3) the sudden cessation of the storm as soon as Jonah hit the surface of the water. It is a story which, if taken literally, is full of the miraculous. The moment anything passes out of the sphere of the natural, that moment it ceases to be susceptible of human measurements or standards of any sort. So the Book of Jonah is not a book of one miracle, but of a series of miracles.

Meantime, what about Jonah? "Yahweh ordained a great fish to swallow up Jonah; and Jonah was in the belly of the fish three days and three nights." Nothing is said here about a whale; the "whale" appears for the first time in Matt. 12:40. If it be insisted that we take this story as literal history, it is evident that we are shut up to no particular variety of fish by this narrative. It was a fish set apart by Yahweh for this particular purpose, and we must suppose that it was adapted to the purpose it was intended to subserve. If necessary, Yahweh was thought quite capable of making a fish to suit his purpose, and that may have been the case here; the language permits this, though it does not definitely say it. In any case, we need not worry ourselves about the dimensions of a whale, no matter how literal we wish to be. The whole episode is miraculous, and can be tied down by no human or piscatorial limitations. In the interior of the fish, Jonah had abundant time and food for thought. The result was that he prayed to Yahweh in contrition and penitence, so that Yahweh spoke to the fish, which at once "vomited Jonah out upon the dry land." Here the series of miracles is again increased.

Jonah, once more upon terra firma, is again ordered to Nineveh, and this time he responds to the call. He entered the city finally and began to send forth his cry: "Yet forty days and Nineveh will be destroyed." The entire city took the threat seriously and betook itself to mourning. From king to slave the whole population entered upon a fast, put sackcloth upon their loins, and cried aloud to God for mercy. Even the beasts of the city were included in the observance of this strict regime. God heard the cry of the city and relented from his dread purpose to destroy the city. But this was too much for Jonah, who was greatly displeased and disappointed by the apparent outcome of his mission. He

therefore prayed God to take his life from him, saying
that he was better off dead than alive. But Yahweh
simply said to him with gentle irony: "Are you very
angry, Jonah?"

Thereupon Jonah went out of the city to the east and
made a booth under which he seated himself, waiting
and hoping against hope that he might, after all, see
the destruction of the heathen city. But Yahweh mi-
raculously provided a gourd which grew up over Jonah's hut and furnished him a grateful protection from
the fierce heat. Scarcely had he had time to appreciate
the gourd when God sent a worm which smote the
gourd, so that it died. To make matters worse, God
sent a sultry, stifling east wind which Jonah found
unbearably trying. Again his sullen cry for death was
heard, and once more came the gentle irony of God.
"Are you very angry on account of the gourd?" And
Jonah replied that he was angry to the point of death.

Then Yahweh turned upon him with crushing force,
saying:

You have had pity on the gourd, for which you did not labor,
nor did you make it grow; it came up over night and perished over
night. And ought I not to have pity on Nineveh that great city,
wherein are more than 120,000 persons who cannot distinguish
their right hand from their left hand; and likewise much cattle?

These 120,000 represent babies.[3] Jonah, the disgrun-

[3] This is the prevalent interpretation among commentators (see the
commentaries of Sellin, Keil and Delitzsch, and G. A. Smith), but
surely the thought is merely of the population of the city as a whole—a
great, teeming mass of mankind who have no special claim on Yahweh's consideration; they are ignorant, "they cannot distinguish their

tled and discredited prophet, sits out there soured upon life because Yahweh has not seen fit to wipe out 120,-000 babies at one fell stroke together with the rest of the great population. What a revolting picture! How narrow, how small, how inhuman Jonah looks!

What is the bearing of the story on the situation in which it was written? The story is a parable, or allegory, of the history of Judah. Jonah represents the people of Judah. They were set in the world to make the goodness and justice of God known to all nations. They failed utterly to realize or accept their task. Therefore, they were cast into exile, where they stayed until they came to some consciousness of their iniquity. Finally, they were brought back home to Judah and given another chance to carry out their world-wide mission. But, like Jonah, they went about their work in a bitter and revengeful spirit, and were therefore open to severe rebuke and criticism.

This story was called forth by the reform movement, which sought to eliminate all non-Jews from Judah and to keep the people of Yahweh pure and unsullied by contact with alien peoples. Instead of desiring the conversion of the nations to Yahweh, they were beseeching Yahweh for destructive vengeance upon the nations. The picture of Jonah frowning upon Nineveh was none too strong for the facts.

The Book of Jonah thus becomes a great missionary

---

right hand from their left hand"; but they are human! And that fact alone is sufficient for the loving-kindness of the Lord (cf. Robinson, *Die zwölf kleinen Propheten: Hosea bis Micha*, p. 126).

tract. It is a plea for a human brotherhood that knows no national barriers and has room for no racial animosities or antipathies. Far from being a mere "fish story" to be laughed at, it is a great missionary challenge. It carries on splendidly the great message of the "Servant of Yahweh Songs." It puts to shame all petty human limitations and confidently declares that

The love of God is broader than the measure of man's mind,
And the heart of the Eternal is most wonderfully kind.

CHAPTER XV

A NEW OUTBURST OF PROPHECY

WE GATHER up here in one bouquet the last fading flowers of prophecy. The books containing them are Joel; Zechariah, chapters 9–14; and Isaiah, chapters 24–27. The dates of them cannot be precisely determined. But that they are all post-Exilic is beyond successful contradiction; and that they all come from the early part of the Greek period of Jewish history is generally conceded. Alexander the Great overthrew Darius III at Issus in 333 B.C., and Greece succeeded to the mastery of the oriental world. The aim of Alexander and his successors was not merely to acquire territory and conquer armies, but rather to conquer minds and cultures. The invasion of arms was but one step in the invasion of thought and life. The aim was to found a new Greece in Asia, to enlarge the Greek world. To this end strenuous efforts were put forth. Greek cities were founded in Asia Minor and Syria and Palestine. Greek customs, language, laws, and religion became the standard. Small comfort was given to the native cultures and faiths. This was all in striking contrast to the attitude of the former Persian government, which had in general shown itself tolerant and kindly to all native institutions. If the Jews had felt themselves under an alien hand when the Persians ruled them, how much more did they so feel under the Greeks! The Jewish and the Semitic world had passed into the hands of men "who knew not Joseph."

In this group of prophecies coming from the Greek period, it is noteworthy that the interests of the prophets are of a quite different sort from those of their great predecessors. The prophets of the days gone by had concerned themselves primarily with current issues. They had sought to encourage their contemporaries in the doing of justice and in acts of mercy. They had wrestled with the problems of national and international politics of their own age. They had tried to build a new social order in which righteousness should reign supreme. But these writers have transferred their interests from the present to the future. They have lost hope in the possibility of remaking the present political and social order and are looking to the days to come for the Golden Age to dawn. Their interests are no longer ethical and social; they are eschatological. They despair of the present, and hope for the future.

The two great topics of the book of Joel[1] are the plague of locusts and the Day of Yahweh. The prophecies were perhaps called forth by the events attending the downfall of the Persian Empire, somewhere in the middle of the fourth century B.C. The two series of sermons on the plague and on the Day of Yahweh have been bound together by editorial hands. The plague of

---

[1] For an introduction to Joel see J. A. Bewer, *Joel* ("International Critical Commentary" [1912]); F. C. Eiselen, *The Prophetic Books of the Old Testament* (1923), II, 380–404; and T. H. Robinson, *Die zwölf kleinen Propheten: Hosea bis Micha* (1936), pp. 55–57.

locusts was itself quite serious enough to have started a prophet to preach. For the prophets the laws of nature were the laws of God; and anything that was at all out of the usual run of things was interpreted as a direct intervention of God in human affairs.

Perhaps his first address is found in chapter 2. Verses 1a, 2, and 9, 10, are the work of the later editor, who sees in the locust plague a threatened Day of Yahweh. But the prophet is here talking about actual locusts and the devastation they were working. He pictures the land as looking like a region that has been swept by fire. He vividly describes the locusts themselves in terms of the movements of an invading army sweeping everything before it. He regards this destructive scourge as a visitation of the wrath of God sent upon the Jewish people in punishment for its sins.[2] He therefore sends forth a call to repentance.[3]

Again, in 1:2–14, 16–20, he gives a vivid and powerful description of the havoc and consternation wrought by the locusts; and once more sends forth his call to an assembly for fasting and prayer:

Hear this, you old men;
And listen, all you inhabitants of the land.
Has there ever been anything like this in your days,
Or in the days of your fathers?

Tell of it to your children,
And your children in turn to their children,
And their children to the following generations.

[2] For a vivid description of the actual plague of locusts that swept over Judah and Jerusalem in 1914 A.D. see the article by John Whiting, *National Geographic Magazine* (December, 1915). It is there pointed out how strikingly accurate in his description of locusts this writer was.

[3] Joel 2:1a, 3, 9, 12–14.

What the cutter left, the destroyer has eaten;
And what the destroyer left, the leaper has eaten;
And what the leaper left, the finisher[4] has eaten.

Wake up, you drunkards, and weep,
And wail, all you drinkers of wine,
For the new wine; for it is cut off from your mouths.

For a nation has come up against my land;
Strong and innumerable.
His teeth are those of the lion;
And he has the fangs of a lioness.

He has made my vine a ruin,
And my fig-tree a dry stick.
He has stripped it bare and cast it out;
Its vines are whitened.

Wail, like a virgin girded with sackcloth,
For the husband of her youth.
Sacrifice and libation are cut off from the house of Yahweh;
The priests, the ministers of Yahweh, mourn.

The field is devastated; the ground mourns;
Because the corn is ruined, the new wine is parched, the olive wilts;
The ploughmen are ashamed, the vinedressers wail,
For the wheat and for the barley,
Because the increase of the field is lost.

The vine is dried up and the fig-tree wilts;
The pomegranate, the palm, and the apple-tree,
All the trees of the field are withered;
So that joy is withered away from the sons of men.

Gird yourselves and lament, O you priests;
Wail, you ministers of the altar.
Come, spend the night in sackcloth, you ministers of my God;
Because sacrifice and libation are withheld from the house of your
God.

[4] These four epithets all are descriptive of the locusts.

Is not the food cut off before our eyes,
From the house of our God, mirth and joy?

Waste are the granaries, ruined are the barns,
Because the corn is dried up;
What shall we put in them?

The herds of cattle wander about,
For there is no pasture for them.
The flocks of sheep, too, are destroyed.

Unto thee, O Yahweh, do I call,
For fire has devoured the pastures of the open country,
And flame has burned all the trees of the field.
The beasts of the field also pant unto thee,
For the streams of water are dried up,
And fire has devoured the pastures of the open country.

In response to the urgent appeal of Joel, the people, led by the priests, called a meeting and proclaimed a fast.[5] They went into this penitential movement with the enthusiasm born of despair, willing to do anything to escape the ills under which they were suffering. In due time, the locusts passed on; and the invincible life-force in nature began to assert itself once more. Over this change of condition the prophet rejoices, and for it he praises God.[6]

The rest of the book is concerned with the terrors of the coming Day of Yahweh. Its dawn will be attended by great psychical disturbances in the minds of men, so that old and young will be seeing visions and dreaming dreams. Thereupon will great wonders be manifested in the heavens and on earth, and great destructive powers let loose from which only those who worship Yahweh will escape.[7]

[5] Joel 2:14 ff.　　[6] Joel 2:18–27.　　[7] Joel 2:28–32.

The great Day will see the gathering in the home-
land of the Jews from all parts of the world. Likewise,
the nations are to be assembled there in the valley of
Jehoshaphat, where Yahweh will enter into judgment
with them for their past sins. As they have done to Judah so shall it be done to them. They sold the Jews into captivity in far countries; they themselves will be
sold in like manner to distant peoples.[8] The nations
will gather in innumerable force for battle in the valley
of Jehoshaphat, where Yahweh will overthrow them
with his cataclysmic terrors. But Judah and Jerusalem
will be recipients of the favor of Yahweh whose abode
will be in Mount Zion.[9] It may be noticed here that
Joel resembles the Book of Ezekiel in this idea of the
concentration of the nations for punishment in the land
of Israel.

The same type of thought and hope appears in Zechariah, chapters 9–14.[10] The questions as to unity and
authorship raised by these chapters cannot be discussed
here. The text is split up into many sections, but the
same general spirit and point of view dominate
throughout. There may be contained in this collection
of chapters oracles from several hands, but they are all
concerned about the same things, and they entertain
the same hopes and fears.

Destruction from Yahweh is foretold for all the peoples of the coastlands; but Judah and Jerusalem are

---

[8] Joel 3:1–8.   [9] Joel 3:9–21.

[10] For discussion of the date of these chapters see H. G. Mitchell,
Haggai and Zechariah (1912), pp. 232–59; F. C. Eiselen, *op. cit.*, II,
560–83; Barnes, *Haggai, Zechariah and Malachi* (1917), pp. xiv–xxii;
Horst, *Die zwölf kleinen Propheten* (1938), pp. 207–8.

guaranteed safety by the presence of Yahweh.[11] The Messiah is coming in triumph, though riding upon an animal emblematic of the peace he has conquered for his people. His dominion will be world-wide. He will make the Jews victorious over the Greeks, and will crown their land with prosperity.[12] Yahweh will bless the land with fertility, and will lead forth his people to victory over their foes. The people of northern Israel, long since carried into exile, and, as a matter of fact, lost by assimilation with the population among whom they had settled down, are nevertheless to be brought back and united with the Jews once more as the people of Yahweh. The great nations are to be overthrown, and the people of Yahweh will dwell in triumphant security.[13]

In chapter 11, we seem to have an allegory in which the prophet is describing conditions as they actually were in his day. He dare not single out the Greek ruler and denounce him openly, but he does it with safety in this cryptic fashion. He seems to have, in part, at least, acted out the part of a shepherd who had been given charge of a flock of sheep, but proved faithless to his charge, leaving the sheep to the cruel mercies of robbers and fleecers. He represents the shepherd as deliberately breaking the staves that were the symbols of his responsibility, and thereby repudiating all responsibility for the welfare of the flock. He then shows the shepherd as claiming his reward from those who had enriched themselves by his connivance, and as having been given only the value of a mere slave. This the

[11] Zech. 9:1–8.   [12] Zech. 9:9–17.   [13] Zech. 10:1–12.

shepherd deposited in the treasury for safekeeping. This was all apparently a picture of the attitude of the king in the prophet's own time, who failed utterly in his duties as protector of his people and left them to the extortions of tax collectors and other underlings. Perhaps the king in question was Ptolemy III (246 B.C.), to whom the Jews were subject.[14] The prophet seems to have passed on from him to his son, Ptolemy IV,[15] and to have represented him as even worse than his father. But after a period of fiery trial[16] the false shepherd will fall, and the sorely afflicted and decimated people will find rest under the protection of Yahweh.

In 12:1—13:6, the familiar thought of the nations being gathered against Jerusalem again appears. But Jerusalem will spell disaster and destruction for all. An interesting light is cast upon the political jealousies of the writer's times when it is said that the countryside of Judah is to be given the priority in the victorious campaign lest Jerusalem and its leaders should get too much glory as compared with the rest of the land. A part of the work of the messianic age is to involve a change of heart in the people of Jerusalem so that they will repent of their wickedness and mourn for their sins. Allusion is made in 12:10 to some victim of the people's violence in days gone by for whom in their new and penitent frame of mind the people will be stricken with grief and remorse. The identity of this

[14] It has been suggested that 11:6 is a gloss and that the three shepherds there symbolize Antiochus III, Seleucus IV, and Heliodorus (see Mitchell, *op. cit.*); but see S. I. Feigin, "Some Notes on Zechariah 11:4–17," *Journal of Biblical Literature*, XLIV, 203–13.

[15] Zech. 11:15 ff.   [16] Zech. 13:7 ff.

victim cannot be recognized; the only thing clear is that the event had already occurred when this prophet wrote. Another fact of interest is the attitude of this prophet toward the prophets of his time. He evidently looked upon them as a bad lot, and foresaw the day as close at hand when their true character would be generally known, with the result that no man would be willing to be known as a prophet, but would blatantly deny the fact if he did belong to that class.

The fourteenth chapter is a collection of apocalyptic wonders and terrors. The city will be attacked and captured by the nations, who will carry into exile half of its population. But Yahweh will take the field against the nations, taking up his position on the Mount of Olives to the east of the city. Thereupon, the Mount of Olives will be cleft asunder, one-half of it moving to the north and the other to the south, thus opening up a valley in the midst of it. Not only so, but the regular order of day and night will be set aside and will give way to continuous daylight. To add to the delights of the new Jerusalem, a perennial stream will spring up therein and will flow in two directions, half of it toward the Mediterranean and half of it toward the Dead Sea. The topography of Jerusalem is also to be changed radically in another particular. Whereas the real Jerusalem was and is surrounded by hills and valleys, the new city is to be the center of a great plain, stretching out from it in all directions. The nations that attacked Jerusalem and vanquished her in the past are to fall a prey to a devastating disease, their bodies rotting away and falling to pieces where they stand. Civil war also will set in among them. So Jerusalem will be rendered secure, and will become the holy center to which all the peoples of the earth that survive will come as pilgrims to keep the Feast of Tabernacles. If they fail to come to that feast, rain will be withheld from upon them; but in Egypt, where rain is unknown, the punishment will be the failure of the Nile to overflow. Everything in and about the Temple of Yahweh will be holy, even the pots and pans. But traders will be unknown in the house of Yahweh.

The third of our prophets is represented by chapters 24–27 of the Book of Isaiah.[17] These chapters are made up of two types of material, viz., prophetico-apocalypse and lyrical poetry. The first of these includes Isa. 24: 1–23; 25:6–8; 26:20—27:1; 27:12, 13 The second stratum is Isa. 25:1–5, 9–12; 26:1–19; 27:2–11. These may be from different authors but the general tone and content of the two strands are very much alike.

The apocalypticist looks for a complete overthrow of the existing social order of the world. This great catastrophe is to be sent upon the earth in punishment of the sins of the nations. But Yahweh will reign supreme in Zion, and his people will be undisturbed. Not merely so, but the prosperity of Jerusalem is to be so great as to make the city the cynosure of all eyes. Best of all, in that city the last great enemy, Death, is to be vanquished.[18] While the great punishment of the nations

[17] For date and authorship see G. B. Gray, *Isaiah* ("International Critical Commentary" [1912]), pp. 397–404; Eiselen, *op. cit.*, I, 167–73; Procksch, *Jesaja, übersetzt und erklärt*, pp. 305–46; Wilhelm Rudolph, *Jesaja 24–27* (1938); J. Lindblom, *Die Jesaja Apokalypse* (1938).

[18] Isa. 24:1–23; 25:6–8.

is taking place, the Jews are to shut themselves up in Jerusalem in their houses and so escape falling under Yahweh's scourge. The exiles will then return home from all countries whither they have been scattered, and will gather to worship Yahweh in Jerusalem.[19]

The lyric poet sings a song of gratitude to Yahweh for the overthrow of the nations that he sees about to come. Moab, in particular, is to be laid low. He rejoices in the strength of Zion made strong by Yahweh's presence. He extols the faith of the pious and exhorts to a continuance thereof. He makes acknowledgment of the people's indebtedness to Yahweh, who has done for them that for which they had waited and hoped so long. The foes of Judah are dead and will stay dead. His mind reverts to the past when Judah had anxiously waited and prayed and nothing seemed to have been accomplished. But he leaps from these sad memories to buoyant hope, and declares that, while the foes of Judah are permanently laid low, the Jews who have died in the long struggle will come to life again and resume their places upon earth in bodily form.[20]

His last song[21] is a reminiscence of Isaiah's "Song of the Vineyard" in Isaiah, chapter 5. But here the vineyard is assured of Yahweh's constant care and protection. All who would encroach upon it are destined to be destroyed; and the vineyard will supply the whole world with fruit. The remaining verses[22] are foreign to the foregoing song and to the following apocalypse, and seem, therefore, an independent fragment. They

[19] Isa. 26:20—27:1 and 27:12 f.   [21] Isa. 27:2–6.
[20] Isa. 25:1–5, 9–12; 26:1–19.   [22] Isa. 27:7–11.

seem to claim that the punishment of Judah was not so severe as that of the foes of Judah. The city and fortress of this foe is to be laid in ruins and turned into pasture land, because the inhabitants refused to be instructed of Yahweh.

It is characteristic of the apocalyptic material and point of view so largely adopted by these three groups of prophecies that they are primarily eschatological in their interpretation of their situation. They have lost hope of any human change in their condition. They are intently looking forward to the intervention of Yahweh by a sudden irruption into human affairs. The existing order is to be done away with. The outlook for the future is throughout universal in that it reckons with both Judah and the world at large. It is clearly recognized that the fate of Judah cannot be settled apart from the lot of the nations. But Judah is destined to take the lead of the new world as representative of Yahweh upon earth. The nations are to receive a well-deserved punishment. But this punishment is revoltingly cruel in some of its features. The old ethical passion of the great prophets has almost wholly disappeared. Ritual comes in for a much larger recognition than it ever received at the hands of the great masters. One outstanding feature of these writers is their absolute disregard of realities. Their pictures of the future are drawn with no reference to the world as it was in their day. They did not even feel themselves bound by geographical and geological limitations. In this, as in other things, they show spiritual kinship with some passages in the Book of Ezekiel.

CHAPTER XVI

DANIEL AND THE MACCABEES

WE CANNOT here take space for a discussion of the arguments for the Maccabean date of the Book of Daniel. We must be content with referring the reader to the excellent discussions of the subject already available.[1] Suffice it to say that the historical inaccuracies in the statements regarding the Exilic and earlier post-Exilic periods, and also in those dealing with the post-Maccabean age, on the one hand, and the minute and detailed knowledge that the book displays of the Maccabean period, on the other hand, combine to make the case for the Maccabean origin of the book practically irrefutable.

The historical situation out of which the Book of Daniel came may be briefly sketched. Antiochus IV was on the throne of Syria, and therefore was the king to whom the Jews were subject. Antiochus was an ambitious but vain ruler. He gloried in the title "Epiphanes," i.e., the Manifest One; but some of his

[1] See, e.g., S. R. Driver, *Daniel* (Cambridge Bible [1900]); R. H. Charles, *Daniel* (1929); J. A. Montgomery, *The Book of Daniel* (1927); Aage Bentzen, *Daniel* (1937); G. B. Gray, *Critical Introduction to the Old Testament* (1913); F. C. Eiselen, *The Psalms and Other Sacred Writings* (1918), pp. 251–88; see also Oesterley and Robinson, *Introduction to the Books of the Old Testament* (1934), pp. 330–40; Eissfeldt, *Einleitung in das Alte Testament* (1934), pp. 562–83. For the traditional point of view see R. D. Wilson, *Studies in the Book of Daniel* (1917); *ibid.* (2d ser., 1938).

suffering subjects preferred to call him "Epimanes," i.e., the Madman. He was desirous of hastening the process of Hellenizing the Orient. That process had already gone far, and was still moving rapidly; but not rapidly enough to satisfy the demand of the vainglorious king. He therefore sought to achieve his end by force. He came to the throne of Syria in 175 B.C. A quarrel arose with Egypt over the possession of Palestine which wound up in war in 173 B.C. Antiochus prevailed and penetrated Egypt itself as far as Alexandria, from the siege of which Antiochus was recalled by matters of pressing importance at home. On the way back, he stopped at Jerusalem. Trouble had broken out there between the party desirous of holding fast to the old Hebrew traditions and the opposing party that sought to liberalize Judaism, and to ape the Greeks as much as possible. Antiochus soon after his accession had deposed Onias, the high priest, a representative of the Hebrew element, and had put in his place Jason, who was more amenable to the desires of Antiochus and had paid him a heavy bribe for the position. Jason had established a Greek gymnasium almost under the shadow of the Temple itself. This became a popular place, and the very priests in their eagerness to participate in the sports neglected their official duties.

The party of Onias naturally resented this sort of thing, and the two groups came to blows. Onias was driven from the city in flight to Egypt. But Jason was not left to enjoy the fruits of his victory. Menelaus, who was not a member of the priestly order, offered Antiochus, who was still in Egypt, a larger bribe than

Jason had given; and Menelaus naturally was given the position. This Jason resented violently, and organizing a force he captured Menelaus and imprisoned him in the citadel. To put these fighting malcontents in their place, Antiochus made his side trip to Jerusalem (170 B.C.). While there he plundered the Temple of its treasure, which was probably his main motive in visiting the city, and put a large number of the citizens to death. But two years later worse things befell the city. Antiochus had invaded Egypt again only to be met by a Roman legate who commanded him in the name of the Senate to return home. The Roman power was too formidable to be openly flouted. Hence Antiochus returned in bad humor to his own land (168 B.C.). Very soon thereafter he turned his attention again to Jerusalem. This time he went to work in earnest to turn the Jews into Greeks, or at least to turn them from the worship of Yahweh to the worship of Zeus. He had a Greek altar erected on top of the altar of burnt-offering (December, 168 B.C.). Here sacrifices were to be made to Zeus. This is what the writer of Daniel calls "the abomination of desolation." He placed a Syrian garrison in the citadel of Jerusalem, and destroyed the walls of the city. He issued decrees prohibiting the practice of circumcision, the offering of sacrifice to Yahweh, the reading and possession of the Jewish Scriptures, the observance of the Sabbath, and other rites of Yahwism. He sent a commission throughout the cities and villages of Palestine to destroy all evidences of Yahwistic practices and to force the population to conform to the new regulations. He caused swine to be sacrificed in the Temple on the Greek altar; and he forced the priests to eat the sacrificed flesh, so that they became unclean and unfit for the discharge of their proper functions.

To the loyal worshipers of Yahweh this situation was intolerable. It would compel them to violate every high and holy ideal and to be untrue to their deepest loyalties. Many of the weaker sort fell in with the royal demands. But the bravest and best refused to conform. Among these was Mattathias, a priest of Modein, a village overlooking the Dead Sea. One day the royal inspector came to Modein and ordered the Jews to celebrate a sacrifice to Zeus. As a renegade Jewish priest was in the act of offering the idolatrous sacrifice, Mattathias leaped upon him and slew him. Then he turned and slew the Syrian officials. Mattathias thereupon fled to the hills with his five stalwart sons, where kindred spirits joined them. Judas Maccabeus, the most vigorous of the sons of Mattathias, took the lead of the band; and the Maccabean revolt gained rapid headway. It was not halted until a Maccabean king sat upon the royal throne in Jerusalem. Meantime, the patriots and zealots recaptured the city of Jerusalem, with the exception of the citadel, and proceeded to cleanse the Temple and to rededicate it to the worship of Yahweh. The dedication took place on the twenty-fifth of Chislev (= December), 165 B.C., just three years from the day upon which the first pagan offerings had defiled it.[2]

[2] Our chief sources of information for the history of the Maccabean period are I Maccabees and Josephus.

The Book of Daniel comes out of the midst of the Maccabean struggle. It was written as a pamphlet for those times. It was an attempt to hearten the Jews in the great conflict. It sought as best it could to sustain the "morale" of the faithful. It did this in two general ways. First, it told a series of stories from the past which furnished encouraging evidence of the fact that Yahweh had taken care of his servants in the past amid all kinds of dangers. Ought he not to be trusted to care for his people again in their time of need? Second, it gave a series of visions ostensibly granted to holy men in days gone by. In these visions the entire history of the Jews in particular and the world in general was foretold down to and beyond the Maccabean period. These visions promised deliverance and glory to the Jews in the days to come. They appeared to foretell accurately the course of history from the Exile to the Maccabean period, at least as far as the ordinary man knew. Could they not, therefore, be trusted in their account of the period yet to come? It was all in the future for Daniel; he has been correct in his predictions for a period covering approximately four hundred years; surely it would be unreasonable to distrust him in his predictions for the next few years!

The stories from the past were admirably selected for the purpose of the Maccabean author. They bore directly and immediately upon the needs and problems of his own day.[3] The first story (chap. 1) relates how

---

[3] It is quite probable that the materials in Daniel, chaps. 1–6, were in existence for some time before the Maccabean period. But the maker of the Book of Daniel recognized their value for his purpose and incorporated them, with the necessary editing, in his book.

Daniel and his three friends were chosen with other young men to undergo a course of training in preparation for entry into the king's service. The best of food and drink was provided for them from the king's table, but Daniel and his friends could not eat and drink these things and be true to the requirements of their own religion. Hence they besought the chief officer and obtained permission to go on trial for ten days, during which time their diet was made up of nothing but pulse and water. At the end of the period of probation their appearance and condition were better than what those who had eaten the royal viands could show. So they were permitted to adhere to this simple diet for the entire period of three years. At the end, they were brought in with the other youths before the king and were found superior to them all, not only in appearance, but also in wisdom and knowledge. They were indeed "ten times better than all the magicians and enchanters that were in all his realm." They therefore were chosen as the king's attendants and advisers. A story like this was great encouragement to a people who were ordered to eat unclean food and were fighting for the privilege of keeping themselves "clean" and undefiled. The God who helped Daniel and his friends in days past would also help his people now in a similar situation.

The second story (chap. 2) represents Nebuchadrezzar as having dreamed a dream which he could not remember. He called all the wise men and magicians of Babylon and ordered them to tell him what the dream was and what it signified. They declared this to be an impossible task and an unheard-of demand. But he insisted and enforced his demand by the threat of death to all the wise men if they failed to furnish the necessary information. At this juncture, Daniel asked for a little time, which was granted. He and his three friends at once betook themselves to prayer, and the dream and its meaning were revealed to Daniel in a vision from Yahweh. Daniel thereupon communicated his information to the king, telling him what he had dreamed and what the dream signified. In doing this he impressed upon the king the fact that none but Yahweh could enable his servants to know and interpret this dream. The king prostrated himself before Daniel in acknowledgment of the power of Daniel's God, and at once appointed Daniel viceroy of the whole of Babylonia, with Shadrach, Meshach, and Abed-nego as his chief officers.[4] In this way, the writer of the book emphasizes the supremacy of Yahweh, the God of Judah, over all the gods of the empire. The interpretation of the king's vision may be indicated, for it is in brief outline the foundation of all the visions in the second portion of the book. Nebuchadrezzar is represented by the head of gold. The next kingdom inferior to his was that of the Persians. The third, or brazen kingdom, was thought of by the writer as the kingdom of the Medes. The fourth kingdom was that of Alexander the Great. The "division" of that kingdom represents the separation of Alexander's great empire into the king-

[4] The similarity to the story of Pharaoh's dream (Gen. 41), and the author's dependence thereon, will be apparent; only in minor details does the narrative diverge from the outline of the older story.

dom of Syria, under the Seleucids, and the kingdom of Egypt, under the Ptolemies. In the days of this divided kingdom, the messianic Kingdom is to come into being and to overthrow all existing powers, after which it will continue in power forever.

The story of the fiery furnace is told in the third chapter. Nebuchadrezzar is said to have set up a golden image on the plain of Dura and to have ordered all men everywhere to bow in worship before it whenever the trumpets should blow. The report was brought to him that Shadrach, Meshach, and Abed-nego refused to worship the image that he had erected. Nebuchadrezzar, filled with rage, sent for the three Jews and ordered them on pain of death by fire to worship his image. To this demand the young Jews replied that if their God was able he would deliver them from the king's power; but if not, yet they would not compromise themselves by worshiping the king's image. The king, thoroughly enraged at this defiance, ordered them hurled into the burning fiery furnace, which had been heated seven times as hot as usual for this especial occasion. Indeed, so fierce was the heat that the men who hurled the youths in were themselves slain by it. But, *mirabile dictu*, the Jewish youths were seen walking in the midst of the flames accompanied by a fourth person who looked like a celestial being. The king in amazement ordered the young men to come forth from the furnace, when it was seen that the fire had failed to touch them in any way, save to burn away the bonds with which they had been bound. There was not even any smell of fire upon them! The result of this extraordinary event was that Shadrach, Meshach, and Abed-nego were promoted and that Nebuchadrezzar issued a decree prohibiting his subjects from saying anything against the God of the Jews, the supreme God. A story of this sort that was believed would, of course, embolden the Jews immeasurably in their loyalty to God. The "if not" of Shadrach and his friends may seem to have required extraordinary faith, but no greater faith than was actually exhibited by the Maccabeans in the great struggle.[5]

The fourth chapter relates King Nebuchadrezzar's experience. He dreamed a dream which none of his counselors could understand. But Daniel understood it and interpreted it as meaning that Yahweh was going to smite Nebuchadrezzar in the midst of his glory and power with madness, so that for seven years he would be an associate of the beasts of the field. After that period was over, he would return to his throne and acknowledge the power of the true God. All this came upon Nebuchadrezzar as foretold, and the restored Nebuchadrezzar became a follower and worshiper of Yahweh. How applicable this story was to the Maccabean situation! Antiochus was commonly regarded as at least half-crazed. What a comfort to feel that he would be brought to his senses and made to see the glory of God!

The feast of Belshazzar is described in the fifth chapter. As the king was celebrating a great feast at which the captured vessels from the Temple of Yahweh in Jerusalem were being used by the king and his wives

[5] See, e.g., I Macc. 1:62 f.; II Macc. 6:18 ff.; 7:1 ff.

and concubines and were thus being desecrated in the vilest manner, the fingers of a hand appeared on a wall of the banqueting hall and wrote some mysterious hieroglyphs thereupon. The king was filled with terror and appealed to the magicians for an interpretation, but in vain. Then the queen came to the rescue, suggesting that Daniel, who had been highly honored by Nebuchadrezzar,[6] should be called, for he had solved such riddles before. Daniel came in response to the summons of the king, and proceeded to deliver a pointed homily to him upon the way in which Nebuchadrezzar had been punished by Yahweh for his failure to acknowledge the lordship of Yahweh, and the fact that Belshazzar seemed to have learned nothing from the experience of his great predecessor. Therefore Yahweh had sent this message to the king. The message consisted of three Aramaic words, the first one being repeated: *Mene, mene, tekel, upharsin.* These are interpreted as meaning: *mene,* "God has numbered your kingdom and brought it to an end"; *tekel,* "You

[6] Nebuchadrezzar is here called "father of Belshazzar"; but the latter was the son of Nabonidus, a Babylonian usurper, hence in no way related to Nebuchadrezzar, who was a Chaldean. Nabonidus, however, married a daughter of Nebuchadrezzar (see R. P. Dougherty, *Nabonidus and Belshazzar* [1929], p. 60). Thus Belshazzar may well have been a grandson of his great predecessor, but, since descent in the Orient was normally reckoned through the male line, this fact falls short of vindicating the accuracy of the author of Daniel at this point. Moreover, Belshazzar was associated with his father on the throne during the later years of his reign (see *ibid.,* pp. 93–104), so there is basis for calling him king. But that our author passes completely over Nabonidus, the real head of the state, is a revealing case of his unfamiliarity with the history of this period.

are weighed in the balances and found wanting";
peres,[7] "Your kingdom is divided and given to the
Medes and Persians." The king at once commanded
that Daniel be decorated and made one of the three
chief rulers of the kingdom. That very night Belshazzar was slain.[8] Belshazzar is but Antiochus Epiphanes
in disguise. The fate dealt out to him is what the Maccabeans ardently desired for Antiochus. His treatment
of the sacred vessels is of one piece with the attitude of
Antiochus toward the Temple and the Jewish religion.
Such a story as this would do much to maintain the
morale of the struggling Jews.

The last of these stories carries us on into the time of
Darius, the Mede.[9] He had given Daniel high place in
the empire, and was contemplating giving him the
chief executive position. This aroused great jealousy
among rival officials, and they set about to compass his
ruin. They realized that the only vulnerable point in
his life was his religion. Consequently, they persuaded
the king to issue a decree that no prayer or request
should be addressed to any other, man or god, save the

[7] This is the singular form, while *upharsin* is the plural form preceded by the conjunction meaning "and."

[8] On the day of Belshazzar's death, the Persians had already captured Babylon and were in possession of the empire. Hence Belshazzar's power to bestow honors of any value was gone.

[9] There was no kingdom of the Medes in control of Babylonia. The
Babylonians were immediately succeeded by the Persians, under Cyrus.
Probably Darius I, the Persian, is really meant. His reign lasted from
521–485 B.C. This would make Daniel to have been almost one hundred years old. However, Darius is thought of here (Dan. 6:29) as
having preceded Cyrus the Persian. But no such king is known. On this
and other historical problems of the Book of Daniel see H. H. Rowley,
Darius the Mede and the Four World Empires in the Book of Daniel (1935).

king for the next thirty days on pain of death for any
such offender. Daniel naturally learned of this, but he
went into his upper room, with windows wide open
toward Jerusalem, and prayed three times a day, as
was his custom. His enemies, who were on the watch,
reported this to Darius and insisted that Daniel should
not be made an exception, but should be cast into a
den of lions, in accordance with the law. The king protested and pleaded in Daniel's behalf, but in vain. The
royal decree could not be set aside. With the king's
reluctant consent, Daniel was taken in the evening and
thrown among the lions. The king spent a bad night,
sleepless and fasting. At break of day he hurried to the
lion's den and called out in anxiety to Daniel to know
whether or not he was alive. Daniel replied that he was
unharmed and had been protected by an angel of God.
He was at once released, and his persecutors, with their
wives and children, were thrown to the hungry lions,
who made short work of them. Then Darius issued an
order that Daniel's God be worshiped and feared
throughout the empire. This victory for Daniel and his
God is said to have been made possible because Daniel
"trusted in his God."[10] The moral for the Maccabean
saints was plain and the promise alluring. Inspired by
such hopes, they remained loyal to their ideals and
faithful to their God through hard and trying experiences, until they reached the desired goal.

The second half of the book is given up to the record
of four great visions seen by Daniel the prophet in the

[10] Dan. 6:25.

first and third years of Belshazzar, the first year of Darius (the son of Ahasuerus),[11] and the third year of Cyrus. They all say the same thing, but in the last vision it is worked out in much greater detail than in the others. The method of the visions is to begin with the Exile period and skip rapidly over the early empires until the Greek Empire is reached. Then the narrative expands into more or less detail and becomes quite specific. But upon passing on into the unknown future, vagueness and generalities become the rule. Indeed, it is surprising that there is as much of the definite and specific in the genuine predictions as there is. If the writer had been primarily concerned to "play safe," he would have given less opportunity for error.

The first vision[12] represents four beasts rising out of the sea. These four beasts are said to stand for four kings, that is, kingdoms or empires, that are to rise to power. Practically nothing is said about the first three, but they were representative of Babylonia, Medea, and Persia, respectively. The fourth beast is described as terrible and dreadful and is given much attention. This was clearly to represent the Macedonian empire achieved by Alexander the Great. The ten horns of this beast represent the kings that should arise out of this empire. They were the successors of Alexander the Great prior to the accession of Antiochus Epiphanes.

[11] I.e., Xerxes; no such king as Darius, the son of Xerxes, is known; but the author, with his amazing facility in garbling history, may here in his confused way be referring to the fact that Darius II succeeded Xerxes II.

[12] Daniel, chap. 7.

These successors were Seleucus I (312–280 B.C.), Antiochus I (279–261 B.C.), Antiochus II (260–246 B.C.), Seleucus II (245–226 B.C.), Seleucus III (225–223 B.C.), Antiochus III the Great (222–187 B.C.), and Seleucus IV (186–176 B.C.).[13] The last three of the ten were "plucked up" by Antiochus IV, and were therefore his contemporaries. Judgments vary as to their identity, but they may have been Heliodorus, prime minister of Seleucus IV, who sought the crown but never held it; Demetrius, son of Seleucus IV and the lawful heir to his father's throne, who was held prisoner in Rome; and Ptolemy VII, king of Egypt, whom some wished to have as king, had not Antiochus supplanted him.[14] Following these ten horns came "a little horn," in which "were eyes like those of a man and a mouth speaking great things." This is none other than Antiochus Epiphanes, who, it is said, will "think to change the seasons and the law" and "will wear out the saints of the Most High." But the vision sees the Ancient of Days upon his throne surrounded by myr-

[13] Obviously, this totals seven, not ten; but this writer is notoriously inaccurate on matters historical (cf. his statement that there were four kings of the ancient Persian empire [Dan. 11:2], though actually there were ten). However, if he intended here to include Heliodorus, the minister of Seleucus IV, who certainly had designs on the throne, and Demetrius and his infant brother, sons of the latter, or both of these to the exclusion of Heliodorus, we come close to his total. Then, too, it is not clear that he meant to omit Alexander, for the horns were all the horns of the beast prior to the rise of the "little horn."

[14] See Driver, *op. cit.*, pp. 101 f., for the varying views. Instead of Ptolemy, the third of this group may have been Seleucus IV, for though his death actually occurred before Antiochus' attempt on the throne, yet the interval was so short that our author may well have represented Seleucus' death as due to Antiochus.

iads of angels. He judges the beasts and condemns the fourth beast to be burned with fire. Not only so, but the seer beholds "one like unto a man," who was brought before the great throne of God and was given dominion forever over all nations and tongues. This is the kingdom of the "saints of the Most High"—in other words, the faithful Jews. It is so superior to the others that it is represented by a man, as distinct from the beasts symbolizing them. However, the dominion of Antiochus is to last for "a time, two times, and half a time," i.e., for three and a half years. This period is best reckoned as lasting from the edict of Antiochus issued in the summer of 168 B.C. to the rededication of the Temple in December, 165 B.C.

The second vision[15] again makes use of animals and horns. First of all, a ram with two horns appeared, the one horn being higher than the other and coming up later. This was later interpreted to Daniel as representative of the two kingdoms of the Medes and the Persians. Then a goat came into view with a conspicuous horn on his head. He overthrew the ram and swept away all opponents. But the horn was finally broken and in place of it came up four horns. This was explained to Daniel as representing the kingdom of Greece with its great world-conqueror, Alexander the Great. He in turn was succeeded by his four generals, under whom the empire was broken up into four kingdoms and correspondingly weakened. Out of them in turn came up a little horn which waxed strong and magnified itself against God. This was, of course, An-

[15] Daniel, chap. 8.

tiochus IV, who did away with the continual burnt-offering in 168 B.C. Daniel heard a voice asking how long this should continue and another voice answering: "Unto two thousand and three hundred evenings and mornings; then will the sanctuary be victorious." This seems to mean that the period during which the continual burnt-offering, that was offered morning and evening, is to cease will be eleven hundred and fifty days. This would be about three years and two months; the actual period, according to I Macc. 1:54; 4:52–53, was three years and ten days. Finally, Antiochus is to be "broken without hand," i.e., by some divine agency, not by human forces.[16]

The third vision[17] came at the conclusion of a long period of prayer on Daniel's part in which he besought Yahweh to intervene in behalf of his afflicted people. It is an outpouring of a penitent soul that is admirable in conception and beautiful in expression. It is one of the great recorded prayers of history. The vision itself is the shortest of all visions. It is wholly chronological in form. "The man Gabriel" informs Daniel that a total period of seventy weeks has been decreed during which the people of Judah are to suffer for their sins. That these "weeks" are to be understood as made up of years instead of days is clear on careful study. Jeremiah is credited with having predicted "seventy years"[18] of punishment; but that period had long since expired; hence the later writers had expanded it to seven times

---

[16] Antiochus died suddenly in 164 B.C. at Tabae in Persia of some mysterious ailment (I Macc. 6:5–16).

[17] Daniel, chap. 9.   [18] Jer. 25:12; 29:10.

seventy years by changing years into septads of years.[19]
This would bring the entire period of four hundred and
ninety years to an end in 97 B.C. The error involved in
this was due to the writer's incomplete knowledge of
the period between the return from exile and his own
times. Gabriel then proceeds to break up the seventy
weeks of years into three periods. The first week of
years is to extend from the fall of Jerusalem in 586 B.C.
to the coming of Cyrus in 538 B.C.—roughly a total of
forty-nine years. Cyrus was called "Anointed" by the
unknown prophet of the Exile.[20] Then for sixty-two
weeks the city is to stand rebuilt, but in continual
trouble. This period is too long; it shows an error in
the writer's calculations. But this error was part of the
common reckoning of his time. All other computa-
tions of the period known to us from the ancient world
show the same or a similar mistake.[21] The date of the
close of this second period of weeks which the writer
had in mind is clearly indicated by the fact with which
he closes the period (vs. 26). The cutting-off of an
anointed one to which he refers is, apparently, the
murder of Onias III at the instigation of his rival
Menelaus in 171 B.C.

The closing week of years beginning in 171 B.C.
would end in 165 B.C. The prince of the period is naturally Antiochus IV. He destroys the city and the
Temple. He makes a firm covenant with many, who
are, of course, the renegades who have gone over body

[19] The foundation of this method of interpretation was laid in Lev.
26:18, 21, 24, 28, and II Chron. 36:20 f.

[20] Isa. 45:1; cf. 44:26, 28; 45:13.

[21] See Driver, *op. cit.*, p. 147.

and soul to Hellenism. He suspends the services of the Temple and the prescribed daily sacrifices for half a week. This Antiochus actually did, so that there was no regular offering from the fifteenth of Chislev, 168 B.C., to the twenty-fifth of Chislev, 165 B.C. During that period the altar of Zeus was "causing appalment" in the Temple. But utter destruction will come upon the king and the abhorrent altar will be destroyed. The Maccabeans restored the Temple rites in 165 B.C., but Antiochus lived until 164 B.C.

The last vision is of extended character.[22] It is more detailed and specific than any of the preceding visions. It covers the years immediately prior to and including the Maccabean revolt with considerable detail and accuracy. But after recording the "little help" of the Maccabean revolt the narrative fades away into generalities about the character of Antiochus and then presently departs completely from the actual facts of history. This vision is represented as having come after a period of fasting and prayer that lasted three weeks. The actual vision that greeted Daniel's eyes as he reports it was that of a glorious being in the form of a man, the sight of whom overcame him. But an intermediary agent strengthened and sustained Daniel so that he was able at length to listen to the words of the glorious one. He is told that there will be yet three more kings of Persia after Cyrus. The fourth king of Persia will stir up a war against Greece,[23] but just then

[22] Daniel, chaps. 10–12.

[23] The identification of this "fourth" king provides an amazing revelation of the author's garbling of history. This king is "far richer than they all: and when he is waxed strong . . . . he shall stir up all

THE PROPHETS AND THEIR TIMES

a "mighty king" arises, who it becomes clear can be none other than Alexander the Great.[24] The career of Alexander, his early death, and the division of his empire among his four generals is briefly sketched, then the prediction passes on to the reorganization of the territory into the kingdoms of Syria and Egypt.[25]

The first king of the southern kingdom was Ptolemy I, of Egypt. The prince who rose up under him and became stronger than his master was Seleucus I, the founder of the Seleucidean dynasty in Syria. The prediction then passes on to the reign of Ptolemy Philadelphus (285–247 B.C.), who sought to end the long struggle with Syria for the possession of Palestine by marrying his daughter, Berenice, to Antiochus II (261–246 B.C.), of Syria, stipulating that Antiochus should divorce the wife he already had and disinherit his two sons. Thus Syria stood in a fair way to become part of the Egyptian domain. But Ptolemy died after two years, and all his plans came to naught. Antiochus took back his first wife and divorced the Egyptian princess, Berenice. Laodice, the first wife, determined to make assurance doubly sure, murdered her husband and induced her own son, Seleucus, to make his own

against the realm of Greece." This can be none other than Darius Hystaspis, who began the so-called "Persian wars" against Greece. And he was actually fourth on the throne of the empire, if we include the pretender Gaumata. But our writer goes on with the astonishing information that it was in the reign of this king that Alexander invaded Persia. Now Alexander's contemporary and opponent actually was Darius. But he was Darius III (335–331 B.C.), not Darius I a century and a half earlier!

[24] Dan. 11:3, 4.   [25] Dan. 11:5 f.

claim to the throne secure by murdering Berenice and her baby.

The murder of Berenice was not unavenged. Her brother, Ptolemy Euergetes (247–222 B.C.), invaded Syria and pushed as far east as Babylon. He was prevented from making himself master of Syria as a whole by disturbances in his own country, which forced his return home. He came back a victor loaded with spoils.[26] Seleucus recovered his territory in 242 B.C., but when he invaded Egypt he was defeated in 240 B.C. and fled back home.

The conflicts of Seleucus III (226–223 B.C.) and Antiochus III (223–187 B.C.), known as "the Great," with Ptolemy IV (222–205 B.C.) and Ptolemy V (205–181 B.C.) are then "foretold."[27] These ended in the great battle at Raphia (205 B.C.), in which Antiochus was completely defeated.[28] After twelve years, during which Antiochus had made his reputation as "the Great" by his conquests in the east, a treaty was made between Syria and Macedonia for a joint attack upon Egypt, now under the rule of an infant king, and a division of its territory. This brought about the end of the power of Egypt in Syria and Palestine. Antiochus made peace with Egypt and cemented it by marrying his daughter Cleopatra, "the daughter of women,"to Ptolemy Epiphanes, king of Egypt (194–193 B.C.). But Antiochus lost the support of Rome which was transferred to Ptolemy. These proceedings are summarized in verses 13–17.

[26] Dan. 11:7–9.   [27] Dan. 11:10–19.   [28] Dan. 11:11, 12.

The downfall of Antiochus III was rapid and complete. He had ambitions toward the west. These brought him into conflict with Rome. He was defeated by the Romans at Thermopylae in 191 B.C., and again at Magnesia in Asia Minor in 190 B.C., where his losses were terrific. This brought his ambitions for westward expansion to a hopeless end. He was followed by his son, Seleucus IV (187–185 B.C.), who was forced to pay heavy tribute for nine years to Rome. This king is evidently referred to here as the one who sends a tax collector throughout the kingdom.[29]

The successor of Seleucus was a "contemptible person," viz., Antiochus Epiphanes (175–164 B.C.). The son of Seleucus was the lawful heir to the throne, but he was a mere child and he was held in Rome as a hostage. Hence Antiochus could and did obtain the crown by "flatteries." He overcame all opposition. One of his first acts was to depose Onias III, the high priest in Jerusalem, spoken of here as "the prince of the Covenant." Antiochus is described here as one who kept no promises, as having risen to power through the support of a small but powerful group, and as being characterized by lavish prodigality with resources obtained by plunder and robbery. This is in keeping with what historians say of Antiochus.[30] This, however, the seer declares, will last only as long as God wills.[31]

The vision then goes on to predict the first campaign

[29] Dan. 11:18–20.

[30] See I Macc. 1:19; 3:30 f.; Polybius xxvi. 10. 9–11; xxxi. 4. 9; henagoras x. 52; Livy xli. 20.

[31] Dan. 11:12–24.

of Antiochus against Egypt (170 B.C.). It foretells the defeat of Ptolemy Philometor, due in part to the defection of his own followers, some of whom, as a matter of fact, did desert to the enemy. Reference is also made to the strained relations between Antiochus and Ptolemy after the latter had fallen into the power of the former, who professed to be his friend, though in reality he was striving to add Egypt to his own dominions. Then the visit of Antiochus to Jerusalem and his desecration and robbery of the Temple are foretold in general just as they occurred.[32] The second expedition against Egypt follows at once in the vision. The prohibition of further advance sent by Rome through Popilius Laena, which caused Antiochus to turn back and vent his spleen upon Jerusalem, is plainly described. The abolition of the continual burnt-offering and the erection of the altar of Zeus in the holy place are clearly mentioned. But the opposition of the faithful and the rise of the Maccabeans are recorded as affording a "little help." The conduct of Antiochus in setting at naught all religions and the one true God and in setting up for himself a "god of fortresses" is next described. This, too, is a transcript from the actual course of conduct adopted by Antiochus.[33]

Finally, a new invasion of Egypt and Palestine is pictured. This is to be successful for a time, but then Antiochus will hear bad news from the north and east; and on his way back will come to his end "between the seas and the beauteous holy mountain."[34] This must mean on the Maritime Plain skirting the Mediter-

[32] Dan. 11:25–29.   [33] Dan. 11:29–39.   [34] Dan. 11:40–45.

ranean. No such further attack upon Egypt actually took place; nor did Antiochus die as described, but in far-off Persia. The sudden change from accurate and somewhat detailed history to complete unreliability can be accounted for only on the grounds that the writer has at this point merged out of accounts of the known past into predictions of the future. In other words, the precise date of his writing is represented by the interval between verses 39 and 40 in this eleventh chapter of his book.

The prediction continues in chapter 12. A time of indescribable trouble is to follow the death of Antiochus. But every faithful Jew whose name is found recorded "in the book"[35] will escape. This is evidently the register of the citizens of the messianic Kingdom. This includes those living on the earth and also those faithful who have passed away. For they will be brought back through a resurrection to share in an everlasting messianic life. On the other hand, the wicked will be brought back to life to receive "shame and everlasting contempt." Daniel is then represented as asking how long until these things should come to pass. He was told that it would be three and a half years. To Daniel's further request for more specific information the answer was made that from the time of

[35] This notion of a divine record was a very old idea in the Orient, and became increasingly at home in Judaism through this post-Exilic period (cf. Mal. 3:16). Its use here is of special interest as revealing the growth of the concept of what we should call "the church," that is, a community of faithful within the national limits, whose religious standing is dependent, not on blood, but on faith and conduct (cf. p. 99 above).

the cessation of the continual burnt-offering until the messianic manifestation should be twelve hundred and ninety days. This would bring the period to an end on June 6, 164 B.C. But the full appearance of the messianic glory will not be seen for another forty-five days after June 6.

It may well seem difficult to understand how these visionary notions could serve any useful purpose, or be of sufficient worth to justify their writing, much less their inclusion in a body of literature that for two milleniums has been regarded as possessing in some special way religious worth and authority. But such hasty mood is soon sobered by consideration of the incredible achievements of those suffering and overwhelmed Jews for whom the Book of Daniel was written. It is true, we lack evidence as to the influence upon them of this book in particular; but they were hopes and visions and faith such as here set forth that sustained and emboldened them; they fought and suffered and died, buoyed up by the conviction that these things were eternally true. And in the strength of their faith they finally threw off the yoke of the Syrian tyrant and re-established the kingdom of Judah in the holy city.[36] Nor is this strange, for the Book of Daniel is one of the great books of religious insight and faith of our priceless heritage of Hebrew sacred scripture. It is a fitting culmination of the great process of discovery which we have been tracing in the work of the prophets. Indeed, it but gathers up and presents in vivid, pictorial form

[36] For the ethical significance of the apocalyptic point of view see J. M. Powis Smith, *The Moral Life of the Hebrews* (1923), pp. 313–18.

the best in their teaching. Here is the familiar prophetic emphasis on righteousness; that it is a righteousness of the law must not hide from us its real significance, for to the pious Jew the ritual was a symbol and expression of his devotion to the whole law of God. Here, too, is the prophets' vision of the God of history. The author of Daniel is one with Isaiah in his certainty that the pomp and armed might of the great empires exist only by the will of God and only to serve that far-off divine event toward which he is ever shaping the course of things in this troubled world. Nor was such belief confined to these two; a moment's reflection will show that this conviction of the supreme power of God in human history was the basic faith of all the seers of Israel, whose work through many a trying age we have been surveying. But the vision of the apocalyptist seems to go beyond them; theirs was a hope and faith, but for him the triumph of right has all the clarity and certitude of a vision of God. He sees the world-empires one after another destroyed in their brutality, until at length the great beast is slain; then the kingdoms of this world become the kingdom of our God. Through all the uncertainty of history, through dreary days when scoffers are prone to cry, "Where is your God?" through times of incredible cruelty of man to man, there runs the divine purpose to bring in "the kingdom of the saints."

In quiet times such as the senior generation can still remember—days when it seemed that brutality and oppression were quickly passing and there was good reason to believe that the world of man would steadily grow better—the Book of Daniel speaks as a remote voice from a long dead past. But twice in our age we have seen it spring to life with meaning and relevance when our placid world was falling to pieces about our ears. For some it has been a source of mystic speculation; its days and weeks and the seeming mysterious "time, times and half a time" have provided for the uninformed a stimulus to guessing the course of the future and calculating the coming of the day when the heavens should be rolled back as a scroll. But when the meaning and message of the book for its own crucial day are understood, it begets a vital faith by the example of this troubled saint who in an age of exulting wickedness rose to certitude such as we have here. In dark days religious people turn naturally to apocalypse; nor is this, save in its morbid expression, a flight from reality. It is the demand of faith for "a conviction of things not seen," in order that it may endure, sustained by a realization of the eternal purposes of God.

As these lines are being written the Nazi military machine has overrun all western Europe, and now, allied in arms with the Fascist dictatorship, stands poised for an assault on Britain, the one remaining bulwark in the Old World of the way of life we have known and treasured. Doubtless we are at this distance incapable of accurate evaluation of the totalitarian ideals and their promise or threat for human life. Yet the undisputed record of Nazi calculated brutalities, of deliberate and purposeful perfidy, of subjection of individual rights to the interests of a nonmoral, if not immoral, state, and withal their hostility toward those values, mediated through the Judeo-Christian tradition, whose spread through more than two thousand years has gauged the level of human advance, leaves no room for doubt that we stand now in one of the great crises of history, with civilization itself swaying on its foundations. Moreover, at the best outcome this terrific struggle now can attain, it has inevitably entailed a protracted period of economic stress and consequent social unrest, if not upheaval. By any calculation there are dark days in store; we are entering a time that will try severely our resources of faith and hope and courage. More than all else we need the apocalyptist's vision of God seated upon his throne, before whom the great beast was slain and its body given to the fowls of the air; and there was brought near one like unto a son of man to whom was given dominion and glory and a kingdom that shall not pass away.

CHAPTER XVII

CONCLUSION

THE prophets were a crowning glory of Israel. They began their course amid the mists of the low-lying valleys; they ended it upon the sunlit mountain tops. Other peoples of the ancient world had seers, soothsayers, and necromancers; Israel alone carried on through these lower levels into the higher altitudes of prophecy. The prophets bore a large share in creating that religious faith and character which were the distinguishing feature of Israel's life. The institutions of the Hebrew industrial and social life were in no essential respect different from or better than the corresponding institutions in the life of her neighbors. The more we learn about the peoples of the world of western Asia in the Hebrew period, the more similarities do we discover between them and the Hebrews. Even the institutionalized ethics of Israel as found in her earliest codes of law are in many respects on the same plane as the ethical principles embodied in the Hittite code of laws. It is not until the prophets by their splendid courage and clear vision had lifted the life of Israel to a higher level that we are able to make comparisons that always redound to the glory of the Hebrews. It is safe to say that had it not been for the prophets the people of Israel would scarcely have been heard of in the world's history. The prophets gave imperishable distinction and value to the record of Hebrew life.

How did they do it? They were not gifted with knowledge or ability in a sufficiently greater degree than that possessed by their contemporaries to furnish the explanation. They shared the world-view of their times with all its limitations in the way of ignorance and superstition. They do not commend themselves to us by their greater intelligence. Nor were they in one respect, at least, better patriots than those whom they criticized and opposed so strenuously. In devotion to the interests of the country, the men who fought to the bitter end and died rather than surrender the liberty of their beloved country, as did the northern Israelites in 720 B.C. and the Jews in 586 B.C., can scarcely be granted lower rank than the prophets who told them their struggle was all in vain, and did their best to get them to lay down their arms. It is not at all necessary to give the prophets credit for greater sincerity and singleness of purpose in the formulation of their policies than those that were possessed by some of their bitterest opponents. The difference between them was rather one of standpoint and direction. The opponents of the prophets were men who were satisfied with the existing order. Their interests were involved in the maintenance of things as they were, and they were unable to see beyond their interests, which at the same time seemed to them in all sincerity to be the interests of the country at large. Disasters did but spur them to greater offerings and more intense efforts to propitiate an angry God. They could imagine nothing else than that Israel's God should glorify his people at the expense of their foes. The prophets, on the other hand, though starting with the same principle as the politicians, viz., that piety and prosperity were almost equivalent terms, probed deeper in their search for the meaning of the disastrous course of events in which they were involved. Supremely it was their genius to see in these events a revelation of the nature of God and of his activity. For reasons we cannot analyze but may only gloss over in our ignorance by reference to their own personal disposition and their noble heritage of Hebrew ideals reaching in a broken line back to Moses or beyond, they were fired with a consciousness of the reality of God and of his righteousness. They were unusual men. They stood out above their age; they stand out across all the ages like Plato and Praxiteles, Dante, Rembrandt, and Bach. They were men of genius. They possessed that peculiar sensitiveness and understanding—that *vision* which is the distinguishing feature of every great artist. But their special interest was the fine art of living—briefly, ethics and religion. The pious tradition of more than twenty centuries has loved to affirm that they were divinely inspired. Nor would our more careful scrutiny in recent times disagree; on the contrary, the wonder of Israel's prophets, far overtopping in moral grandeur and religious insight all that ancient world, demands no less explanation. They were men who heard the voice of God. That theirs was a true inspiration the test of long, subsequent centuries has shown.

Yet the mood of European theology in popular

vogue at this moment compels us to guard well our affirmation. Theirs was no invidious exclusive experience, the like of which is denied to other men. Our study has sufficed to show how commonplace—in the better sense of this much abused term—was the experience from which they came with flaming certitude to announce, "Thus saith the Lord." They heard and saw God in the common things of every day. But so have hosts of men done in all ages and all races; only bigotry could bring us to deny an equal validity with the prophets of Israel in the religious vision of men such as Zoroaster or Ikhnaton or, on a lower level, the unnamed thinkers of ancient Babylonia. The Hebrew sages have themselves given us the best theory and interpretations of divine inspiration. They conceived of a divine "wisdom" pervasive through the world, calling to men everywhere to accept her instruction (Prov. 1:20-23; 8:1-11; 9:1-6). The inspiration of Israel's prophets was one with that of men the world over who have earnestly sought and eagerly found truth. Their uniqueness is to be tested alone by the results of their search. But from such comparison we need not shrink, who love the heritage of Israel; they, supremely, heard and uttered the voice of God.

The prophets set themselves the task of interpreting the history of their times in terms of God. It is a remarkable aspect of their work, not sufficiently realized by the modern student. Beneath all their fulminations against current evils and their threat of impending ruin was the basic conviction that God is at work in the world; rather, that the mightiest reality in a dynamic,

troubled age is not the things of sense, not armed might
or vested self-seeking, but the power of God and the
purposes of God; human history is a record of the ways
of God! Isaiah stated this in epigrammatic antitheses:

> Now the Egyptians are men, and not God
> And their horses are flesh, and not spirit.[1]

We have recently been discussing the same thought as
presented through the strange visions of the Book of
Daniel. But the point to realize is that it is the common conviction, variously expressed, of all Israel's
prophets; indeed, one might generalize still further and
say that this is one of the great themes of the Old Testament as a whole; it is a remarkable body of literature
in this regard, as in so many others.

But the prophets' concept of history entailed a con-
sequence which they did not hesitate to accept. It
made them critics of their own people. Their vision of
a righteous God and the demands of his righteous purposes threw a lurid light upon the self-seeking and
motley wickedness that made up so large a part of the
life of their time, as of ours. The popular prophets were
not so, or the soothsayers and diviners of other lands,
whose function was to "prophesy smooth things." We
glimpse their mentality in the four hundred prophets of
Ahab's court, who supported his scheme with the oracle, "Go up to Ramoth Gilead and prosper" (I Kings
22:12), or in the historic Jonah who prophesied the
recovery of Israel's lands "from the entrance of
Hamath to the sea of the Arabah" (II Kings 14:25).

[1] Isa. 31:3.

But the true prophets surveyed their nation and their age objectively and passed judgment upon it. In its lack of conformity to the will of God lay the key to the misfortunes of the times; these came not by chance or malevolence, but through Israel's sin. The prophets did not primarily blame others; they blamed their own people. This was an astonishing attainment for the ancient world, and set a pattern that was to become characteristic of Jewish life throughout the dreary ages of its dispersion. For the Jew misfortune has been a call to penitence and reform.

With such a task the prophets were forced by the disasters that befell Israel to do some hard and painful thinking. They were forced by the history of their own times to revise their messages again and again in order to keep pace with the progress of the age. The Assyrians and Babylonians forced them to revise their conception of Yahweh from time to time until they finally made him God of the universe. The tragedies of Hebrew history challenged their best efforts and caused them to abandon the doctrine that goodness always pays substantial dividends in the coin of the world and to move forward to the conviction that goodness and the fear of God are in and of themselves supreme blessings and are to be cherished for their own sake, no matter what the course of events may be. They started with a message that gave little attention to the needs and interests of the individual, but concentrated itself upon the welfare of the state and the community. They ended by making the individual person's fate a matter of vital interest to God, and by looking forward to a Kingdom of God made up of re-generated individuals. They began their career by making Israel the favorite of God, and by looking upon all other peoples as destined to minister to Israel's glory. They ended by making Israel the "Servant of God," upon whom great sufferings were imposed by God in order that the spectacle of the suffering servant might open the eyes of the nations to their sins and lead them to repentance and grateful recognition of the goodness of God. When the national history of Israel came to a disastrous end, they refused to surrender their faith and persisted in painting pictures of a glorious future, sometimes conceived in terms of recom-pense to Israel, but by the greater seers thought of as the time when Israel should be faithful, and the nations would come thronging to the worship of God.

When we seriously consider and thoroughly appre-ciate what the prophets did for Israel and through Israel for humanity; we inevitably share the sentiment breathed forth by an ancient student of prophecy:

Would God that all the Lord's people were prophets!

BIBLIOGRAPHY

A. PROPHECY

GORDON, A. R. *The Prophets of the Old Testament*. New York: Hodder & Stoughton, 1916.

GRAHAM, WILLIAM C. *The Prophets and Israel's Culture*. Chicago: University of Chicago Press, 1935.

GUILLAUME, ALFRED. *Prophecy and Divination among the Hebrews and Other Semites*. New York: Harper & Bros., 1938.

ROBINSON, T. H. *Prophecy and the Prophets in Ancient Israel*. New York: Charles Scribner's Sons, 1923.

SKINNER, JOHN. *Prophecy and Religion*. Cambridge (England): At the University Press, 1922.

SMITH, J. M. POWIS. *The Prophet and His Problems*. New York: Charles Scribner's Sons, 1914.

B. HEBREW RELIGION AND SOCIETY

ALBRIGHT, W. F. *From the Stone Age to Christianity: Monotheism and the Historical Process*. Baltimore: Johns Hopkins Press, 1940.

GRAHAM, WILLIAM C., and MAY, H. G. *Culture and Conscience: An Archaeological Study of the New Religious Past in Ancient Palestine*. Chicago: University of Chicago Press, 1936.

HOOKE, S. H. *Myth and Ritual: Essays on the Myth and Ritual of the Hebrews in Relation to the Culture Pattern of the Ancient East*. London: Oxford University Press, 1933.

———. *The Labyrinth: Further Studies in the Relation between Myth and Ritual in the Ancient World*. New York: Macmillan Co., 1935.

JACK, J. W. *The Ras Shamra Tablets: Their Bearing on the Old Testament*. Edinburgh: T. & T. Clark, 1935.

LESLIE, ELMER A. *Old Testament Religion in the Light of Its Canaanite Background*. New York: Abingdon Press, 1936.

OESTERLEY, W. O. E., and ROBINSON, T. H. *Hebrew Religion*. New York: Macmillan Co., 1930.

PEDERSEN, J. *Israel: Its Life and Culture*. London: Oxford University Press, 1926.

SMITH, J. M. POWIS. *The Moral Life of the Hebrews*. Chicago: University of Chicago Press, 1923.

C. HISTORY AND GEOGRAPHY

BREASTED, J. H. *A History of Egypt from the Earliest Times to the Persian Conquest*. 2d ed. New York: Charles Scribner's Sons, 1924.

HALL, H. R. *The Ancient History of the Near East*. 8th ed. London: Methuen & Co., 1932.

KITTEL, RUDOLF. *Great Men and Movements in Israel*. New York: Macmillan Co., 1929.

LODS, ADOLFE. *Israel from Its Beginnings to the Middle of the Eighth Century B.C.* Trans. S. H. HOOKE. London: K. Paul, Trench, Trubner & Co., 1932.

―――. *The Prophets and the Rise of Judaism*. Trans. S. H. Hooke. New York: E. P. Dutton, 1937.

MEEK, T. J. *Hebrew Origins*. New York: Harper & Bros., 1936.

Noyes, C. *The Genius of Israel*. Boston: Houghton Mifflin Co., 1924.

OESTERLEY, W. O. E., and ROBINSON, T. H. *A History of Israel*. 2 vols. Oxford: Clarendon Press, 1932.

OLMSTEAD, A. T. *History of Assyria*. New York: Charles Scribner's Sons, 1923.

―――. *History of Palestine and Syria to the Macedonian Conquest*. New York: Charles Scribner's Sons, 1931.

SEMPLE, ELLEN CHURCHILL. *The Geography of the Mediterranean Region: Its Relation to Ancient History*. New York: H. Holt & Co., 1931.

SMITH, GEORGE ADAM. *Jerusalem*. 2 vols. New York: A. C. Armstrong & Sons, 1908.

―――. *Atlas of the Historical Geography of the Holy Land*. New York: Hodder & Stoughton, 1915.

―――. *The Historical Geography of the Holy Land*. 25th ed. New York: R. Long & R. R. Smith, Inc., 1932.

INDEX OF BIBLICAL PASSAGES[1]

Italic figures indicate page numbers.

SUBJECT INDEX